ICONS

D0353965

WEB DESIGN: NAVIGATION

Ed. Julius Wiedemann

TASCHEN
HONG KONG KÖLN LONDON LOS ANGELES MADRID PARIS TOKYO

CONTENTS

CASE: 01

Publicis & Hal Riney

Matthew Clugston

June 2008: "We want to see something that's never been done before". It's a situation many an agency has found themselves in at one time or another, and this was exactly what was asked of digital design agency Clusta when San Francisco-based ad outfit Publicis & Hal Riney wanted a fully-functional website which could be navigated solely through hand movement. No mouse. No keyboard. No problem?

The philosophy behind said idea was that with the US business community being fervent early technology adopters – the widespread ownership of the hugely popular iPhone in the States meant touch navigation was already becoming the norm – a touch-less solution was the inevitable next step.

The brief itself was relatively closed, with the ultimate aim of rejuvenating the agency's image with a website which incorporated a stunning aesthetic with a forward-thinking, innovative interface. The agency wanted 1) a website which would allow users, with the aid of a simple webcam, to move through the site with only simple movements of the hand, and 2) to develop a unique 'fluid ink' animation which would offer a visual representation of the navigation.

So how to approach building a never-before-attempted commercial site without a previous blueprint? Clusta knew the answer lay in the technology, which first saw the light of day on the PlayStation 2 gaming system. The EyeToy, Sony's USB camera peripheral first introduced in late 2003, had proved a huge hit with gamers who for the first time could ditch their controllers and play games using basic body movements.

Clusta used the EyeToy as its initial inspiration, opting to use Flash-player 8 because of its enhanced scripting and video capabilities (Flash 7 would have been unable to support the level of video compression or overlays required, while Flash 9 did not have a sufficient level of penetration amongst web users).

Clusta then went to work on making the 'virtual navigation' technique a reality by incorporating a small webcam video screen in the bottom right-hand corner of the home page, containing a superimposed body outline enveloping the live image of visitors to the site.

From this small screen, movement 'hotspots' (which can detect changes in colour values or pixel movements) in the top, bottom, left and right of the video acted as the navigation points, allowing users to virtually touch or swipe with their hands to navigate to various areas of the site.

As a creative director at Clusta, I was acutely aware of the many pitfalls ahead when looking to perfect the Flash navigation's execution. The level at which movement sensitivity was set was crucial: too sensitive, and even the slightest movement could result in accidental navigation; if too much movement was required, the site would appear slow, cumbersome and generally unresponsive.

The team spent time tweaking the sensitivity, opting for a system where the site would sense a gradual build-up of movement, albeit in a relatively short time-frame, before registering a navigational command.

So, having perfected the hands-free navigation aspect of the site, Clusta moved on to the considerable task of developing the fluid ink effect which would lead people to different areas. It ended up being the toughest part of the project...

Enter the custom-built glass tank – which was brought into the studio for the job of filming the red dye dropped into water which would eventually find its way

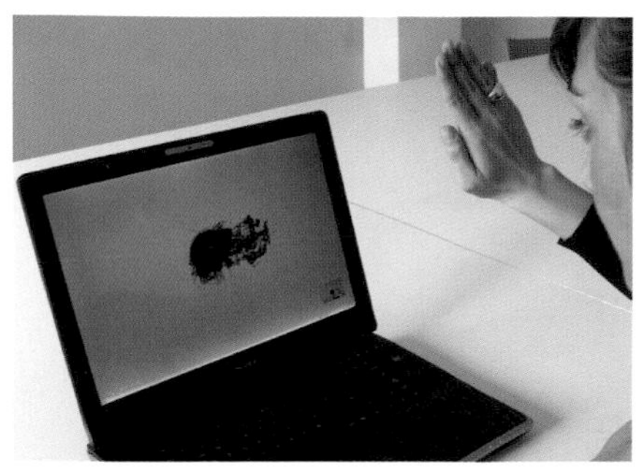

on to the site. The tank brought with it its own particular challenges: each shot would take on average 35 minutes, with each set-up requiring a fresh tank of water, and air bubbles invariably finding themselves clinging to the tank surfaces and having to be removed each time before photography could begin.

A lot of work was also done on optimisation – rather than having hundreds of ink variants, a small selection of ink flows were used that looked different enough from each other and wouldn't cause the site to slow down because of major download times.

Over 50 different ink drops were shot from multiple angles (20 were eventually used following added effects and edits) to provide the desired overlaid, organic, morphing effect.

With the webcam technology and the fluid ink effect completed, all that was left was to add content and prepare for the eventual launch (a mouse driven option was also built in as a failsafe should users not have access to a webcam).

If anyone was concerned about how the site would be received, they needn't have worried: following its launch, the site was almost immediately championed by tech bloggers wowed by the innovative use of the webcam/Flash interface and this was followed up with national and international media interest. Various news reports suggested that the motion-activated technology may eventually lead to helping typists suffering from RSI (Repetitive Strain Injury) as well as disabled computer users with severe co-ordination difficulties.

Clusta has already developed the technology to recognise gesturing and the direction or speed of movements. Does this spell the beginning of the end of the keyboard? Certainly not yet, but the fictional world represented in futuristic blockbusters such as Steven Spielberg's *Minority Report* is one step closer to becoming real.

Matthew Clugston's primary role in Clusta is creative director. This involves design on several levels in several disciplines: print, video, branding, web design and implementation, photo re-touching, DVD authoring, animation, and branding. During the last year of his degree Matthew began setting up **Clusta** with a small group of colleagues. A short time after finishing his degree he was nominated for the Flash Forward Film Festival for a website he had designed. It was also at this time that he developed Clusta's second website which was subsequently to receive international recognition and put Clusta on the design map. Matthew has continued to develop Clusta's brand over the last 10 years. **<www.clusta.com>**

CASE·01

Publicis & Hal Riney

Matthew Clugston

Juni 2008: „Wir wollen etwas sehen, das es noch nie gab." Vor dieser für Designagenturen nicht seltenen Herausforderung stand die Digitalagentur „Clusta", als sie von der in San Francisco ansässigen Werbeagentur „Publicis & Hal Riney" den Auftrag erhielt, eine voll funktionsfähige Website zu kreieren, die ausschließlich durch Handbewegungen gesteuert werden sollte. Keine Maus. Keine Tastatur. Kein Problem?

Die Grundidee hinter diesem Konzept war die Annahme, dass Geschäftsleute in den USA stets auf die neuesten technischen Errungenschaften zugreifen: Der hohe Beliebtheitsgrad des iPhone in den USA zeigte, dass die Touch Navigation (die Navigation durch leichte Berührungen) sich bereits durchgesetzt hatte. Eine berührungslose Technologie war nur der nächste logische Schritt.

Der Auftrag war klar: Ziel sollte es sein, mithilfe der Firmen-Website das Image von Publicis & Hal Riney zu verjüngen. In der Website sollte eine beeindruckende Ästhetik mit einer zukunftsweisenden, innovativen Oberfläche vereinigt werden. Die Agentur wünschte einerseits eine Webseite, die es dem Benutzer erlaubte, sich mithilfe einer normalen Webcam und einfachen Handbewegungen durch die Site zu bewegen, und andererseits die Entwicklung einer einzigartigen „Fluid Ink"-Animation, durch die die Navigation visuell dargestellt werden sollte.

Wie aber sollte man eine noch nie in die Tat umgesetzte Idee für eine Firmenwebsite realisieren, ohne dafür ein Vorbild zu haben? Bei Clusta verstand man sofort, dass die Antwort in der Technologie der PlayStation 2 lag. Die von Sony Ende 2003 auf den Markt gebrachte USB-Kamera „EyeToy" hatte in der Spieler-Community wie eine Bombe eingeschlagen: Erstmalig war es möglich, Konsolen, Joysticks und andere Geräte einfach wegzulassen und das Spiel mit Körperbewegungen zu steuern.

Das EyeToy diente bei Clusta als erste Inspiration. Man entschied sich dafür, den Flash-Player 8 einzusetzen, weil dieser über ein sehr hohes Leistungsvermögen verfügte (Flash 7 war für die hohe Videokompression und die Overlays nicht weit genug entwickelt, und Flash 9 hatte noch nicht genug Verbreitung gefunden).

Clusta setzte nun die „virtuelle Navigation" in die Tat um. In der unteren rechten Ecke der Homepage wurde ein kleiner Webcam-Videobildschirm integriert, in dem der Körperumriss des Besuchers in Echtzeit erschien.

In diesem kleinen Bildschirm wurden oben, unten, rechts und links des Videos „Hotspots" eingesetzt, die als Navigationspunkte dienten und es dem Benutzer erlaubten, seine Hände virtuell einzusetzen und sich damit durch die Site zu bewegen.

Als Kreativdirektor bei Clusta musste ich vor allem darauf achten, dass sich bei der Erstellung der Flash-Navigation keine Fehler einschlichen. Vor allem war die Empfindlichkeit gegenüber den Bewegungen ausschlaggebend: War sie zu empfindlich, würde bereits die leichteste Bewegung ungewollt eine Reaktion auslösen. Mussten die Bewegungen zu stark sein, würde die Site langsam, schwerfällig und reaktionsschwach wirken.

Unser Team verbrachte viel Zeit damit, die Empfindlichkeit der Site auszutesten. Ziel war es dabei, einen graduellen Toleranzrahmen gegenüber Bewegungen zu schaffen, die Reaktion auf einen Befehl aber trotzdem schnell erfolgen zu lassen.

Nachdem die Navigationsmethode für die Seite perfekt war, musste Clusta nun die zweite wichtige

Aufgabe erfüllen: die Entwicklung des „Fluid Ink"-Effekts, der den Benutzer in verschiedene Bereiche leitet. Dies schien der schwierigste Teil des Projekts zu sein ...

Ein extra angefertigter Glastank wurde für die Aufnahmen des roten, sich im Wasser bewegenden Farbstoffes ins Studio gebracht. Dies barg einige Herausforderungen: Jede Aufnahme dauerte etwa 35 Minuten, und für jede neue Aufnahme musste der Tank neu befüllt werden. Luftblasen sammelten sich an der Glaswand, die jedes Mal vor dem Aufnahmestart mühsam entfernt werden mussten.

Viel Arbeit wurde außerdem in die Optimierung des Konzepts gesteckt. Statt Hunderter verschiedener Tintenformen sollte eine kleine Auswahl von Tintengebilden gewählt werden, die jede für sich komplett anders aussah und vor allem die Site nicht durch lange Ladezeiten verlangsamen durfte.

Über 50 verschiedene Tintentropfen wurden aus unterschiedenen Winkeln abgeschossen (20 davon wurden letztendlich verwendet), um den gewünschten organischen Morphing-Effekt zu erzielen.

Nach der Umsetzung der Webcam-Navigation und des „Fluid Ink"-Effekts mussten nun nur noch die Inhalte eingefügt werden. Außerdem wurde für Benutzer ohne Webcam die Option integriert, die Site mit der Maus zu steuern.

Schon sehr bald waren alle Sorgen ausgeräumt, dass die Seite beim Publikum eventuell nicht angenommen werde: Sofort nach ihrer Veröffentlichung wurde die Seite von der TechBlogger-Szene für ihr innovatives Konzept und die Webcam/Flash-Oberfläche gelobt, dem dann ein nationales und internationales Medieninteresse folgte. In zahlreichen Berichten spekulierte man darüber, ob die bewegungsgesteuerte Technologie irgendwann Menschen helfen könne, die unter dem RSI-Syndrom (Repetitive Strain Injury Syndrom) oder einer Behinderung leiden.

Clusta hat bereits eine Technologie entwickelt, mit der Gesten, Bewegungsrichtung und Bewegungsgeschwindigkeit erkannt werden können. Ist damit das Ende der Tastatur nahe? Sicherlich noch nicht ganz, aber die fiktionale Zukunftswelt einiger Filme wie zum Beispiel Steven Spielbergs *Minority Report* ist nun tatsächlich ein Stückchen Realität geworden.

Matthew Clugstons Hauptaufgabe bei Clusta ist seine Arbeit als Kreativdirektor, bei der es um Design auf verschiedenen Ebenen und in unterschiedlichen Disziplinen geht: Druck, Video, Branding, Webdesign und die Umsetzung von Websites, Fotobearbeitung sowie DVD-Entwicklung und -Animation. In seinem letzten Studienjahr gründete Clugston zusammen mit einigen Kommilitonen die Agentur **Clusta**. Kurz nach seinem Studium wurde eine von ihm designte Website auf dem Flash Forward Film Festival nominiert. Zur gleichen Zeit arbeitete er bereits an der Entwicklung der zweiten Clusta-Website, die internationale Anerkennung erlangte und Clusta in der Designwelt bekannt machte. Clugston arbeitete in den letzten zehn Jahren kontinuierlich an der Entwicklung der Marke Clusta. <www.clusta.com>

Publicis & Hal Riney

Matthew Clugston

Juin 2008 : « Nous voulons voir quelque chose qui n'ait encore jamais été fait. » Cette situation, plus d'une agence l'a vécue à un moment ou un autre, et c'est exactement la demande que l'agence de design numérique Clusta a reçue de Publicis & Hal Riney, un groupe publicitaire installé à San Francisco, qui voulait un site Web complet dont la navigation répondrait uniquement aux mouvements de la main. Pas de souris. Pas de clavier. Pas de problème ?

Derrière cette idée, la philosophie était la suivante : dans un monde des affaires américain fait de fervents consommateurs précoces de technologie (avec l'acquisition à grande échelle du très populaire iPhone aux États-Unis, la navigation tactile était en passe de devenir la norme), une solution sans contact s'imposait comme l'étape suivante.

Le brief a été en soi assez fermé : l'objectif final était de rajeunir l'image de l'agence avec un site Web affichant une esthétique surprenante et une interface novatrice et ouverte à la réflexion. L'agence voulait i) un site Web qui permettrait aux utilisateurs, à l'aide d'une simple webcam, de naviguer grâce aux mouvements de la main et ii) développer une animation unique « d'encre liquide » qui offrirait une représentation visuelle de cette navigation.

Comment aborder alors la construction d'un site commercial jusqu'alors jamais tenté et sans plan préalable ? Clusta savait que la réponse résidait dans la technologie, d'abord apparue avec la console de jeu PlayStation 2. L'EyeToy, une caméra USB périphérique lancée par Sony à la fin de l'année 2003, avait connu un franc succès auprès des joueurs qui, pour la première fois, pouvaient laisser tomber les manettes de jeu et jouer grâce à de simples mouvements du corps.

Clusta a pris l'EyeToy comme inspiration initiale, en optant pour Flash-player 8 en raison de ses fonctions vidéo et script avancées (Flash 7 ne pourrait pas prendre en charge le niveau de compression vidéo et de chevauchement requis, alors que Flash 9 n'avait pas un niveau de pénétration suffisant parmi les utilisateurs Web).

Clusta a ensuite essayé de faire de la technique de « navigation virtuelle » une réalité en incorporant un petit écran vidéo de webcam dans l'angle inférieur droit de la page d'accueil, avec un cadre superposé autour de l'image en direct des visiteurs du site.

Dans cet écran, les « points sensibles » des mouvements (capables de détecter les changements de valeurs de couleurs ou de déplacements de pixels) en haut, en bas, à gauche et à droite de la vidéo ont servi de points de navigation, permettant aux utilisateurs de toucher ou de taper virtuellement avec les mains afin d'atteindre diverses zones du site.

En tant que directeur de la création chez Clusta, j'étais extrêmement conscient des nombreux écueils qui nous rencontrerions pour perfectionner la navigation Flash. Le niveau de sensibilité des mouvements était déterminant : trop élevé, le moindre mouvement risquait d'entraîner une navigation accidentelle ; s'il fallait beaucoup de mouvements en revanche, le site serait perçu comme lent, lourd et peu réactif.

L'équipe a passé du temps à ajuster la sensibilité, adoptant un système dans lequel le site détecterait une accumulation progressive des mouvements, bien que dans un temps relativement court, avant d'enregistrer une commande de navigation.

Aussi, après avoir résolu la navigation mains-libres du site, Clusta s'est-elle attelée au développement de l'effet d'encre fluide qui conduirait les utilisateurs

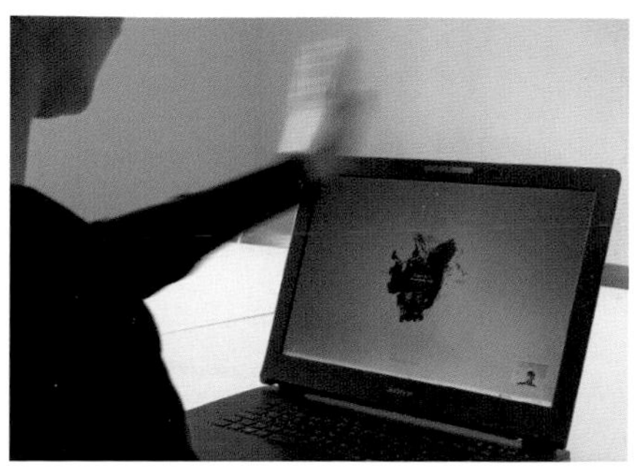

à différentes zones, énorme tâche qui s'est avérée la partie la plus ardue du projet.

Nous avons pour cela eu recours à un réservoir en verre, fabriqué spécialement et transporté au studio pour y filmer la teinture rouge qui tombait dans l'eau et qui serait finalement intégrée au site. Le réservoir a posé quelques difficultés particulières : chaque prise devait prendre 35 minutes en moyenne, or il fallait pour chaque montage remplir le réservoir d'eau propre et, avant chaque séance photo, éliminer les bulles d'air qui se formaient systématiquement à la surface.

L'optimisation a également demandé une bonne dose de travail. Au lieu d'avoir des centaines de types d'encre, une petite sélection a été utilisée, suffisamment différentes entre elles et ne risquant pas de ralentir le site en raison des temps de téléchargement.

Plus de 50 chutes d'encre différentes ont été filmées depuis divers angles (20 ont finalement été utilisées après l'ajout d'effets et des montages) pour créer l'effet superposé, organique et de morphing souhaité.

Une fois la technologie de la webcam et l'effet d'encre fluide résolus, il ne restait plus qu'à ajouter du contenu et à se préparer pour le lancement final (une option avec souris a également été développée comme sécurité pour les utilisateurs n'ayant pas accès à une webcam).

Si quelqu'un s'inquiétait de savoir comment le site allait être reçu, c'était chose inutile : après son lancement, il a presque immédiatement été acclamé par les bloggers du domaine, emballés par l'utilisation inédite de l'interface webcam/Flash ; l'intérêt des médias nationaux et internationaux a suivi. Plusieurs articles ont évoqué la possibilité que la technologie activée par mouvements puisse au final aider les personnes souffrant de troubles musculo-squelettiques (TMS) et celles atteintes d'un handicap associé à de graves difficultés de coordination.

Clusta a déjà mis au point la technologie reconnaissant les gestes, ainsi que le sens et la vitesse des mouvements. Est-ce là le début de la fin du clavier ? Pas encore, évidemment, mais le monde imaginaire dépeint dans des superproductions futuristes comme *Minority Report* de Steven Spielberg se rapproche un peu plus de la réalité.

Le rôle principal de **Matthew Clugston** chez Clusta est celui de directeur de la création, ce qui le fait toucher au design à plusieurs niveaux et dans diverses disciplines : impression, vidéo, design et implémentation Web, retouche photo, création de DVD, animation et branding. La dernière année de ses études, Matthew a constitué **Clusta** avec un petit groupe de collègues. Peu de temps après, diplôme en poche, il a été nominé au festival Flash Forward pour un site Web de son cru. À cette époque, il a développé le deuxième site Web de Clusta, qui allait être reconnu au niveau international et faire de l'agence une référence dans le monde du design. Matthew a continué à développer la marque de Clusta au cours des 10 dernières années. <**www.clusta.com**>

HELP

You don't need a mouse to move through our site.
Just your hands and a webcam.
USE WEBCAM
USE MOUSE
PUBLICIS & HAL RINEY

HELP

USING YOUR WEBCAM

SPACE BAR

To move through content, swipe your hand to the left or right side of the screen.
To return to the homepage, wave your hand towards the top of the screen.
To play and pause TV spots or launch interactive work, just press the space bar.

Please keep the area around you free of moving people or objects.

Press 'SPACE BAR' to continue

www.hrp.com

HELP

LEADERSHIP

NEWS

CONTACT
[PRESS SPACE BAR]

WORK

PHILOSOPHY

PUBLICIS & HAL RINEY

HELP

PRINT

BERINGER
Vineyard
2 of 2

HOME | WORK | PRINT

CASE·02

Torchwood Hub Interface

Mark Johnson

When producing multiplatform-work TV shows, a large part of our job is to create supporting material that extends the lifespan, reach and recognition of the show, but in the case of *Torchwood*, a stylish sci-fi drama for the BBC, our job was also to recreate and extend the fictional world depicted in the show.

We had a number of prerequisites from the producers of the series: 1) we needed a way of retrieving classified "Torchwood" information from the archives; 2) those archives would be "damaged"; 3) that "damage" would cause unpredictable things to happen; 4) the archive core was powered by alien bio-technology and the whole thing is actually "alive". Easy we thought.

Based on the brief, we began exploring various options in terms of information architecture and navigation. The immediate thought was that the navigation should be reasonably "free-form" and that we would move away from traditional menu structures wherever possible, and so we prototyped a number of navigation interfaces before settling on the final approach.

Our final creative brief went something like this: "Torchwood have obtained a piece of highly advanced alien bio-tech which can be used for data storage, analysis and retrieval, and now we're going to make it work for us. What follows is a clumsy human intervention of inserting probes, wires, connections and all manner of contraptions in an attempt to get the bio-tech working, and the results are a mix of alien elegance and peak human-user interface – the 'window' GUI!"

Now that we had our underlying driver we decided that the key to bringing this concept to life lay in the navigation – we pushed the "alien" interface towards fluid and free-form with the live "squid" bio-tech floating in the background and with the site content presented as being three layers deep: Torchwood Case > Case Folder > Case File.

This information architecture gave us a fairly "flat" structure, but because of the free-form nature of the navigation it was quite easy to add as much or as little content as required – a small amount of content would have room to "breathe" while a large amount would provide the option for "exploration" – a vital component in the show's fiction.

The interface and navigation also had to encompass a large amount and variety of content ranging from video, still, rich media, instant messaging, texts, etc., so the "window" GUI served this very well. In terms of managing this content everything was produced as stand-alone SWFs and then managed using CMS-generated XML files to determine where content would sit in the overall architecture and when it would go live.

The content itself ranged from simple character bios to wholly extended fictions using reworked video footage, specially commissioned pieces such as the fictional "instant message" exchanges, and the historic "Torchwood" so that the audience would feel a sense of complete immersion and inclusion within the show's fictional world.

Production-wise the build was relatively straightforward with the interface and navigation being worked out very early on, and with a huge bank of assets from the BBC our greatest task was deciding what to leave out.

The site launched in conjunction with *Torchwood* Episode 1 and was immediately a hit with the show's growing fan-base, who seemed to love the exploratory nature of the interface and the extended content. We had successfully found our target audience and there were many forum and blog discussions surround-

www.sequence.co.uk/torchwood

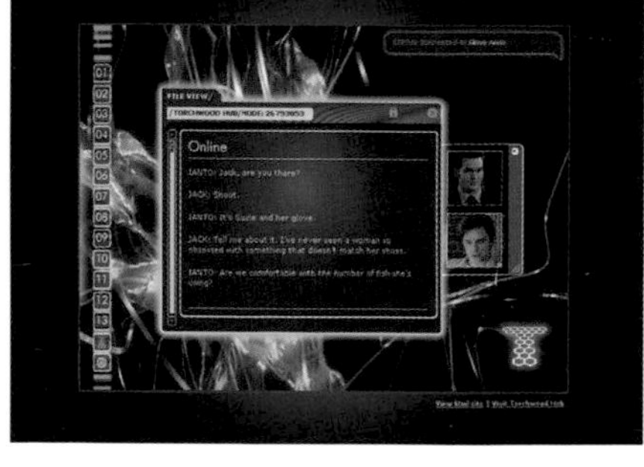

ing the site with audience members comparing notes on content, interfaces, secret details revealed on the site, etc., etc. The vast majority seemed to really enjoy the completely "extended" approach and the alternative navigation... which was, after all, what it was all about – producing entertaining work that would attract, involve and engage the audience both during and long after broadcast.

Credits:
Client: BBC New Media
James Goss (Producer)
Rob Francis (Assistant Producer)
Creative Agency: Sequence
Mark Johnson (Creative Direction/Design)
Leo Yeung (Design/Flash Authoring)
Mick McNicholas (Flash Programming)
Richard Shearman (Producer)
Reuben Whitehouse (HTML Coding)

Mark Johnson is Creative Director at **Sequence**, a UK-based and award-winning digital creative agency serving clients such as the BBC (*Doctor Who*, *Torchwood*, *Blue Peter*, CBBC, BBC4), Storm Models, Rachel's Organics, Welsh National Opera, Wales Millennium Centre, Panasonic, and Wales Assembly Government.
<www.sequence.co.uk>

CASE·02

Torchwood Hub Interface

Mark Johnson

Bei plattformübergreifenden Fernsehsendungen besteht ein großer Teil unserer Arbeit daraus, Begleitmaterial zu liefern, das über die Sendung selbst hinausgeht und ihre Lebensdauer übersteigt. Im Falle von *Torchwood*, der populären Science-Fiction-Serie der BBC, ging unsere Arbeit allerdings noch weiter: Wir mussten die gesamte fiktionale Welt der Sendung neu erschaffen und sogar noch erweitern.

Die Produzenten stellten eine ganze Reihe von Bedingungen: 1. Wir mussten einen Weg finden, um an geheime Archivinformationen über Torchwood zu kommen. 2. Die Archive sollten „beschädigt" sein. 3. Dieser Schaden sollte unvorhergesehene Dinge verursachen. 4. Das Archiv wurde von einer außerirdischen, „belebten" Biotechnologie betrieben. Wir dachten, das sei alles kein Problem.

Mit diesen Kriterien im Hinterkopf erforschten wir, welche Möglichkeiten wir bezüglich der Informationsstruktur und der Navigation hatten. Unsere erste Idee war, die Navigation relativ frei zu gestalten und sich so weit wie möglich von traditionellen Menüstrukturen zu entfernen.

Unser endgültiger kreativer Auftrag sah in etwa folgendermaßen aus: „Im Torchwood Institute hatte man eine hoch entwickelte außerirdische Biotechnologie erbeutet, die Daten speichern, analysieren und beschaffen kann. Diese Technologie sollte nun für uns arbeiten. Sonden, Kabel, Verbindungen und alle möglichen technischen Vorrichtungen wurden eingesetzt, um diese Biotechnologie zum Laufen zu bringen. Das Ergebnis ist eine Mischung aus außerirdischer Eleganz und einer hypermodernen Benutzeroberfläche: der ‚Window-GUI' (Graphical User Interface)!"

Jetzt, da wir das Grundgerüst gefunden hatten, wurde uns klar, dass die Navigation der Schlüssel dazu war, dieses Konzept in die Tat umzusetzen. Die „außerirdische" Benutzeroberfläche bekam eine flüssige, freie Form. Dahinter sollte die lebendig wirkende, verschlungene Biotechnologie schweben. Der Seiteninhalt wird auf drei Ebenen präsentiert: Torchwood-Fall > Fallordner > Falldatei.

Die Informationsstruktur war somit relativ „flach", aber dank der frei gestalteten Navigation konnten wir Inhalte in beliebigem Umfang hinzufügen. Ein kleiner Teil des Inhalts konnte „atmen", während der größte Teil – eine ganz wesentliche Komponente der Serie – zur „Erkundung" zur Verfügung stand.

Die Benutzeroberfläche und die Navigation mussten außerdem einer recht großen und vielseitigen Menge an Inhalten Platz bieten. Diese Inhalte reichen von Videos und Fotos über Rich Media, Instant-Messaging-Fenster bis hin zu Text und anderen Formen. Das „Window-GUI" eignete sich dafür perfekt. Sämtliche Inhalte wurden als unabhängige Flash-Animationen (SWF) gestaltet, die mithilfe von XML-Dateien in einem CMS verwaltet werden. So konnte genau festgelegt werden, wo sich die einzelnen Inhalte befinden sollten.

Die Inhalte selbst umfassen einfach gestaltete Lebensläufe und ausführliche Geschichten mit eigens aufbereitetem Videomaterial, präsentieren spezielle Bestandteile wie fiktionale Instant-Message-Dialoge und informieren über das historische „Torchwood". So kann der Besucher der Seite komplett in die fiktionale Welt der Sendung eintauchen. Die Umsetzung dieses Konzepts gestaltete sich relativ unkompliziert: Benutzeroberfläche und Navigation standen bereits sehr früh fest, und wir hatten ein großzügig bemessenes Budget der BBC. Probleme bereitete uns allerdings die Entscheidung, was wir weglassen sollten. Die Seite ging gleichzeitig mit der Ausstrahlung von *Torchwood*,

www.sequence.co.uk/torchwood

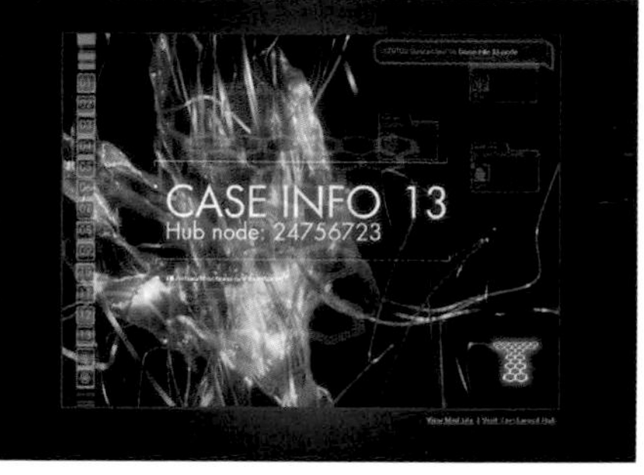

Episode I, online. Sie hatte vom ersten Tag an eine begeisterte, stets wachsende Fangemeinde. Vor allem die Möglichkeiten der „Erkundung" der Oberfläche und der Inhalte sorgten für Begeisterung. Wir hatten ein treues Zielpublikum für uns gewonnen. In zahlreichen Foren und Blogs diskutierte man die Website, ihre Inhalte, die Benutzeroberfläche, die Entdeckung versteckter Details etc. Man lobte vor allem die freie und außergewöhnliche Navigation. Wir hatten unser Ziel erreicht: die Schaffung eines Unterhaltungswerts, der das Publikum während und nach der Ausstrahlung der Sendung begeistert und fesselt.

Mitwirkende:
Kunde: BBC New Media
James Goss (Produzent)
Rob Francis (Produktionsassistent)
Kreativagentur: Sequence
Mark Johnson (Kreativchef/Design)
Leo Yeung (Design/Flash-Entwicklung)
Mick McNicholas (Flash-Programmierung)
Richard Shearman (Produzent)
Reuben Whitehouse (HTML-Programmierung)

Mark Johnson ist Kreativdirektor bei der britischen Kreativagentur **Sequence**. Die preisgekrönte Digitalagentur arbeitet unter anderem für Kunden wie BBC (*Doctor Who*, *Torchwood*, *Blue Peter*, CBBC, BBC4), Storm Models, Rachel's Organics, Welsh National Opera, Wales Millennium Centre, Panasonic und Wales Assembly Government. **<www.sequence.co.uk>**

CASE:02

Interface pour la série Torchwood

Mark Johnson

Lors de la production de séries TV pour plusieurs plates-formes, grande partie de notre travail consiste à inventer une base de matériel qui en augmente la durée de vie, la portée et la reconnaissance. Dans le cas de *Torchwood* toutefois, un drame de science-fiction chic pour la BBC, nous devions aussi recréer et développer le monde fictif dépeint.

Les producteurs de la série nous avaient fixé une série de conditions : 1. Il fallait trouver la façon de récupérer dans les archives des informations classées sur « Torchwood » ; 2. Ces archives seraient « endommagées » ; 3. Ces « dommages » auraient des conséquences imprévisibles ; 4. La base de l'archive était alimentée par une biotechnologie extraterrestre et l'ensemble est en fait « vivant ». Un jeu d'enfants.

À partir de ces instructions, nous avons commencé à travailler sur plusieurs solutions d'architecture des informations et de navigation. La toute première idée a été que la navigation devait être plutôt « libre » et que nous éviterions chaque fois que possible les structures traditionnelles de menus. Nous sommes ainsi arrivés à une série de prototypes d'interfaces de navigation avant de nous concentrer sur l'approche finale.

Notre dernier brief créatif donnait à peu près ceci : « Torchwood s'est procuré un composant de biotechnologie extraterrestre très sophistiqué qui peut permettre le stockage, l'analyse et la récupération de données, et nous allons maintenant le faire fonctionner pour nous. S'ensuit une intervention humaine lourde, avec insertion de sondes, de câbles, de connexions et de toutes sortes de choses pour faire fonctionner cette biotechnologie. Résultat : un mélange d'élégance extraterrestre et d'interface utilisateur hautement humaine, l'interface graphique ! »

Nous avions déjà notre moteur sous-jacent ; nous avons décidé que la navigation était la clé pour que ce concept prenne vie. Nous avons donc transformé l'interface « extraterrestre » en un élément fluide et libre, la biotechnologie « squid » flottant en arrière-plan, le contenu du site simulant trois couches d'informations : Cas Torchwood > Dossier du cas > Fichier du cas.

Cette architecture des informations nous a offert une structure assez « plate », mais grâce à la navigation libre, il était assez facile d'ajouter autant de contenu que souhaité. Un petit volume de contenu aurait de la place pour « respirer », une quantité plus importante laisserait la chance « d'explorer », composant vital dans la fiction de la série.

L'interface et la navigation devaient également inclure un contenu important et varié, de type vidéo, photos, média enrichi, messagerie instantanée, textes, etc., fonction que l'interface graphique de la fenêtre a parfaitement remplie. Pour gérer ce contenu, tout a été pensé comme des éléments autonomes au format SWF, puis géré à l'aide de fichiers XML générés par un SGC pour savoir où intégrer le contenu dans l'architecture globale et à quel moment il s'animerait.

Le contenu en soi allait de simples biographies des personnages à des fictions complètes à base de matériel vidéo retravaillé, notamment des créations sur commande, comme les échanges de « messages instantanés » fictifs et l'historique « Torchwood ». Le but était que le public ait l'impression d'une immersion totale et d'une plongée dans le monde imaginaire de la série.

Sur le plan de la production, la tâche était relativement simple car l'interface et la navigation ont été résolues très rapidement. Avec l'énorme banque de

données de la BBC, le plus difficile a été de décider ce que nous ne garderions pas.

Le site a été lancé en même temps que le premier épisode de *Torchwood* et a remporté un succès immédiat auprès de la base croissante de fans de la série, qui ont apparemment adoré l'aspect de découverte de l'interface et le contenu étendu. Nous avons réussi à capter notre public cible et un grand nombre de forums et de discussions dans des blogs ont gravité autour du site, les membres comparant des notes sur le contenu, des interfaces, des détails secrets révélés sur le site, etc. Visiblement, la grande majorité a vraiment apprécié l'approche totalement « étendue » et la navigation différente, ce qui était justement notre objectif : offrir un résultat amusant qui attire, implique et retienne le public pendant, mais aussi après la diffusion.

Crédits :
Client : BBC New Media
James Goss (producteur)
Rob Francis (assistant de production)
Agence de création : Sequence
Mark Johnson (direction de la création/design)
Leo Yeung (design/création Flash)
Mick McNicholas (programmation Flash)
Richard Shearman (réalisation)
Reuben Whitehouse (codage HTML)

Mark Johnson est directeur de la création chez **Sequence**, une agence de création numérique primée installée au Royaume-Uni. Parmi ses clients, elle compte la BBC (*Doctor Who*, *Torchwood*, *Blue Peter*, CBBC, BBC4), Storm Models, Rachel's Organics, l'Opéra national du Pays de Galles, le Wales Millennium Centre, Panasonic et le Wales Assembly Government. **<www.sequence.co.uk>**

CASE·03

Navigation Systems
Dylan Tran

Our philosophy on website design and navigation is strongly influenced by the principles we've learned from our traditional art and design disciplines. Fahrenheit.com is the third generation of our company website and it features our portfolio of identity systems, web & interactive design, print graphics, interior design and motion graphics. Our site is visited by creative and marketing directors, educators and designers worldwide, and our main objective is to build our firm's reputation and attract new clients.

For us, the challenge has always been to create a user experience that shows off our creativity and skills, but loads quickly and is easy to navigate. Our prospective clients have limited time to engage, and the immediate impact of our presentation has to grab their attention and keep them interested. Furthermore, they need to be able to drill down and get the information they're searching for quickly and easily.

We've always understood the web as an immersive environment that is very much like a city, and sites as being like buildings and spaces. In fact, many of the problems central to urban design and architecture are central to designing for the web: What is the purpose of the environment? What is its character and story? How do you move through it, and how does that experience move you? How do you know where you are, and how do you figure out where to go next?

Also, many of the tenets of page design come into play. Since the online experience is bounded by the edge of the browser, our mind automatically deduces that we are looking at a 'page'. The composition of the page – type layout, font style, colour scheme, imagery and motion – contributes overall to create a singular mood, a sense of place and narrative.

When we design a site, we don't think about the navigation as being a discrete element. Instead, we see it as a system of events and conditions that are organically linked to every other element of the site. Clickable objects such as words, pictures, shapes and animations operate in concert with the environments they're linked to.

It should, therefore, not be surprising that Fahrenheit.com's home page is 75 % navigation. Each 'tab' occupies an eighth of the page and vibrates visually as the cursor rolls over it. The tab offers a glimpse into the environment beyond and establishes a clear path for gaining access to our portfolio or company information. The home page sets the mood for the next step of the journey: reviewing our work, our credentials or contacting us.

Each area is coded with a different colour, texture, and animation, giving the different sections a distinctive identity. After clicking to enter the internal pages, a cinematic transition moves the main navigation from being vertically centred on the page to the top of the page, becoming the persistent nav bar for the site.

Sub-navigation systems, as exemplified in the portfolio section, allow visitors to browse or go directly to an image for rapid-fire review. Although there are several layers of information to navigate through – from section to category to project – by distinguishing the elements in a visual manner, we were able to keep the composition balanced and the information elegantly organised.

When you mouse your cursor across the page, every navigational element animates during roll-over and there is a click transition as well. This is the Fahrenheit Studio touch. Our animations flirt with and beckon the visitor to explore further. We want them to experience

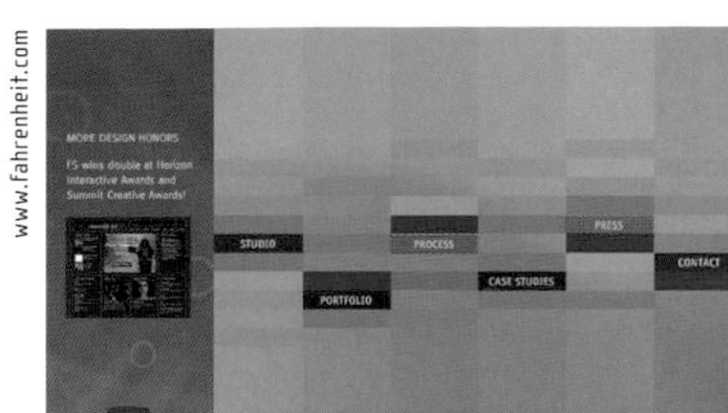

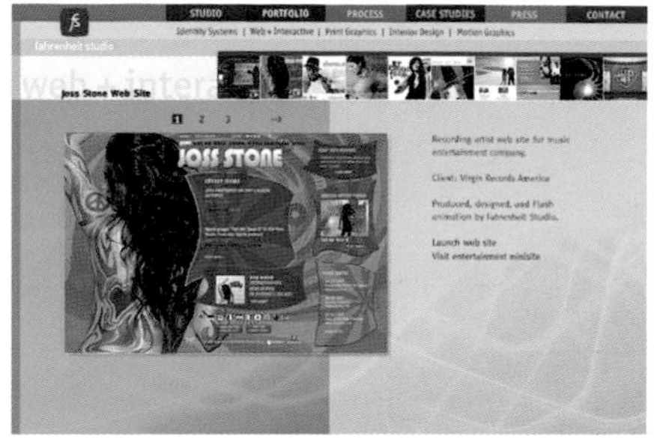

an environment that is a living demonstration of our attitudes towards interface design, navigation and narrative.

The navigation design for Fahrenheit.com is woven into the site's fabric and sets the rhythm for the site's architecture. More importantly, it captivates, involves and entices the visitor to play. Its driving force is delight and curiosity, and its components are designed to tell a story of craft, joyous colour, and simple harmonic page design.

Ideally, site navigation wants to be both apparent and transparent. Like great film-editing, it's best when it's seamless. When artfully integrated into a well-crafted interface, it does more than move the visitor through the site – it inspires them to explore deeper and drives the overall attitude and narrative.

Dylan Tran is the creative director and founding partner of **Fahrenheit Studio**, a Los Angeles-based new media design firm founded in 1995 with Robert Weitz. Fahrenheit specialises in branding and web development for high-profile clients such as Virgin Records, Navellier & Associates, IBM, Warner Music Group, Sony Music Entertainment, Warner Bros. Online, Mattel Interactive, and artists such as The Rolling Stones, Korn, Ben Harper and KT Tunstall. **<www.fahrenheit.com>**

CASE·03

Navigation Systems

Dylan Tran

Unsere Philosophie beim Website-Design ist stark von den Prinzipien der traditionellen Kunst- und Design-Disziplinen geprägt. Fahrenheit.com, bereits die dritte Generation unserer Website, stellt unser Firmen-Portfolio vor: Identity Systems, Web- und interaktives Design, Druck und Grafik, Innenarchitektur und Motion Graphics. Unsere Seite wird von Kreativ- und Marketingdirektoren, Ausbildern und Designern aus der ganzen Welt besucht. Unser Hauptziel ist es, unser Unternehmen bekannt zu machen und neue Kunden anzuziehen.

Für uns lag die größte Herausforderung stets darin, dem Benutzer eine Erfahrung zu bieten, die unsere Kreativität und unser Geschick widerspiegelt, bei gleichzeitig kurzen Ladezeiten und einer schnellen Navigation. Unsere potenziellen Kunden haben keine Zeit, sich lange mit unserer Seite zu beschäftigen. Daher muss unser Auftritt beim ersten Blick Aufmerksamkeit erregen und den Benutzer fesseln. Außerdem müssen alle wichtigen Informationen schnell und einfach abrufbar sein.

Wir haben das Internet schon immer als inspirierende Umgebung verstanden, die gewisse Ähnlichkeiten mit einer Stadt aufweist – Websites stehen dabei für Gebäude und Räume. In der Tat sind zahlreiche Fragestellungen des Städtebaus und des urbanen Designs von großer Wichtigkeit für das Internet: Welchen Zweck hat eine Umgebung? Welchen Charakter? Welche Geschichte? Wie bewege ich mich am besten darin, was bewegt mich dabei? Wie kann ich mich orientieren, und woher weiß ich, wohin ich als Nächstes gehen muss?

Außerdem spielen zahlreiche Grundsätze der traditionellen Seitengestaltung im Print-Design eine wichtige Rolle. Da die Online-Erfahrung durch die Ränder des Browsers beschränkt wird, suggeriert uns unser Gehirn, dass wir eine „Seite" vor uns haben. Die Gesamtkomposition der Seite – Satz, Layout, Schriftstil, Farben, Bilder und Bewegung – stellt eine ganz bestimmte Stimmung, ein Gefühl von Raum und Geschichte dar.

Wenn wir eine Seite kreieren, ist die Navigation für uns kein abstraktes Etwas. Sie bildet im Gegenteil ein System, das mit jedem einzelnen Element der Seite verbunden ist. Objekte, die angeklickt werden können, so etwa Wörter, Bilder und Animationen, befinden sich in einem harmonischen Zusammenspiel mit ihrer Umgebung.

Es ist keine Überraschung, dass die Homepage Fahrenheit.com zu 75 % aus Navigation besteht. Jedes „Tab" nimmt ein Achtel der Seite ein und beginnt sich zu bewegen, wenn sich der Cursor darüberbewegt. Die Tabs ermöglichen einen Einblick in verschiedene Bereiche und bieten Zutritt zu unserem Portfolio oder zu Firmeninformationen. Die Homepage macht Lust auf den nächsten Schritt: die Betrachtung unserer Arbeiten und Referenzen oder eine direkte Kontaktaufnahme.

Jeder Bereich wird in einer anderen Farbe, Struktur und Animation dargestellt – somit erhält jeder Abschnitt eine eigene Identität. Nach Eintritt in den „inneren" Bereich wird die Hauptnavigation durch einen filmisch wirkenden Übergang aus der Vertikalen im Zentrum an den oberen Rand der Seite bewegt und in eine feststehende Navigationsleiste umgewandelt.

Über die Untermenüs – wie im Portofolio-Abschnitt – können Benutzer sich über Pfeile durch die Seite bewegen oder direkt auf die Bilder klicken. Obwohl die Site aus mehreren Informationsebenen besteht (Abschnitt, Kategorie, Projekt), konnten wir durch die unterschiedliche Gestaltung der Elemente eine

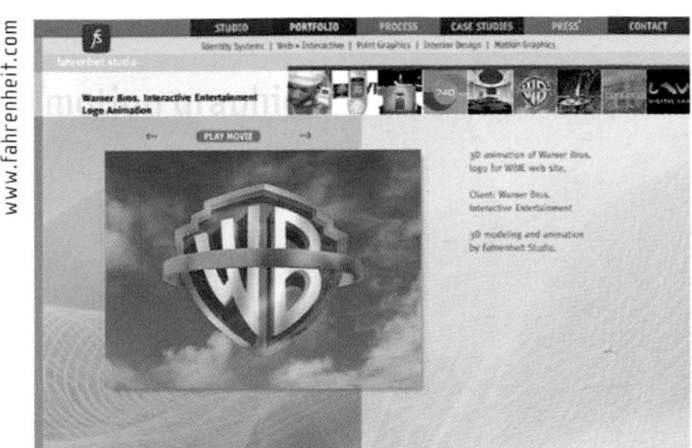

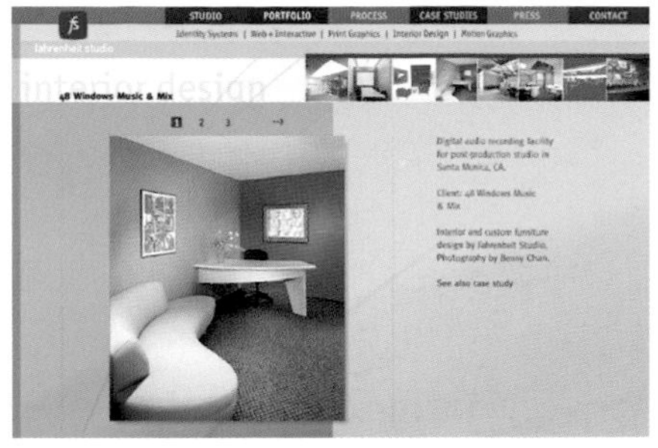

ausbalancierte und wohlorganisierte Komposition erreichen.

Bei der Bewegung des Mauszeigers über die Seite und beim Anklicken werden die Navigationselemente animiert. Genau das ist der spezielle Fahrenheit-Touch. Unsere Animationen flirten mit dem Besucher und laden dazu ein, weiterzumachen. Wir wollen, dass der Besucher eine Website sieht, die er als realistische Demonstration unserer Haltung gegenüber Oberflächendesign, Navigation und Geschichtenerzählen erlebt.

Das Navigationsdesign von Fahrenheit.com harmoniert perfekt mit der gesamten Gestaltung der Seite und gibt ihre Struktur vor. Ganz wichtig ist dabei, dass der Besucher dazu animiert wird, mit der Seite zu spielen. Vergnügen und Neugier sind die treibenden Kräfte. Jedes einzelne Element erzählt seine Geschichte und steht dabei für Kunstfertigkeit, lebhafte Farben und ein einfaches und harmonisches Design.

Idealerweise ist die Navigation einer Internetseite klar und transparent. Genau wie der Filmschnitt sollte sie sich nahtlos in das Medium einfügen. Kunstvoll integriert in eine wohlgestaltete Oberfläche bietet die Navigation mehr als die bloße Bewegung durch die Website – sie lädt den Besucher zum Eintauchen ein und wirkt dabei als führendes Element.

Dylan Tran ist Kreativdirektor und Gründungsmitglied der zusammen mit Robert Weitz 1995 gegründeten, in Los Angeles ansässigen Designagentur für neue Medien **Fahrenheit Studio**. Fahrenheit ist spezialisiert auf Branding und Webseiten-Entwicklung für bekannte Kunden wie Virgin Records, Navellier & Associates, IBM, Warner Music Group, Sony Music Entertainment, Warner Bros. Online, Mattel Interactive sowie für zahlreiche Künstler, darunter die Rolling Stones, Korn, Ben Harper und KT Tunstall. **<www.fahrenheit.com>**

CASE:03

Systèmes de navigation
Dylan Tran

En matière de conception et de navigation de sites Web, notre philosophie est fortement influencée par les principes que les disciplines artistiques et de design traditionnelles nous ont enseignés. Fahrenheit.com est la troisième génération du site Web de notre entreprise ; il présente notre portfolio de systèmes d'identité, de design Web et interactif, de design graphique, de design d'intérieur et d'animations. Notre site est visité par des directeurs de la création et de marketing, des éducateurs et des designers du monde entier, notre principal objectif étant de renforcer la notoriété de notre marque et de capter de nouveaux clients.

Pour nous, le défi a toujours été de créer une expérience utilisateur qui mette en valeur notre créativité et nos compétences, mais dont le chargement soit rapide et la navigation simple. Nos clients potentiels ont peu de temps pour s'impliquer, aussi l'impact immédiat de notre présentation doit-il capter leur attention et maintenir leur intérêt. Par ailleurs, ils doivent pouvoir explorer et obtenir les informations recherchées aussi vite que facilement.

Nous avons toujours considéré le Web comme un environnement immersif très comparable à une ville, les sites formant les immeubles et les espaces. En fait, bon nombre de problèmes propres au design et à l'architecture en milieu urbain sont aussi ceux de la conception pour le Web : quel est le but de l'environnement ? Quel est son caractère et quelle est son histoire ? Comment s'y déplace-t-on et comment cette expérience fait-elle progresser ? Comment sait-on où on se trouve et comment comprend-on où aller ensuite ?

En outre, bon nombre des principes du design de pages entrent en jeu. Sachant que l'expérience en ligne se limite au cadre du navigateur, notre esprit déduit automatiquement que nous sommes face à une « page ». Sa composition (disposition, style de police, schéma de couleurs, images et animation) contribue à créer une ambiance particulière, une notion de lieu et de récit.

Lorsque nous concevons un site, nous n'envisageons pas la navigation comme un élément discret, mais plutôt comme un système d'événements et de conditions liés de façon organique au reste des éléments du site. Les objets sur lesquels cliquer, tels les mots, photos, formes et animations, fonctionnent de concert avec les environnements auxquels ils sont liés.

Pas étonnant dès lors que la page d'accueil de Fahrenheit.com soit navigable à 75 %. Chaque « onglet » occupe un huitième de la page et vibre visuellement lorsque le curseur passe dessus. L'onglet offre un aperçu de l'environnement qu'il renferme et montre le chemin à suivre pour accéder à notre portfolio ou aux informations sur l'entreprise. La page d'accueil détermine la teneur de l'étape suivante du voyage : consulter notre travail, nos références, nous contacter.

Chaque zone est codée avec une couleur, une texture et une animation différentes, ce qui donne une identité propre à chaque section. Dès qu'on clique pour entrer dans les pages internes, une transition cinématique déplace vers le haut la navigation principale, jusqu'alors verticale et au centre de la page, qui devient ainsi la barre de navigation permanente pour le site.

Des systèmes de sous-navigation, tels qu'illustré dans la section du portfolio, permettent aux visiteurs de parcourir ou d'aller directement à une image et de la consulter en mode rafale. Même avec plusieurs couches d'informations à parcourir (des sections aux catégories, puis aux projets), nous avons réussi, en distinguant visuellement les éléments, à conserver une composition équilibrée et une organisation élégante des informations.

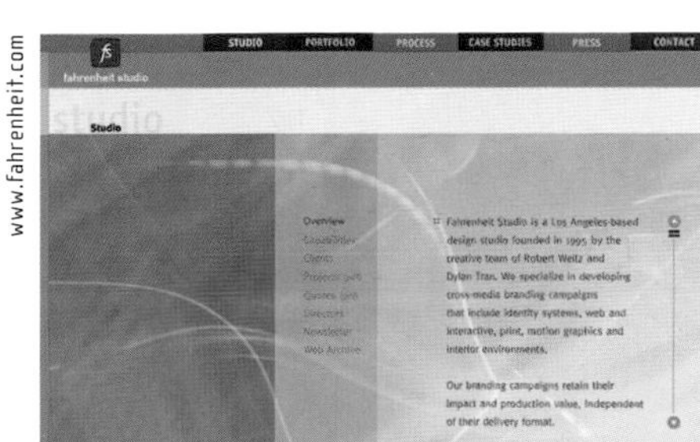

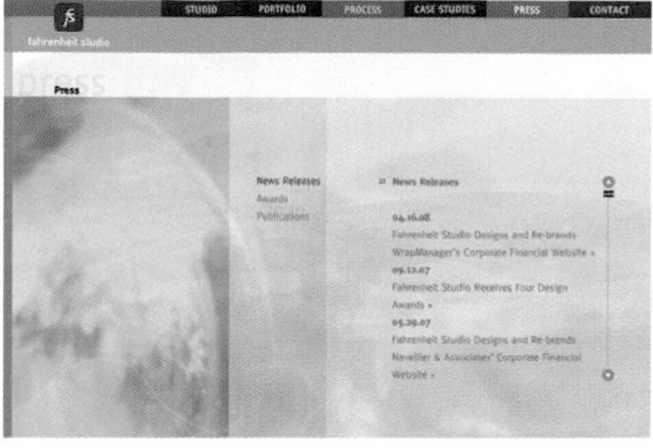

Lorsqu'on déplace le curseur dans la page, chaque élément de navigation s'anime au moment où l'on passe dessus et une transition se fait après un clic. Tel est le signe distinctif de Fahrenheit Studio. Nos animations flirtent avec les visiteurs et les invitent à explorer. Nous voulons qu'ils expérimentent l'environnement, celui-ci étant une démonstration vivante de notre manière de concevoir le design d'interfaces, la navigation et le récit.

La navigation conçue pour Fahrenheit.com est étroitement liée au tissu même du site et elle bat la mesure de son architecture. Plus encore, elle captive, implique et pousse le visiteur à jouer. Sa force de conviction repose sur le plaisir et la curiosité, et ses composants sont pensés pour raconter une histoire de design de pages artistique, joyeusement coloré et harmonieux.

Idéalement, la navigation d'un site se veut à la fois visible et transparente. Comme les meilleurs montages de films, plus elle est fluide, plus elle est réussie. Ingénieusement intégrée à une interface bien pensée, elle fait plus que promener le visiteur dans le site : elle le motive à explorer davantage, en profondeur, et transmet l'attitude et la narration dans leur ensemble.

Dylan Tran est directrice de la création et partenaire fondatrice de **Fahrenheit Studio**, une entreprise de design de nouveaux médias installée à Los Angeles et fondée en 1995 avec Robert Weitz. Fahrenheit est spécialisée dans le branding et le développement Web pour des clients influents comme Virgin Records, Navellier & Associates, IBM, Warner Music Group, Sony Music Entertainment, Warner Bros. Online, Mattel Interactive et des artistes comme The Rolling Stones, Korn, Ben Harper et KT Tunstall.
<www.fahrenheit.com>

ABSOLUT BRAZIL

BRAZIL

www.absolutbrasil.com.br

2008

Concept

The website is the showcase for 12 artists from Brazil, and 2 limited-edition bottles from amongst their work. The user can flick through the images horizontally and can access all the information about the competition, as well as buy the bottles. /// Diese Website dient als Showcase für zwölf brasilianische Künstler, aus deren Werk zwei Flaschen als *Limited Edition* ausgewählt wurden. Der User kann horizontal durch die Bilder blättern. Er bekommt alle Informationen über den Wettbewerb und kann die Flaschen auch kaufen. /// **Le site Web sert de vitrine à 12 artistes du Brésil et à 2 bouteilles d'édition limitée parmi leurs travaux. L'utilisateur peut faire défiler horizontalement les images et accéder à toutes les informations sur la concurrence, ainsi qu'acheter les bouteilles.**

Info

Design Studio: Gringo <www.gringo.nu>. /// **Design:** Gringo. /// **Programming:** Gringo. /// **Others:** Danilo Almeida (3D); Gaia (Sound Design). /// **Client:** Absolut Vodka. /// **Tools:** Adobe Creative Suite, 3D Studio Max. /// **Cost:** 3,5 months.

DANIEL
SENISE

ABSOLUT
BRASIL.

SENISE

Daniel Senise was born in Rio de Janeiro. His first individual exposition was shown in 1984. He participated in the collective expositions "Como vai você, geração 80?" (1984), in Parque Lage (Rio de Janeiro), and "Latin American Artists of the XXth Century", presented in Europe and the United States from 1992-1993. He participated in the Bienal Internacional de São Paulo in 1985, 1989, and 1998, XLIV Biennale di Venezia (1990) and Liverpool Biennial (1999). Daniel Senise is considered one of the most famous names of the "80s generation".

His art, composed of figures modelled with resins and collagen, represents through pieces, Brazilian things that exist and that are in transformation. "Transformation means, Brazil."

BUY THE BOTTLE

COMMENTS

CLOSE

LEAVE YOUR COMMENT

WALLPAPER

SEE THE EXHIBITION

I ♥ ABSOLUT

SOUND OFF | TERMS & CONDITIONS | PRIVACY POLICY | PORTUGUÊS

CAMPAIGNS | DRINKS | ABOUT ABSOLUT | PRESS | THE BLOG

ABSOLUT NEW ORLEANS

The new limited edition in the true spirit of New Orleans.

VISIT SITE

SOUND ON

ABSOLUT BRASIL

SHARE YOUR OPINION

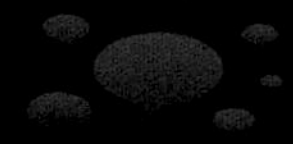

ABSOLUT CITRON MOJITO

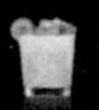

3 parts Absolut Citron
2 parts Lime Juice
1 part Syrup De Gomme
Lime
Mint Leaf
See whole recipe here

FIND DRINKS

What's your pleasure?
Get the perfect recipe right here.

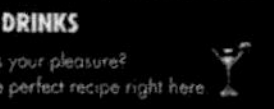

SEARCH

Terms & Conditions | Privacy Policy | Responsibility Statement

©2000-2008 V&S VIN & SPRIT AB, ALL RIGHTS RESERVED.

ADIDAS Y-3 LIGHTBOX

GERMANY

www.neue-digitale.de/projects/y-3_fw2008

2008

Concept

The site may be explored from several different angles in double-screen size expansion. The navigation concept is a grid of light boxes by which the user can "browse" products intuitively without the series reaching an end. /// Die Site kann aus verschiedenen Winkeln erforscht werden. Der anwählbare Screen ist doppelt so groß wie der Bildschirm und scrollt automatisch. Das Konzept der Navigation besteht aus einem sich endlos wiederholenden Lightbox-Raster, in dem der User die Produkte betrachten kann. /// **Le site peut être exploré sous plusieurs angles dans un affichage double écran. Le concept de navigation est une grille de cases via laquelle l'utilisateur peut parcourir les produits de façon intuitive, sans jamais atteindre la fin de la série.**

Info

Design Studio: Neue Digitale GmbH <www.neue-digitale.de>. /// **Design:** Elke Klinkhammer (Creative Direction); André Bourguignon (Senior Art Direction/Motion Design). /// **Programming:** Tom Acland (Technology Direction), Martin Anderle (Flash), Marius Bulla (Technology Project Management). /// **Others:** André Bourguignon, Britta Seidel (Concept Developmen); Christoph Riebling (Sound Design); Maximilian Schäfer (Project/Account Management). /// **Client:** adidas AG. /// **Tools:** Adobe Photoshop, Cinema 4D, Adobe After Effects, Adobe Flash. /// **Awards:** FWA (Site of the Day).

adidas
SPRINT BABY 670410

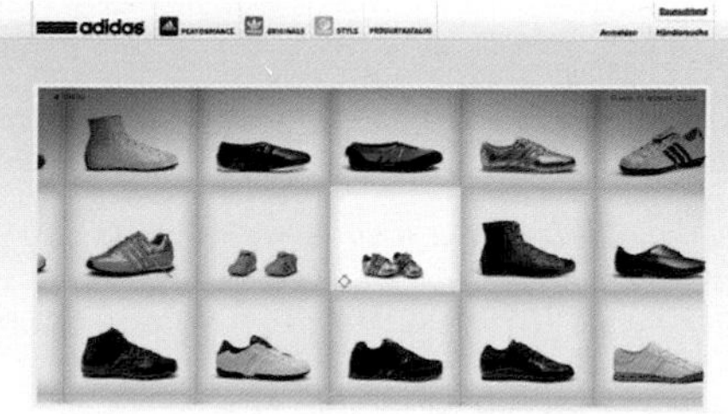

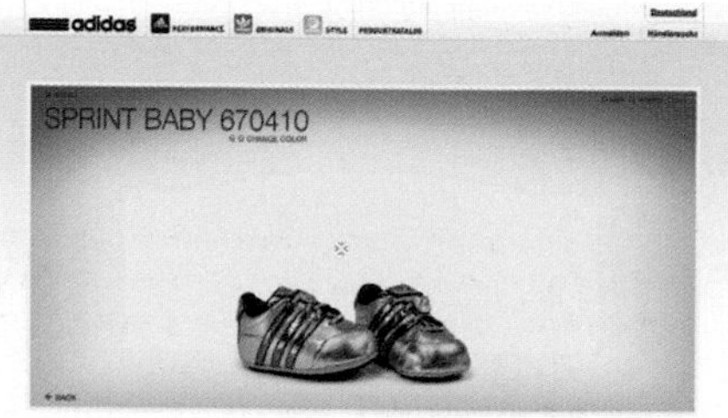

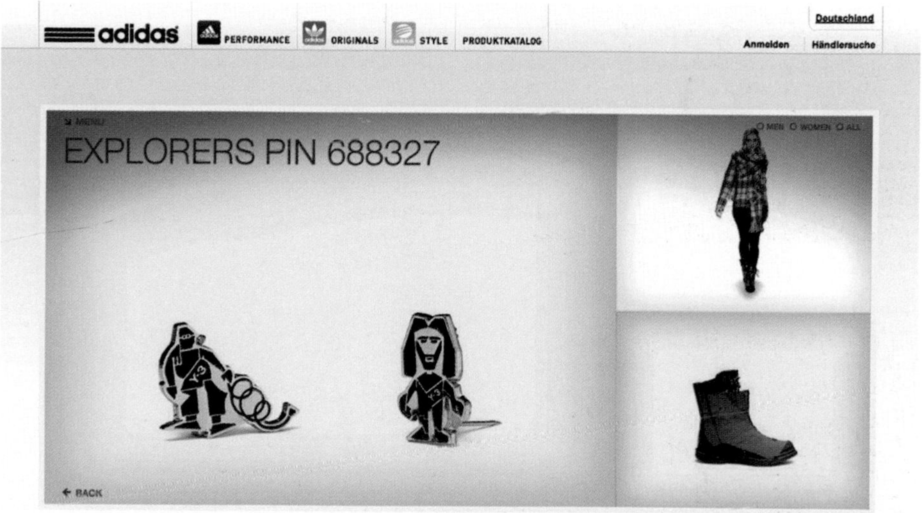

adidas
PERFORMANCE
ORIGINALS
STYLE
PRODUKTKATALOG
Deutschland
Anmelden
Händlersuche
MENU
EXPLORERS PIN 688327
MEN
WOMEN
ALL
BACK

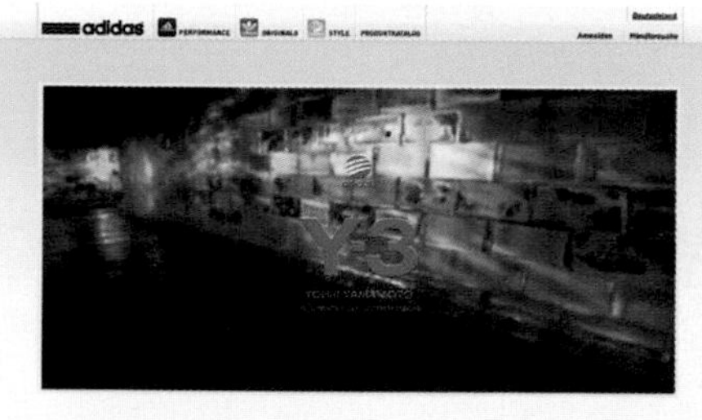

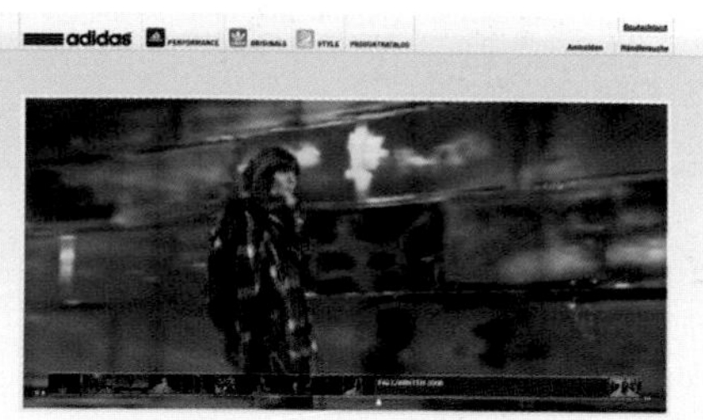

ADOBE CREATIVE MIND

UK

www.unit9.com/creativemind

2006

Concept

The original approach to this project had one simple rule, to speak to designers in their own language. The design was able to communicate on an informal level and immersed the user in a surreal environment of creativity and possibility. /// Der Ausgangspunkt dieses Projekts war die einfache Regel, dass Designer in ihrer eigenen Sprache angesprochen werden sollten. Dieses Design wurde auf einer informellen Ebene vermittelt, und der User kann in eine surreale Umgebung voller Kreativität und bunter Möglichkeiten eintauchen. /// **L'approche originale de ce projet répond à une règle simple : s'adresser aux designers dans leur propre langage. Le design a permis de communiquer en toute simplicité et de plonger l'utilisateur dans un environnement surréaliste de créativité et de possibilités.**

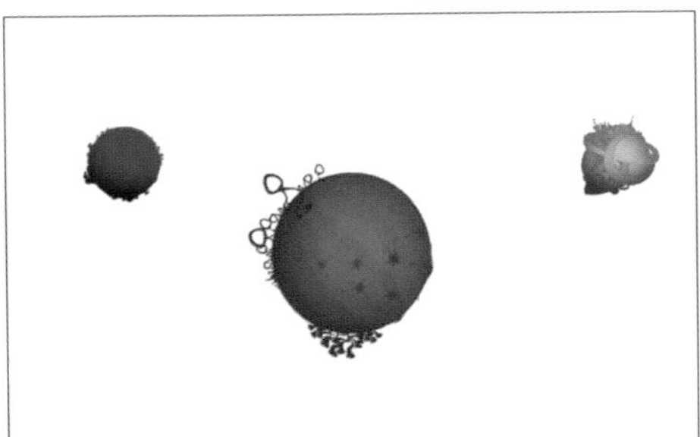

Info

Design Studio: Goodby Silverstein & Partners <www.gspsf.com>; unit9 <www.unit9.com>. /// **Design:** Goodby Silverstein & Partners: Keith Anderson, Mark Sikes, Spencer Riviera; unit9: Alex Jenkins, Robert Bader. /// **Programming:** unit9; Yates Buckley (Technical Director). /// **Client:** Adobe Systems Inc. /// **Tools:** Adobe Creative Suite. /// **Awards:** Webby, FWA (Site of The Month), FITC, FlashForward, Communication Arts Annual, Art Directors Club, Creative Review Annual, Bima, One Show, Clio Awards, Campaign Digital. /// **Cost:** 12 weeks.

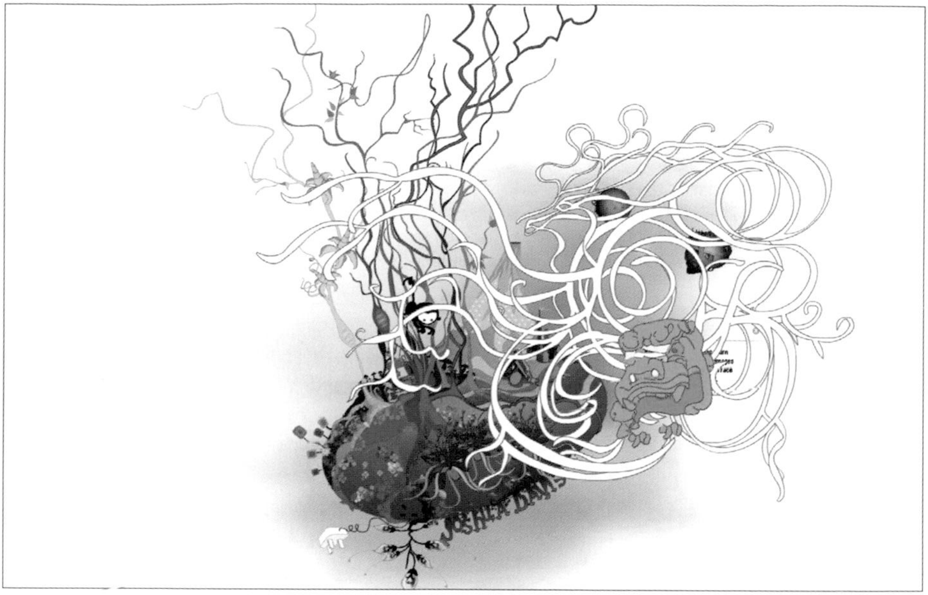

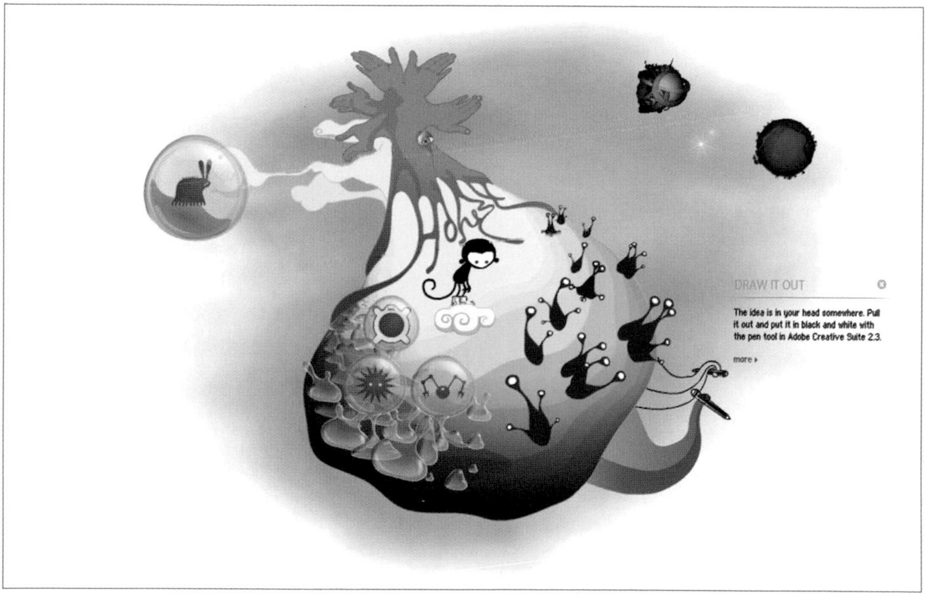

DRAW IT OUT

The idea is in your head somewhere. Pull it out and put it in black and white with the pen tool in Adobe Creative Suite 2.3.

more ›

&CO

CANADA

www.andco.com

2007

Concept

By the use of storytelling, the site aims to rethink the way this architecture company and its architects may be represented, and the way their work philosophy can be communicated on the Internet. /// Durch Storytelling erfindet die Site die Art neu, wie dieses Architekturbüro mit seinen Architekten dargestellt und wie deren Philosophie im Internet vermittelt wird. /// Par le biais de la communication narrative, le site se propose de repenser le mode de représentation de ce cabinet d'architecture et de ses architectes, et la façon dont leur philosophie de travail peut être exposée sur Internet.

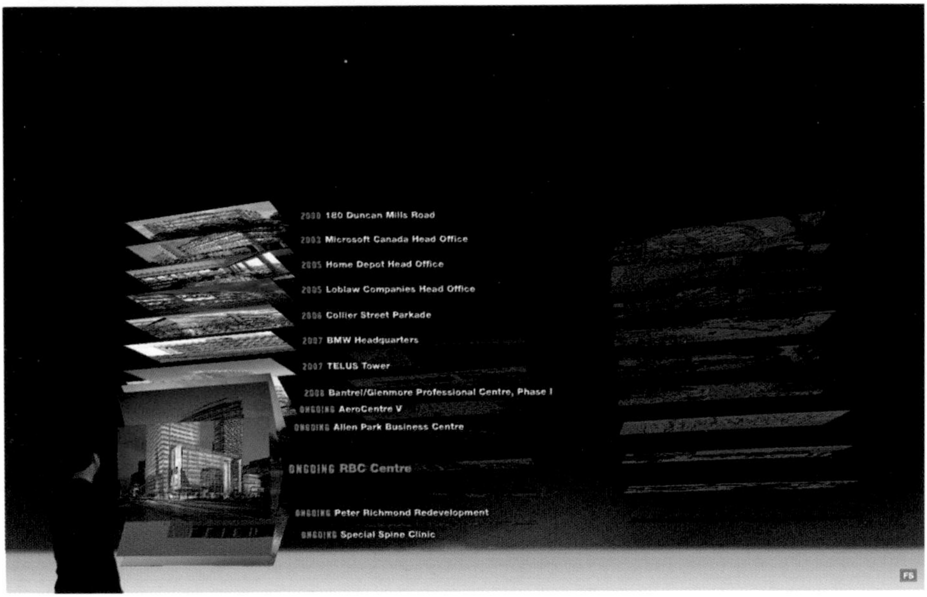

Info

Design Studio: HELLOHELLO!! <www.HelloHello.BZ>. /// **Design:** Thierry Loa, Anthony Murray. /// **Programming:** Thierry Loa (Front-end/Flash AS); Clayton Partridge (Back-end/CMS). /// **Others:** Production/Creation/Direction: Thierry Loa; Anthony Murray (3D). Richard Devine (Music/Sound); Jorge Weisz (DOP); Karl and Jordan Jenkins (Lighting). /// **Client:** &Co Architects. /// **Tools:** Adobe Flash, ActionScript, Papervision 3D, Premiere, After Effects, Lightware 3D, Sound Forge, Adobe ColdFusion, Flash Remoting. /// **Awards:** FWA (Site of the Day), Webby Awards, ADCC Awards 2008. /// **Cost:** 5 months.

ANGELA DOBRICK

GERMANY

www.angela-dobrick.de

2008

Concept

Very intuitive and easy to use. Also a nice mixture between rollovers, scrolling, and clicking. /// Mit ihrer schönen Mischung aus Rollover, Scrolling und Klicken ist diese Site sehr intuitiv und einfach zu benutzen. /// **Très intuitif et simple d'emploi. Avec, également, un mélange réussi d'effets de survol, de défilements et de clics.**

ANGELA DOBRICK | GESTALTUNG
NEWS
MAGAZIN
CORPORATE
BUCH
INFORMATION
KONTAKT

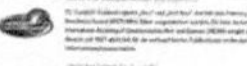

ANGELA DOBRICK | GESTALTUNG
MAGAZIN
FLOW – EUROPCAR

ANGELA DOBRICK | GESTALTUNG
BUCH

HARDCOVER

Info

Design Studio: Tilt Design Studio <www.tiltdesignstudio.com>. /// **Design:** Marc Antosch (Art Direction/Design), Felix Schultze (Animation Concept/Flash Effects). /// **Programming:** Felix Schultze. /// **Client:** Angela Dobrick. /// **Tools:** Adobe Flash, ActionScript. /// **Cost:** ca. 160 hours.

APPLETISER

UK

www.appletiser.co.uk

2007

Concept

This product website is composed of a simple yet effective vertical menu, slightly animated, and with well-chosen music in the background. /// Diese Produkt-Website besteht aus einem einfachen, aber sehr effektiven vertikalen Menü mit dezenten Animationen und einer passend gewählten Hintergrundmusik. /// Le site Web de ce produit compte un menu vertical aussi simple qu'efficace, avec quelques animations et un accompagnement musical bien choisi en arrière-plan.

Info

Design Studio: magneticNorth <www.madebymn.co.uk>. /// **Design:** magneticNorth. /// **Programming:** magneticNorth. /// **Client:** Coca-Cola Enterprises Limited. /// **Tools:** Adobe Flash, Adobe Photoshop, XML, ActionScript.

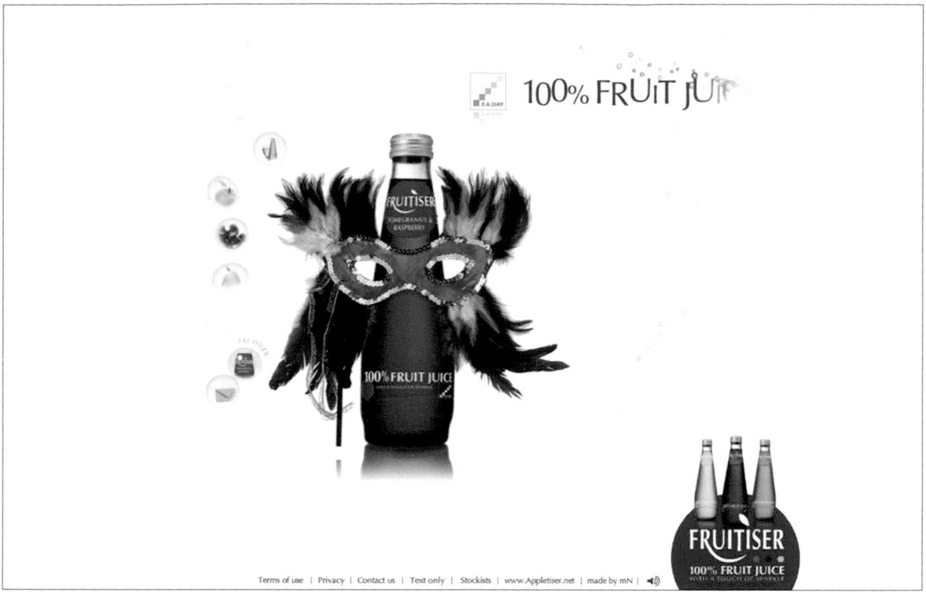

100% FRUIT JUI

FRUITISER
POMEGRANATE & RASPBERRY
100% FRUIT JUICE

FRUITISER
100% FRUIT JUICE

Terms of use | Privacy | Contact us | Text only | Stockists | www.Appletiser.net | made by mN |

ARTERIAL

BRAZIL

www.arterial.tv

2008

Concept

A minimalist interface for this multidisciplinary design studio, with few elements to click. The clickable areas are all within the images, which are grouped separately and are fully interactive with zoom and drag. /// Ein minimalistisches Interface für dieses interdisziplinäre Designstudio, auf dem es nur wenige anklickbare Elemente gibt. Diese Bereiche befinden sich alle in den Bildern, die separat gruppiert und durch Zoomen und Ziehen komplett interaktiv sind. /// Une interface minimaliste pour ce studio de design multidisciplinaire, avec de rares éléments sur lesquels cliquer. Les zones à sélectionner sont toutes intégrées aux images, regroupées séparément et totalement interactives via le zoom et par glissement.

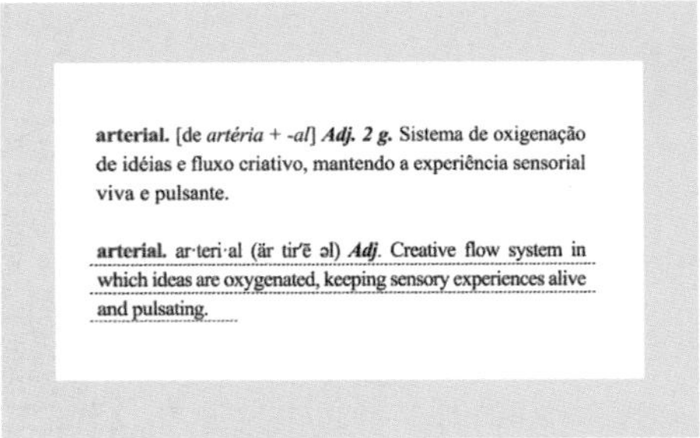

arterial. [de *artéria* + *-al*] ***Adj. 2 g.*** Sistema de oxigenação de idéias e fluxo criativo, mantendo a experiência sensorial viva e pulsante.
arterial. ar·teri·al (är tir′ē əl) ***Adj.*** Creative flow system in which ideas are oxygenated, keeping sensory experiences alive and pulsating.

ARTERIAL
CONTACT
STRANGE
BE A FRIEND TO ART
CALABASH
KUAT
KUAT
regular

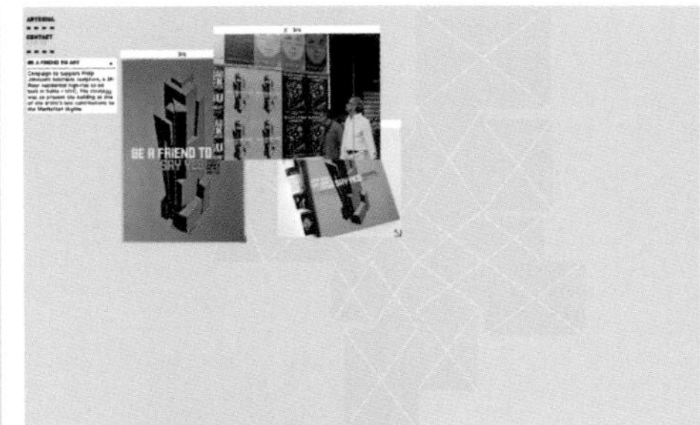

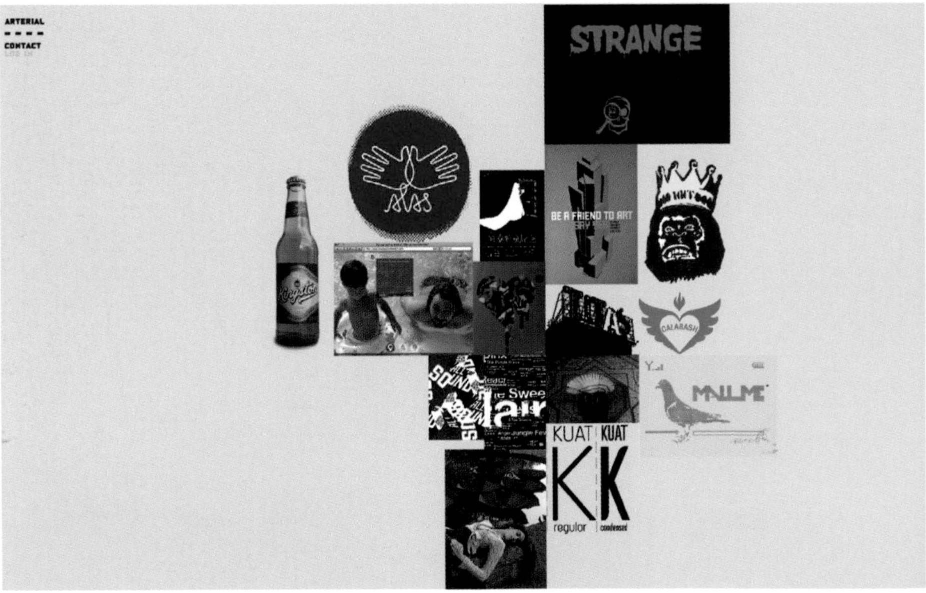

Info

Design Studio: Arterial <www.arterial.tv>. /// **Design:** Chris Calvet, Marcos Leme. /// **Programming:** Luciano Bonachela <www.bonacode.com>. /// **Others:** Renata Perrone (Translation); Marc Van Lengen (Photography). /// **Client:** Arterial. /// **Tools:** Adobe Flash, ActionScript, PHP. /// **Cost:** 4 weeks.

ARTERIAL
CONTACT
LOG IN
DUB VISIONS
Drawing for the DUB VISIONS collective exhibit held in Rio. It constructs a bridge between Upsetter's Super Ape album, Jamaica's sound system and New York's hip-hop culture.
3/3
play video
MACACOS ME MORDAM
1/1
DUB NA PAREDE
ARTERIAL
CONTACT
LOG IN
MARIA FILÓ VERAO 06
Direction, concept and development of visual identity and catalogs for a fashion brand from Rio.
MORE
MARIA FILÓ VERAO 07
MARIA FILÓ OUT 06
2/2
FELIZ ANIVERSÁRIO!
Maria Filó
2/12
2/4

ASYLUM

FRANCE

www.asylum.fr

2008

Concept

Double dash-board navigation throughout, with full-screen image display. /// Die Navigation erfolgt über ein zweiteiliges Dashboard, die Bilder werden bildschirmfüllend dargestellt. /// **Une navigation à partir d'un tableau de bord double et un affichage plein écran.**

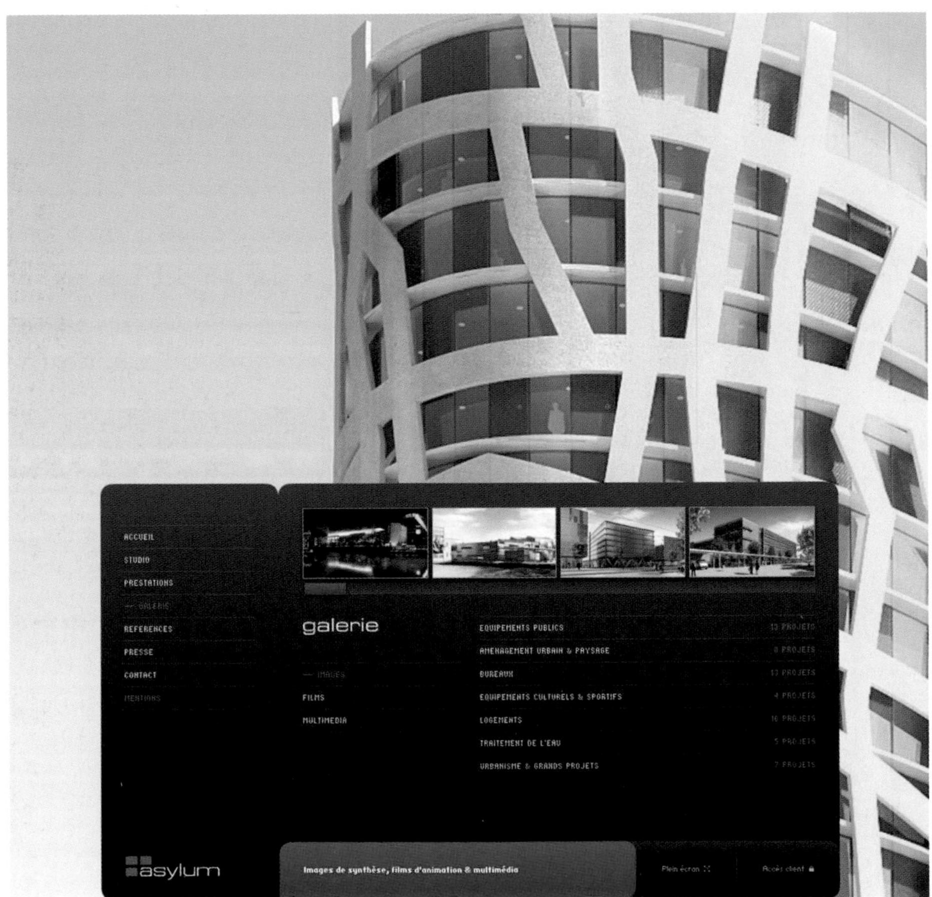

Info

DESIGN STUDIO: Danka Studio <www.dankastudio.fr>. /// **DESIGN:** Guillaume Bonnecase. /// **PROGRAMMING:** Grégoire Gerardin. /// **OTHERS:** João Cabral (Project Manager). /// **CLIENT:** Asylum. /// **TOOLS:** Adobe Photoshop, Flash, XML, Php. /// **AWARDS:** FWA Site of the Day. /// **COST:** 150–200 hours.

Arte Charpentier
LE COURS
OXYGENE
asylum
Images de synthèse, films d'animation & multimédia

asylum
Images de synthèse, films d'animation & multimédia

AXE SAÔNE ARCHITECTS

FRANCE

www.axesaone.fr

2007

Concept

A real Flash 3-D poetic-wandering navigation through a field of poppy flowers. Each poppy is a section or a project of the agency. /// Die poetische und bewegliche Navigation in echtem Flash-3-D findet in einem Mohnblumenfeld statt. Jede Mohnblüte stellt einen Bereich oder ein Projekt der Agentur dar. /// **Une véritable navigation d'itinéraire poétique 3D en Flash au milieu d'un champ de coquelicots. Chaque fleur correspond à une section ou un projet de l'agence.**

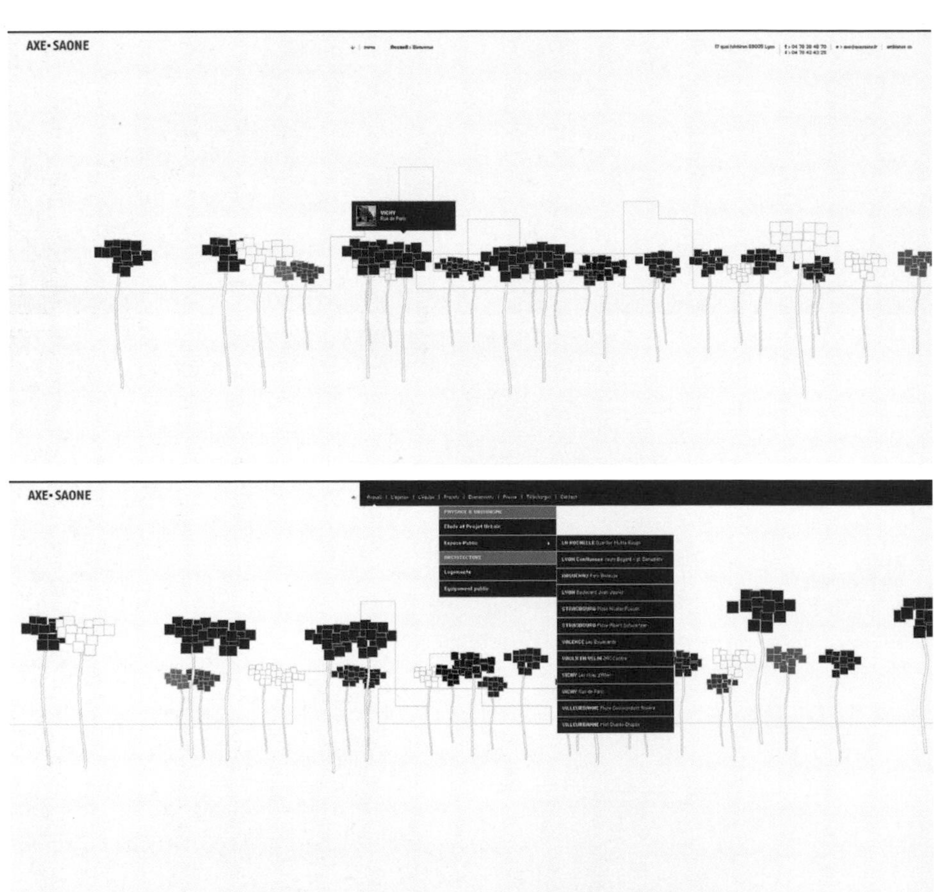

Info

Design Studio: Danka Studio <www.dankastudio.fr>. /// **Design:** Guillaume Bonnecase. /// **Programming:** Grégoire Gerardin. /// **Others:** João Cabral (Project Manager). /// **Client:** Axe Saône Architects. /// **Tools:** Adobe Photoshop, Flash, XML, Php. /// **Awards:** FWA Site of the Day. /// **Cost:** 150–200 hours.

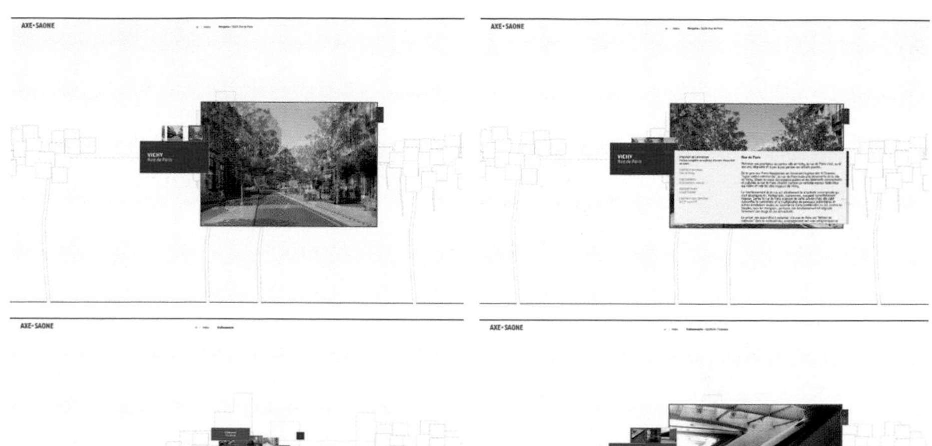
AXE•SAONE
VICHY
Rue de Paris
AXE•SAONE
VICHY
Rue de Paris
Rue de Paris

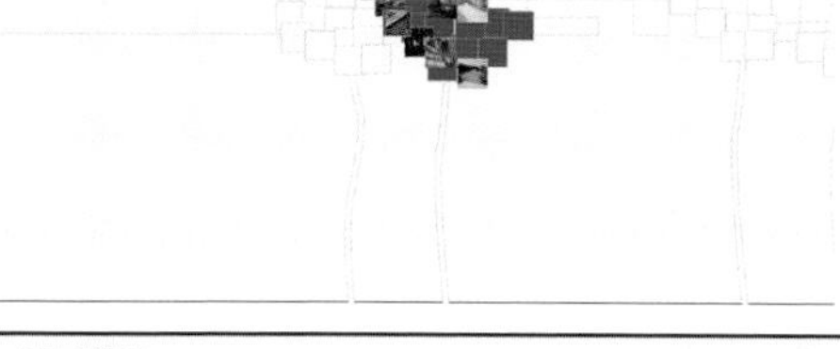
AXE•SAONE

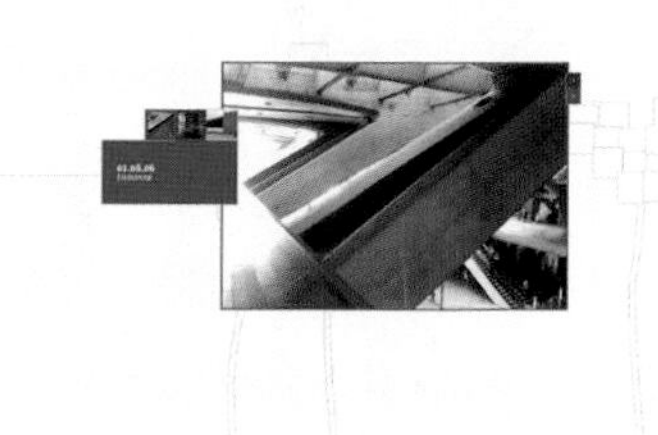
AXE•SAONE

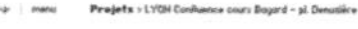

AXE•SAONE
menu
Projets › LYON Confluence cours Bayard - pl. Denuzière
LYON Confluence
cours Bayard - pl. Denuzière
Sous les pries

B_CUBE ARCHITECTS

FRANCE

www.bcube.fr

2007

Concept

An unfolding site-map combined with strong zoom-in and zoom-out camera movements. /// Diese Site-Map entwickelt sich, indem an die Menüpunkte weitere Unterpunkte angestückt werden, und setzt beim Hinein- und Herauszoomen flotte Kamerafahrten ein. /// **Un plan du site qui se développe, assorti d'importants mouvements de caméra avec des zooms avant et arrière.**

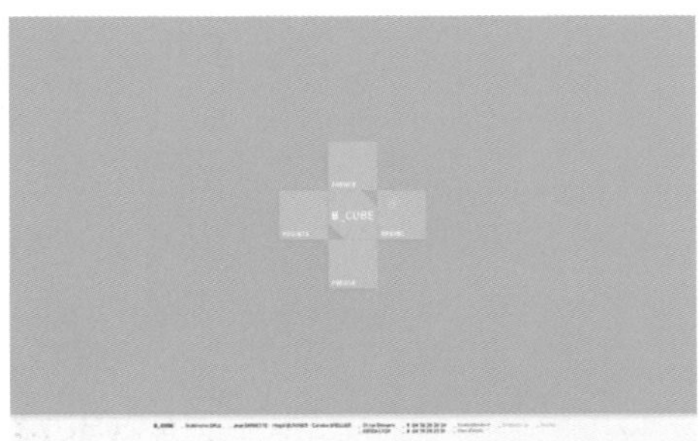

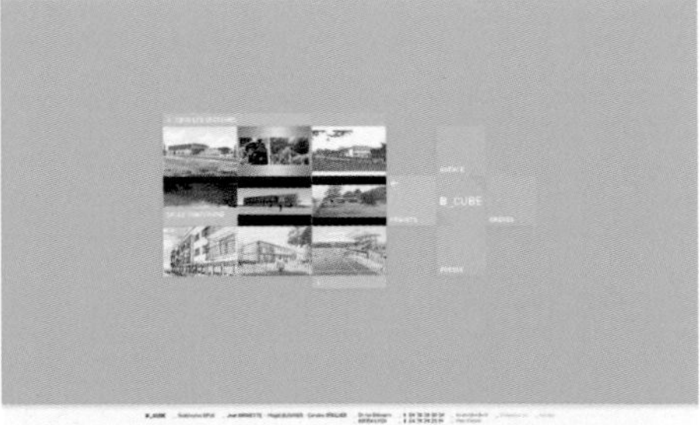

Info

Design Studio: Danka Studio <www.dankastudio.fr>. /// **Design:** Guillaume Bonnecase. /// **Programming:** Grégoire Gerardin. /// **Others:** João Cabral (Project Manager). /// **Client:** B_Cube Architects Agency. /// **Tools:** Adobe Photoshop, Flash, XML, Php. /// **Awards:** FWA Site of the Day. /// **Cost:** 150–200 hours.

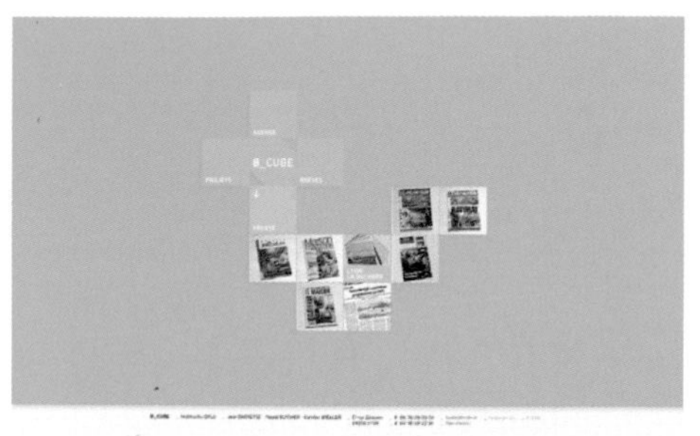

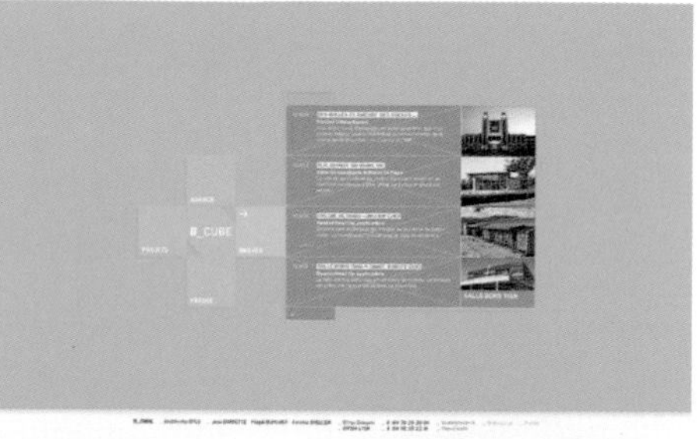

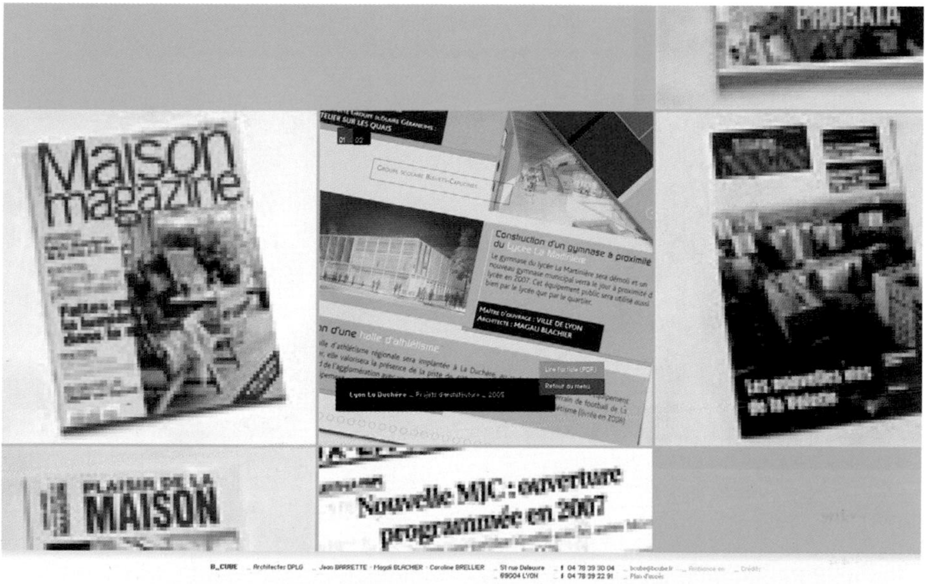

Maison magazine

Construction d'un gymnase à proximité du Lycée La Martinière

Maître d'ouvrage : VILLE DE LYON
Architecte : MAGALI BLACHIER

Lyon La Duchère _ Projets d'architecture _ 2005

PLAISIR DE LA MAISON

Nouvelle MJC : ouverture programmée en 2007

B_CUBE _ Architectes DPLG _ Jean BARRETTE · Magali BLACHIER · Caroline BRELLIER _ 51 rue Deleuvre _ 69004 LYON _ t 04 78 39 30 04 _ f 04 78 39 22 91 _ bcube@bcube.fr _ Plan d'accès

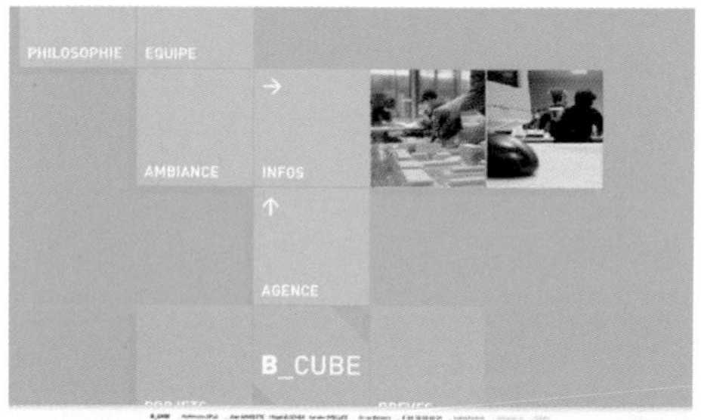

BLOOM

UK

www.bbc.co.uk/bloom

2008

Concept

A website for sustainability education, Bloom allows the user to learn about a carbon neutral life in a playful environment. /// Auf Bloom (einer Lern-Webseite zum Thema Nachhaltigkeit) erfährt der User in einer spielerischen Umgebung mehr über ein CO_2-neutrales Leben. /// Site Web pour l'apprentissage du développement durable, Bloom permet à l'utilisateur de découvrir une vie sans carbone dans un environnement ludique.

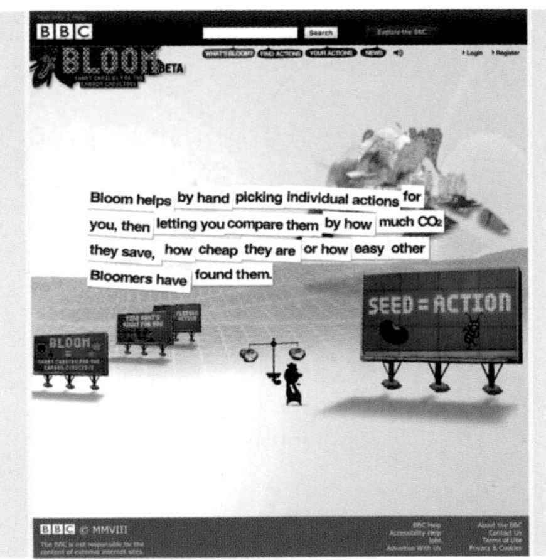

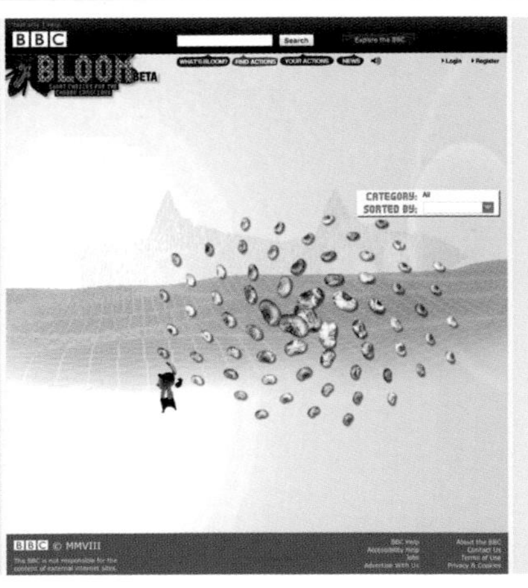

Info

DESIGN STUDIO: magneticNorth <www.madebymn.co.uk>. /// **DESIGN:** magneticNorth. /// **PROGRAMMING:** magneticNorth; BBC in-house. /// **OTHERS:** Daniel Brown (Digital Artist). /// **CLIENT:** BBC. /// **TOOLS:** Adobe Flash, Adobe Photoshop, Javascript, XML, ActionScript. /// **AWARDS:** FWA (Site of the Day), IVCA Clarion Awards (Winner 2008), Y Design Awards (winner 2008), Pixel Awards (Nominee 2008).

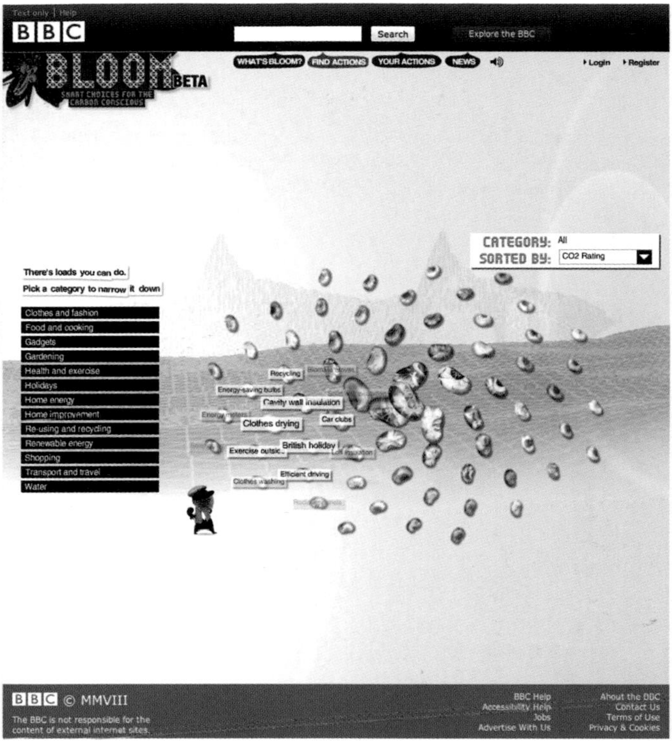

Text only | Help
BBC
Search
Explore the BBC
BLOOM BETA
SMART CHOICES FOR THE CARBON CONSCIOUS
WHAT'S BLOOM?
FIND ACTIONS
YOUR ACTIONS
NEWS
Login
Register
CATEGORY: All
SORTED BY: CO2 Rating
There's loads you can do.
Pick a category to narrow it down
Clothes and fashion
Food and cooking
Gadgets
Gardening
Health and exercise
Holidays
Home energy
Home improvement
Re-using and recycling
Renewable energy
Shopping
Transport and travel
Water
Recycling
Energy-saving bulbs
Cavity wall insulation
Clothes drying
Car clubs
British holiday
Efficient driving
Clothes washing
BBC © MMVIII
The BBC is not responsible for the content of external internet sites.
BBC Help
Accessibility Help
Jobs
Advertise With Us
About the BBC
Contact Us
Terms of Use
Privacy & Cookies

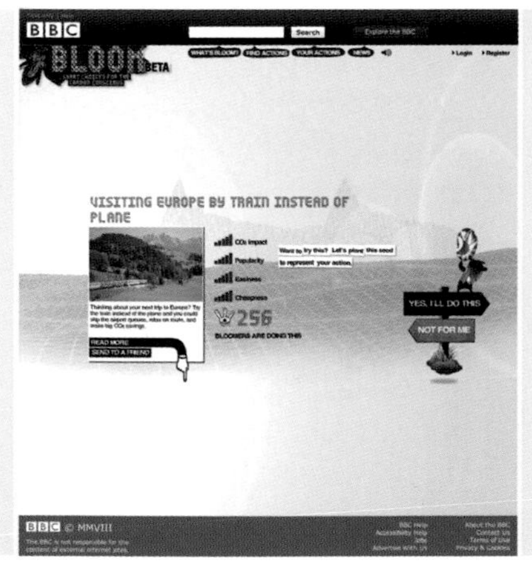
BBC
BLOOM BETA
VISITING EUROPE BY TRAIN INSTEAD OF PLANE
YES, I'LL DO THIS
NOT FOR ME
256
BBC © MMVIII

BBC
BLOOM BETA
VISITING EUROPE BY TRAIN INSTEAD OF PLANE
CLOSE
256
EASINESS
RELATED ACTIONS
BBC © MMVIII

BMW – RELEARN TO DRIVE

USA

www.relearntodrive.com

2008

Concept

BMW's Performance Center is the only privately owned driving school from a premium car manufacturer and this website offers a playful insight into what the driving challenge would be like there. /// Das Performance Center von BMW ist die einzige privat geführte Fahrschule eines großen Autoherstellers. Die Website ermöglicht auf spielerische Weise Einsichten darüber, worin die Herausforderung beim Autofahren besteht. /// **Le centre de performances de BMW est la seule école de conduite privée d'un constructeur automobile. Ce site Web offre une vision amusante de ce à quoi y ressemblerait l'épreuve de conduite.**

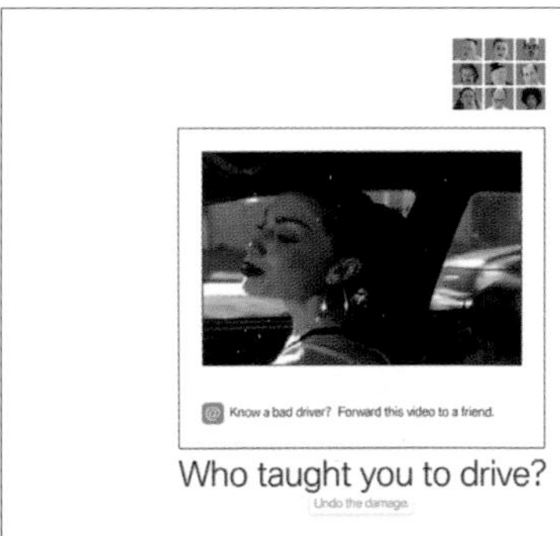

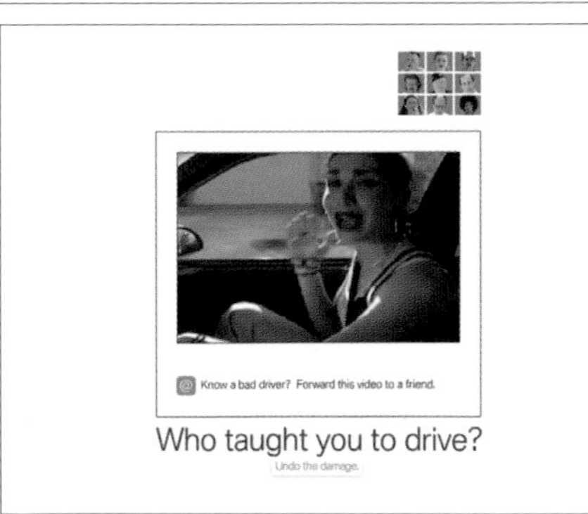

Info

DESIGN STUDIO: JUXT Interactive <www.juxtinteractive.com>. /// **DESIGN:** Scott Staab, Chad Laughlin, Mark Ray, Ryan Martindale. /// **OTHERS:** Aaron Kovan (Broadcast Producer), Jeff Bond (Interactive Producer), Kelly Harris (Account Supervisor), Nick Gesualdi (Account Manager), Lani DeGuire (Creative Project Manager). /// **CLIENT:** BMW. /// **TOOLS:** HTML, Adobe Photoshop, Adobe Flash, Adobe Illustrator, Adobe InDesign, Final Cut, Adobe After Effects. /// **AWARDS:** OC Ad Club Award, Webby Award (People's Voice), Creativity Award, Create Award. /// **COST:** 12 months.

CHIMNEY POT PARK

UK

www.urbansplash.co.uk/chimneypotpark

2006

Concept

For this real-estate sales Internet page, the interface is a pop-up book, fully 3-D, with different pages opening for each page of the menu, as well as a zoom in-and-out feature for more detailed information. /// Bei dieser Internetseite für Immobilienangebote besteht das Interface aus einem komplett dreidimensionalen Popup-Buch, aus dem heraus sich für jeden Menüpunkt neue Seiten öffnen. Ergänzt wird es durch das Feature, in die Detailinfos hinein- und herauszoomen zu können. /// Pour cette page Internet de vente immobilière, l'interface est un livre en incrustation, entièrement 3D, avec des pages différentes qui s'ouvrent pour chaque section du menu, ainsi qu'une fonction de zoom avant et arrière pour des informations plus détaillées.

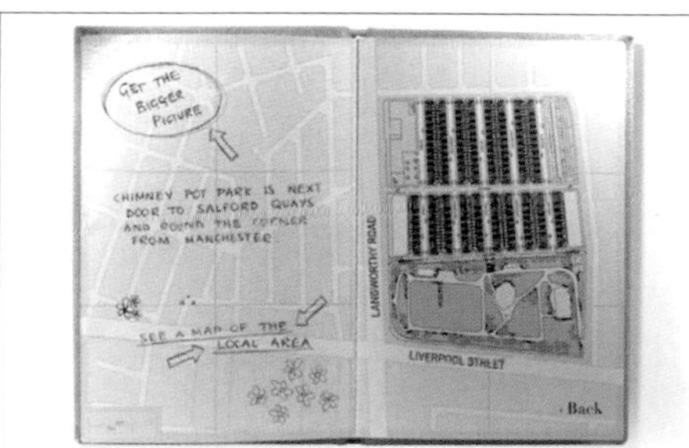

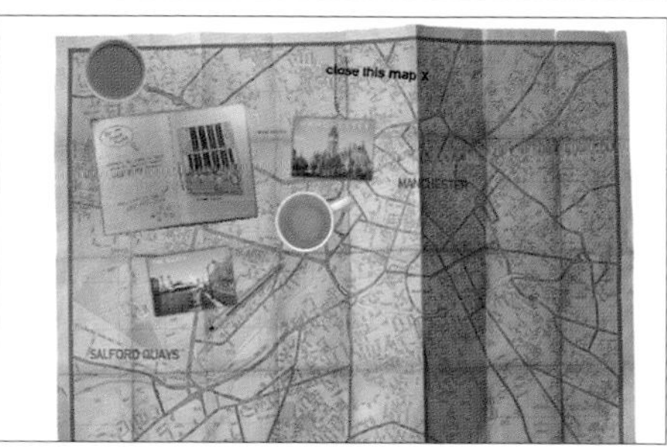

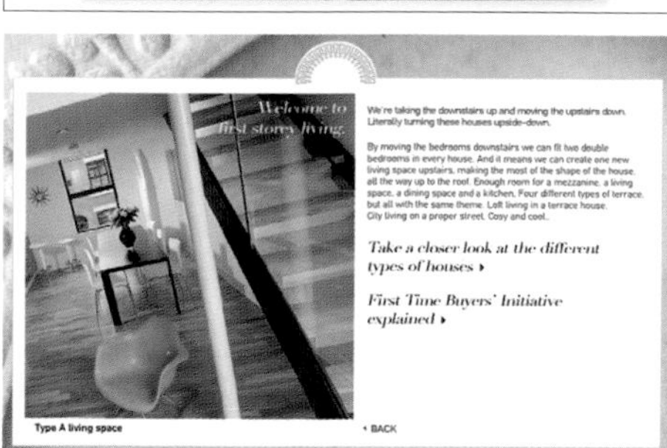

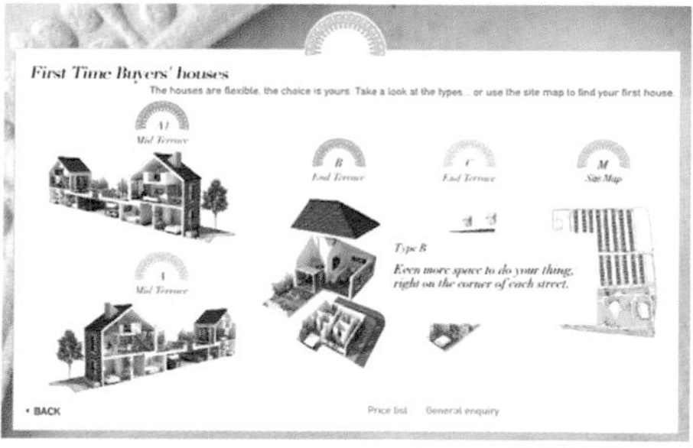

Info

Design Studio: magneticNorth <www.madebymn.co.uk>. /// **Design:** magneticNorth. /// **Programming:** magneticNorth. /// **Client:** Urban Splash. /// **Tools:** Adobe Flash, Adobe Photoshop. /// **Awards:** The Roses Design Awards 2006 (Best Website – Gold).

CENTERPLAN

UK

www.centerplan.dk

2007

Concept

From the start the main menu loads directly from the cursor, letting the user control the action. By way of rewarding curiosity, the site draws the user deeper into the carefully layered content. /// Gleich zu Anfang wird das Hauptmenü direkt über den Cursor geladen, sodass der User alle Aktionen steuert. Seine Neugier wird belohnt, indem die Site ihn immer tiefer in den sorgfältig geschichteten Content zieht. /// Dès le début, le menu principal se charge directement depuis le curseur, ce qui laisse le contrôle à l'utilisateur. Pour récompenser sa curiosité, le site plonge l'utilisateur dans un contenu soigneusement organisé en couches.

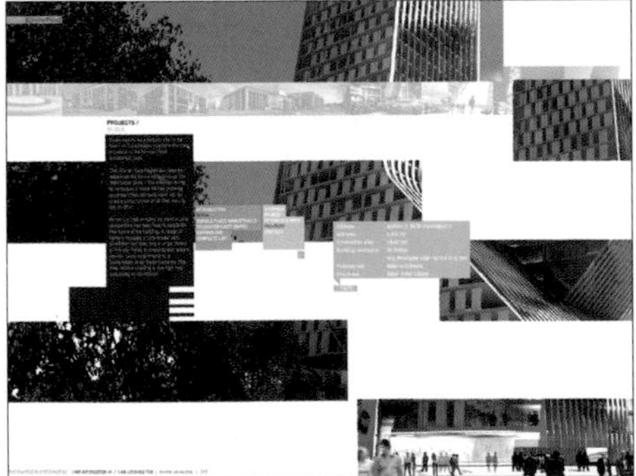

Info

Design Studio: Jaques Vanzo <www.jaquesvanzo.com; unit9 <www.unit9.com>. /// **Design:** Luisa Vanzo (Jaques Vanzo); Robert Bader (unit9). /// **Programming:** unit9; Yates Buckley (Technical Director). /// **Client:** Centerplan.dk. /// **Tools:** Adobe Creative Suite. /// **Awards:** Design Week (Finalist), BIMA (Finalist), Webby (Honoree). /// **Cost:** 8 weeks.

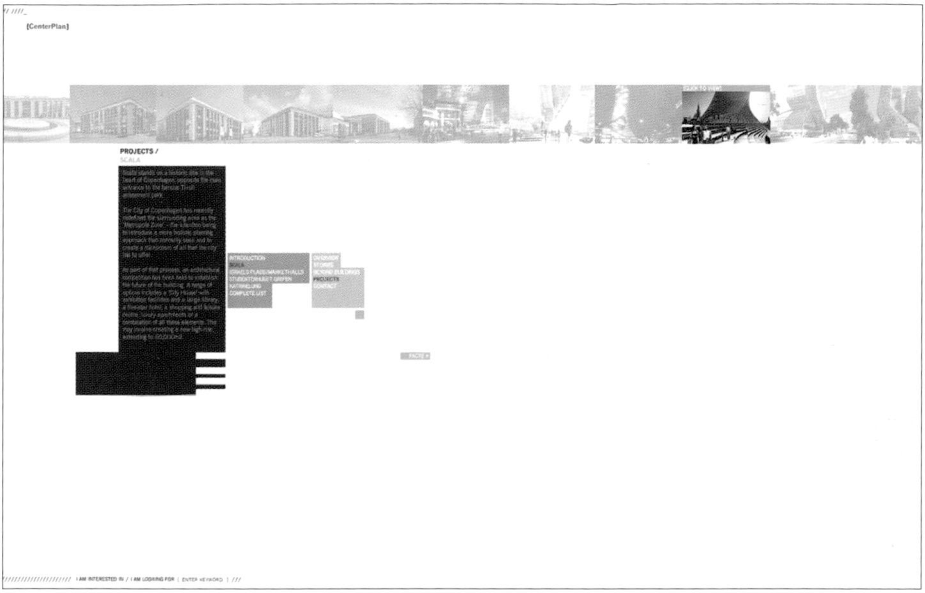

// ////_

[CenterPlan]

PROJECTS /
SCALA

INTRODUCTION
SCALA
ISRAELS PLADS/MARKETHALLS
STUDENTERHUSET GRIFFEN
KATRINELUND
COMPLETE LIST

OVERVIEW
STORIES
BEYOND BUILDINGS
PROJECTS
CONTACT

//////////////////////// I AM INTERESTED IN / I AM LOOKING FOR | ENTER KEYWORD | ///

// ////_

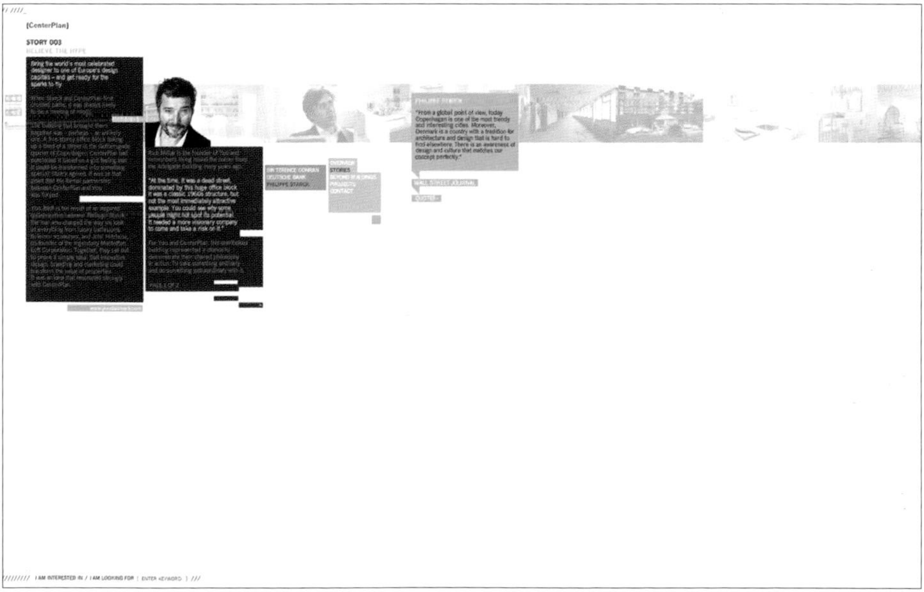

[CenterPlan]

STORY 003
BELIEVE THE HYPE

Bring the world's most celebrated designer to one of Europe's design capitals – and get ready for the sparks to fly.

"At the time, it was a dead street, dominated by this huge office block. It was a classic 1960s structure, but not the most immediately attractive example. You could see why some people might not spot its potential. It needed a more visionary company to come and take a risk on it."

SIR TERENCE CONRAN
DEUTSCHE BANK
PHILIPPE STARCK

OVERVIEW
STORIES
BEYOND BUILDINGS
PROJECTS
CONTACT

"From a global point of view, today Copenhagen is one of the most trendy and interesting cities. Moreover, Denmark is a country with a tradition for architecture and design that is hard to find elsewhere. There is an awareness of design and culture that matches our concept perfectly."

WALL STREET JOURNAL

//////// I AM INTERESTED IN / I AM LOOKING FOR | ENTER KEYWORD | ///

CHRIS WOODS

CANADA/USA

www.chriswoods.ca

2008

Concept

Once a user jumps into the portfolio, everything but the item chosen is hidden. The user can either hover over any edge of the browser (top, right, bottom, left) to reveal the navigation, or can use the arrow keys on the keyboard. /// Betritt der User das Portfolio, wird alles außer dem ausgewählten Element versteckt. Er kann mit der Maus an den äußeren Rändern des Browsers (oben, unten, links, rechts) die Navigation erscheinen lassen oder mit den Pfeiltasten weiterblättern. /// Lorsqu'un utilisateur entre dans le portfolio, tout, à l'exception de l'élément sélectionné, est masqué. Il peut survoler n'importe quel bord du navigateur (haut, droite, bas, gauche) pour afficher la navigation, ou bien utiliser les touches fléchées du clavier.

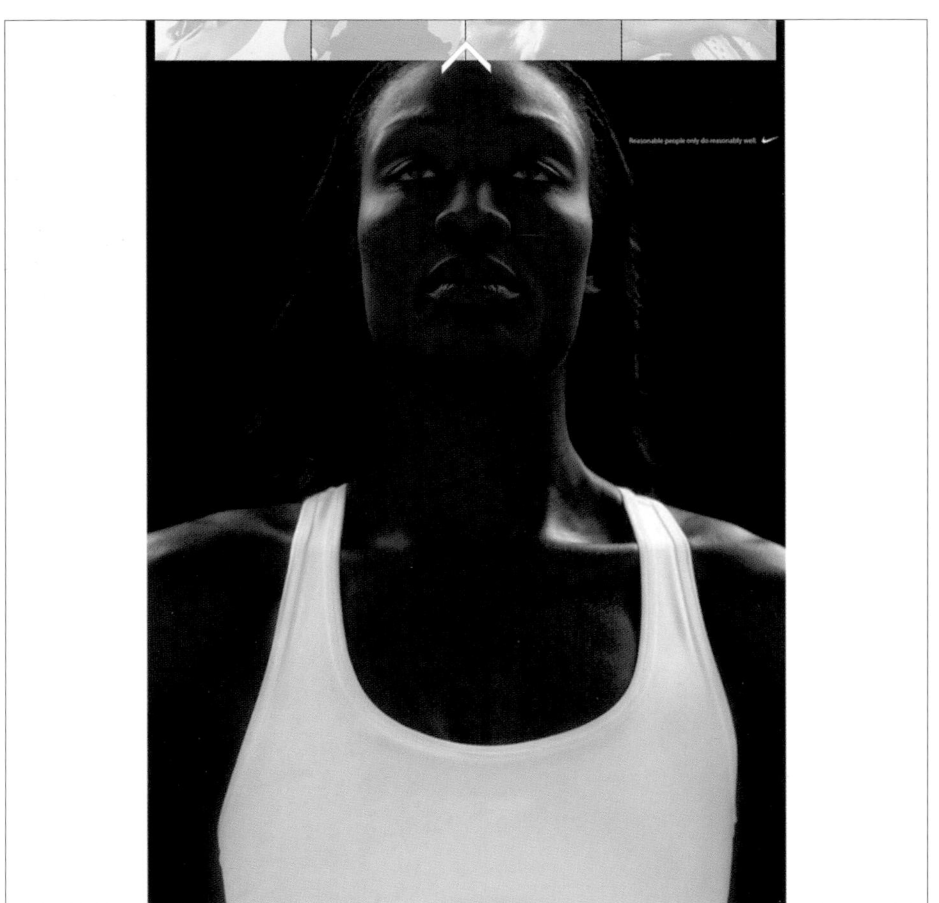

Info

Design Studio: GRAND Creative Inc. <www.wearegrand.com>. /// **Design:** Luke Canning. /// **Programming:** Matthew Quinn. /// **Client:** Chris Woods. /// **Tools:** Adobe Creative Suite. /// **Cost:** 225 hours.

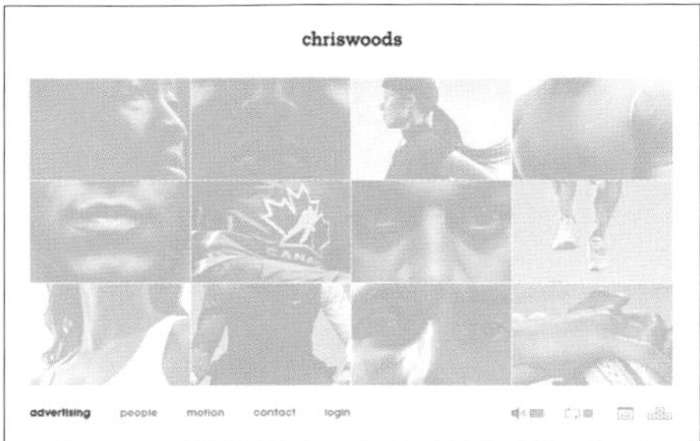
chriswoods
advertising
people
motion
contact
login

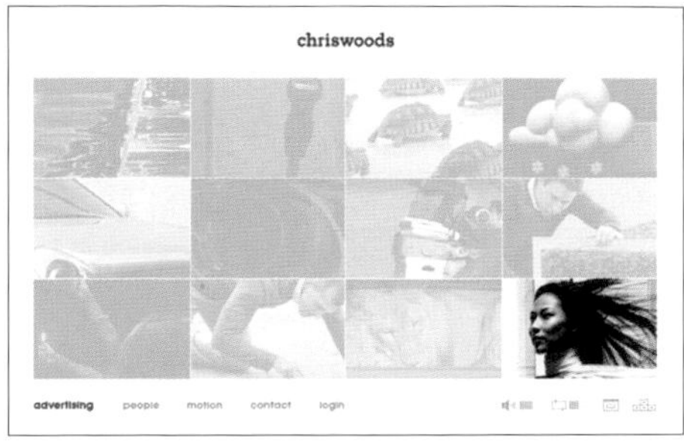
chriswoods
advertising
people
motion
contact
login

VOLVO OF TORONTO.
AN EXPERIENCE UNLIKE ANY OTHER.
VOLVO
for life

COCA-COLA LIGHT FLAVOURS

BRAZIL

www.cocacolalight.com.br/sabores

2008

Concept

In this navigation you can turn the planet round and discover what the flavors are in other parts of the world. The home-page is also carefully illustrated and animated. /// Bei dieser Navigation wird die Erde gedreht, um zu entdecken, wie Coca Cola in anderen Gegenden der Welt schmeckt. Die Homepage ist schön illustriert und enthält viele Animationen. /// Dans cette navigation, vous pouvez faire tourner la planète et découvrir des odeurs d'autres pays du monde. La page d'accueil est illustrée et animée avec soin.

Info

DESIGN STUDIO: Gringo <www.gringo.nu>. /// DESIGN: Gringo. /// PROGRAMMING: Gringo. /// OTHERS: Santa (3D); Gaia (Sound Design). /// CLIENT: Coca-Cola. /// TOOLS: Adobe Creative Suite, 3D Studio Max. /// COST: 2,5 months.

TEMOS O MELHOR LUGAR DO MUNDO PARA VOCÊ. CONFIRA O BALÃO VERMELHO.

TEMOS O MELHOR LUGAR DO MUNDO PARA VOCÊ. CONFIRA O BALÃO VERMELHO.

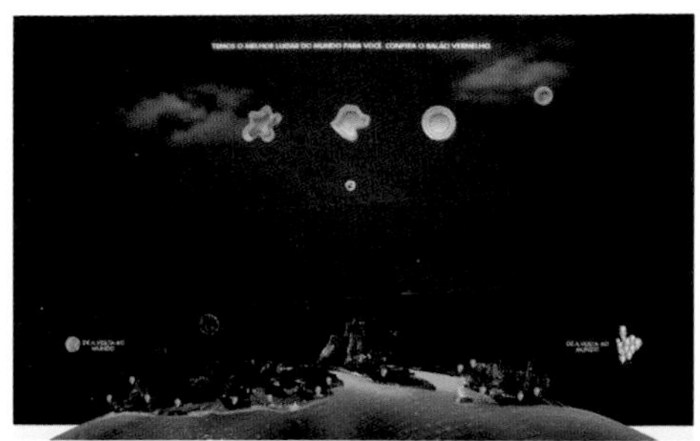

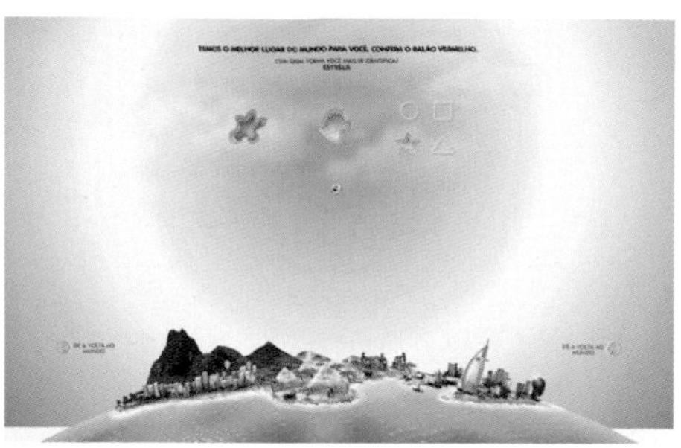

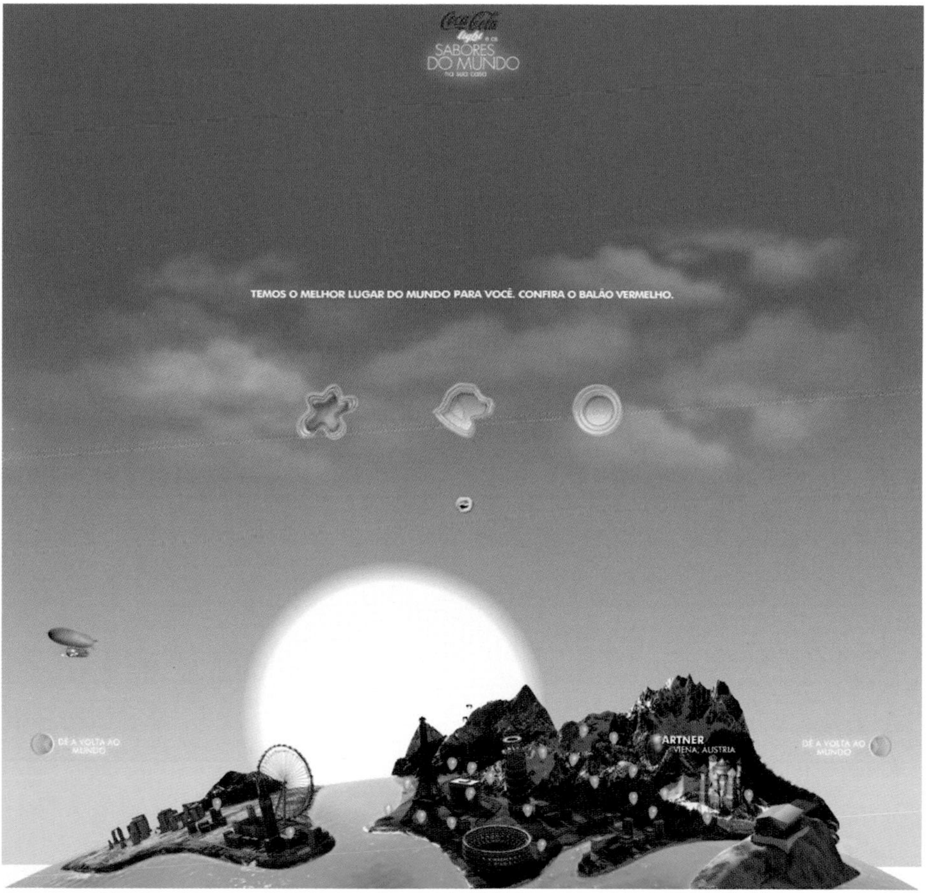

Coca-Cola
light e os
SABORES
DO MUNDO
na sua casa
TEMOS O MELHOR LUGAR DO MUNDO PARA VOCÊ. CONFIRA O BALÃO VERMELHO.
DÊ A VOLTA AO MUNDO
ARTNER
VIENA, AUSTRIA
DÊ A VOLTA AO MUNDO

COME INTO THE CLOSET LET'S DANCE

SWEDEN

2008

http://demo.fb.se/e/ikea/letsdance/site

Concept

Campaign to promote IKEA's wardrobe solutions. All the movements on the website are controlled by sound and music. Users can change songs, upload their own music, play on the keyboard, or sing into the microphone. /// Diese Kampagne wirbt für die Garderobenlösungen von IKEA. Die Bewegungen auf der Website werden komplett über Klänge und Musik gesteuert. Die User können andere Songs auswählen, eigene Musik hochladen, auf dem Keyboard spielen oder in ihr Mikrofon singen. /// **Campagne pour la promotion de solutions de rangements de vêtements d'IKEA. Tous les mouvements dans le site Web sont contrôlés par des sons et de la musique. Les utilisateurs peuvent changer les chansons, télécharger leur propre musique, jouer sur le clavier et chanter dans le microphone.**

Info

DESIGN STUDIO: Forsman & Bodenfors <www.fb.se>. /// DESIGN: Forsman & Bodenfors. /// PROGRAMMING: Kokokaka Entertainent. /// CLIENT: IKEA. /// TOOLS: Adobe Video Production Suite, RED Camera Software.

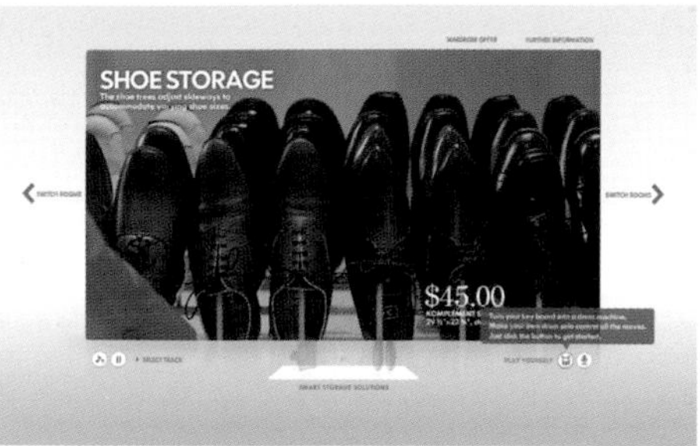
SHOE STORAGE
$45.00

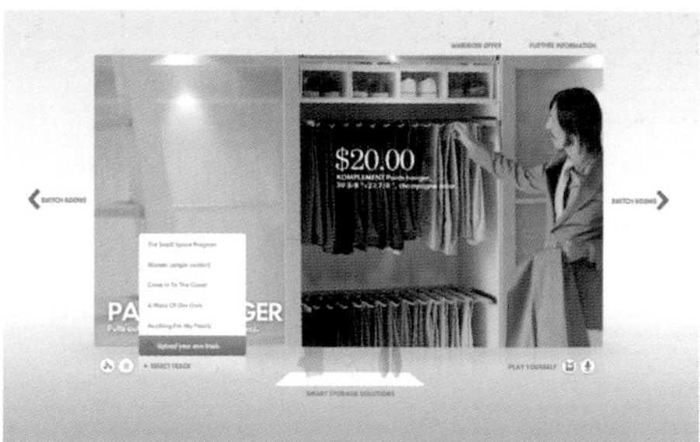
$20.00

$1450.99

$2150.69

$19.99 / 3 pack
BOXES

$5.00
CLOTHES RAIL

$9.99 / 4 pack
SHOE BOXES

$1508.99
750:-

COWSHED PRODUCTIONS

SOUTH AFRICA

www.cowshedproductions.co.uk

2008

Concept

Showcase for Cowshed PR services website, with highly illustrated zoom in-and-out navigation, also featuring a hidden menu at the bottom to display all the options. /// Diese Website dient als Showcase für Cowshed PR mit einer höchst anschaulichen Zoom-Navigation und einem am unteren Rand versteckten Menü, das alle Optionen enthält. /// **Vitrine pour le site Web des services de Cowshed PR, avec une navigation riche en illustrations et dotée d'un zoom avant et arrière, ainsi que d'un menu dissimulé au bas pour afficher toutes les options.**

Info

DESIGN STUDIO: HelloComputer <www.hellocomputer.net>. /// **DESIGN:** Mark Tomlinson, Simon Spreckley. /// **PROGRAMMING:** Shaun Smith. /// **CLIENT:** Cowshed Productions. /// **TOOLS:** Adobe Flash, Adobe Photoshop, Adobe Illustrator, Maya, JSP, XML, HTML. /// **AWARDS:** Loerie Award (Experiential/Digital – Bronze). /// **COST:** 320 hours.

DADDY'S HOUSE

FRANCE

www.daddy.fr

2007

Concept

This website immerses the user in a loft-like house of six rooms, each room being one major section. The user has to take doors, stairs and even secret passages in order to navigate. /// Auf dieser Website betritt der User ein loftähnliches Haus mit sechs Zimmern. Jedes Zimmer stellt einen Hauptbereich der Site dar. Der User nutzt Türen, Treppen und sogar Geheimwege zum Navigieren. /// Ce site Web plonge l'utilisateur dans l'atmosphère d'une maison de type loft comptant six pièces, chacune correspondant à une section principale. L'utilisateur doit ouvrir des portes, emprunter des escaliers et même des passages secrets pour naviguer.

Info

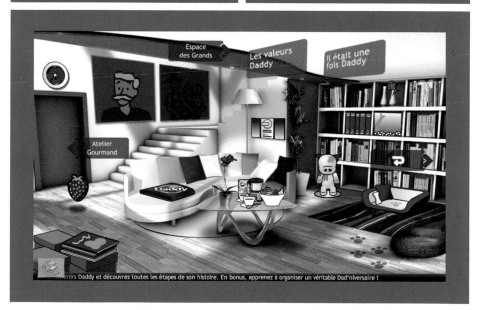

Design Studio: Les Chinois <www.leschinois.com>. /// **Design:** Ludovic Roudy (Creative Direction); Julien Clavier (Art Direction). /// **Programming:** Julien Bennamias (Lead Developer). /// **Client:** Daddy (Eurosugar). /// **Tools:** Adobe Flash, Adobe Photoshop. /// **Cost:** 3 months.

DESIGN YOUR OWN ECO-CAR

SWEDEN

http://demo.fb.se/e/volvo/c30/designyourownecocar

2008

Concept

Re-launch website for the Volvo C30, positioning it as a sporty, compact car for design-focused drivers. There is no ordinary navigation bar on the site. Here the navigation is the site. /// Relaunch der Website für den Volvo C30, auf der dieser Wagen als sportlicher Kompaktwagen für Fahrer vorstellt wird, die besonders aufs Design achten. Hier gibt es keine gewöhnliche Navigationsleiste, sondern die Navigation *ist* die Site. /// Site Web de relance pour la Volvo C30, positionnant le véhicule comme une voiture compacte sportive pour les conducteurs privilégiant le design. Le site ne comporte pas de barre de navigation standard : la navigation est le site en soi.

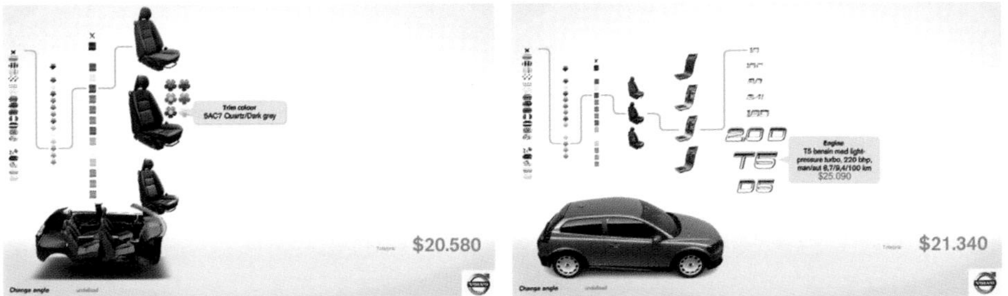

Info

DESIGN STUDIO: Forsman & Bodenfors <www.fb.se>. /// **DESIGN:** Forsman & Bodenfors. /// **PROGRAMMING:** Kokokaka Entertainent; Framfab. /// **CLIENT:** Volvo. /// **TOOLS:** Adobe Flash, Adobe Photoshop, Adobe Illustrator, Maya.

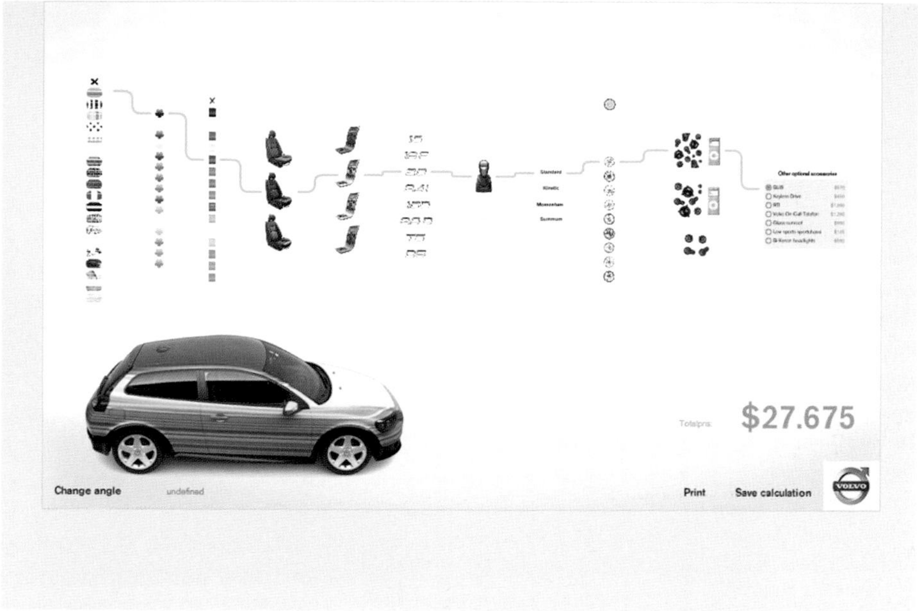

Standard
Kinetic
Momentum
Summum

Other optional accessories

Totalpris: $27.675

Change angle undefined

Print Save calculation

VOLVO

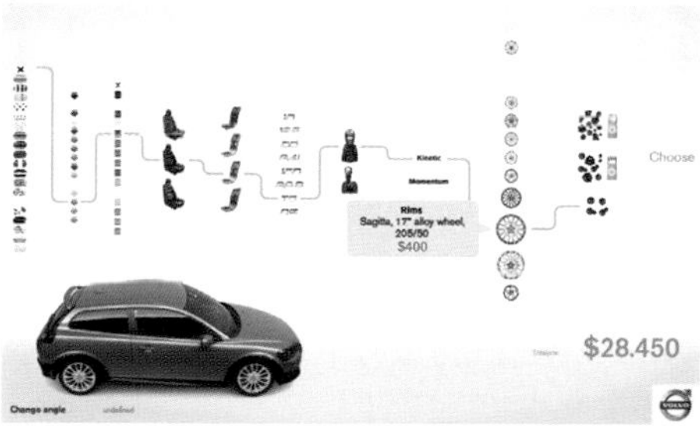

Kinetic
Momentum

Rims
Sagitta, 17" alloy wheel, 205/50
$400

Choose

$28.450

Change angle undefined

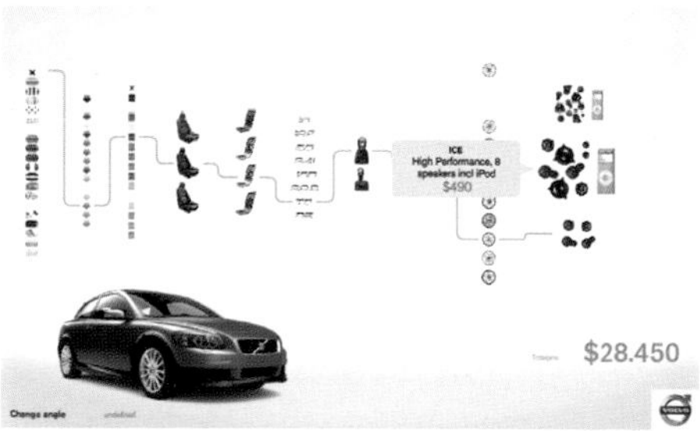

ICE
High Performance, 8 speakers incl iPod
$490

$28.450

Change angle undefined

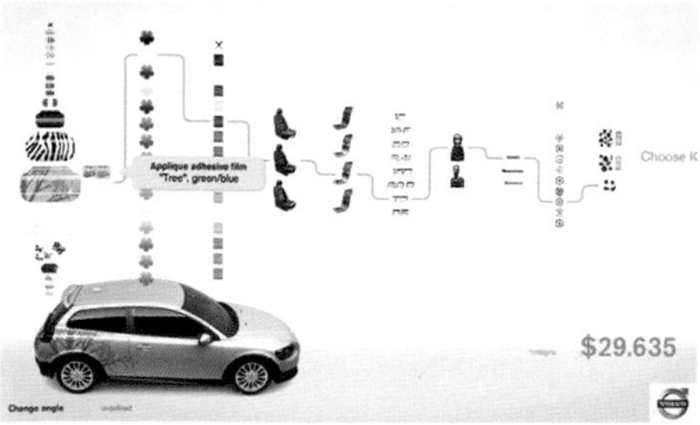

Applique adhesive film
"Tree", green/blue

Choose IC

$29.635

Change angle undefined

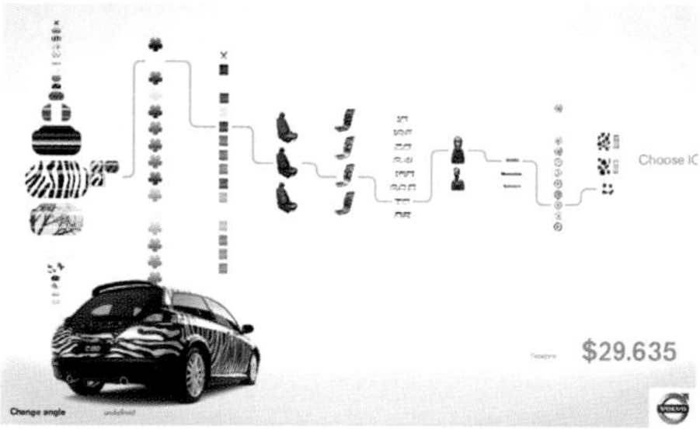

Choose IC

$29.635

Change angle undefined

DANKA STUDIO

FRANCE

www.dankastudio.fr

2008

Concept

Circular navigation using mouse-wheel moves the user by thumbnails through the projects and news. /// In kreisförmigen Bewegungen kann der User per Mausrad anhand von Vorschaubildern durch Projekte und News navigieren. /// **Navigation circulaire à l'aide de la molette de la souris qui fait défiler devant l'utilisateur des vignettes sur les projets et les informations.**

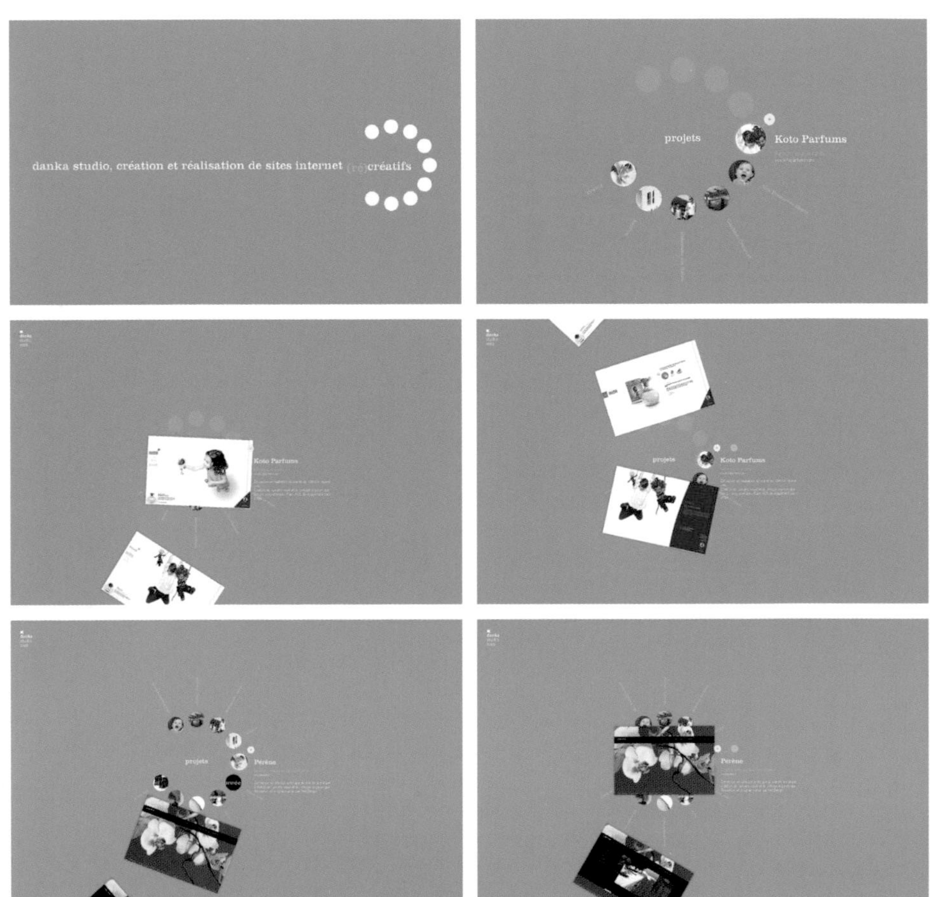

Info

DESIGN STUDIO: Danka Studio <www.dankastudio.fr>. /// **DESIGN:** Guillaume Bonnecase. /// **PROGRAMMING:** Vincent Perrier-Perrery. /// **OTHERS:** João Cabral (Project Manager). /// **CLIENT:** Danka Studio. /// **TOOLS:** Adobe Photoshop, Flash, XML. /// **COST:** 150–200 hours.

EAST PHOTOGRAPHIC

UK

www.eastphotographic.com

2008

Concept

East needed a site that was intuitive, clear, and displayed the images to their best advantage. In addition to these considerations, the online gallery "Go East" exhibits work from creatives outside the agency. /// East wollte eine intuitiv und klar strukturierte Site, die die Bilder möglichst vorteilhaft darstellt. Neben diesen Überlegungen präsentiert die Online-Galerie „Go East" Arbeiten von externen Kreativen. /// East avait besoin d'un site intuitif, clair et présentant les images sous leur meilleur jour. Outre ces considérations, la galerie en ligne « Go East » montre le travail de créateurs externes à l'agence.

Info

DESIGN STUDIO: No Days Off <www.nodaysoff.com>; Pumkin <www.pumkin.co.uk>. /// **DESIGN:** Patrick Duffy. /// **PROGRAMMING:** Alex Charlton. /// **CLIENT:** East Photographic. /// **TOOLS:** Adobe Flash, PHP. /// **COST:** 240 hours.

EARTHCOTE

SOUTH AFRICA

www.earthcote.co.za

2008

Concept

The site allows users to create a customized palette of their favorite Earthcote products, which could then be printed out and taken to a supplier. /// Auf dieser Site können die User eigene Farbpaletten mit ihren Lieblingsprodukten von Earthcote zusammenstellen, die ausgedruckt und an Händler weitergeleitet werden können. /// Le site permet aux utilisateurs de créer une palette personnalisée de leurs produits Earthcote favoris, qu'ils peuvent ensuite imprimer et remettre à un fournisseur.

Info

Design Studio: HelloComputer <www.hellocomputer.net>. /// **Design:** Mark Tomlinson, Simon Spreckley. /// **Programming:** Shaun Smith. /// **Client:** Midas Earthcote. /// **Tools:** Adobe Photoshop, Flash, Adobe Illustrator, PHP, JSON, HTML. /// **Cost:** 240 hours.

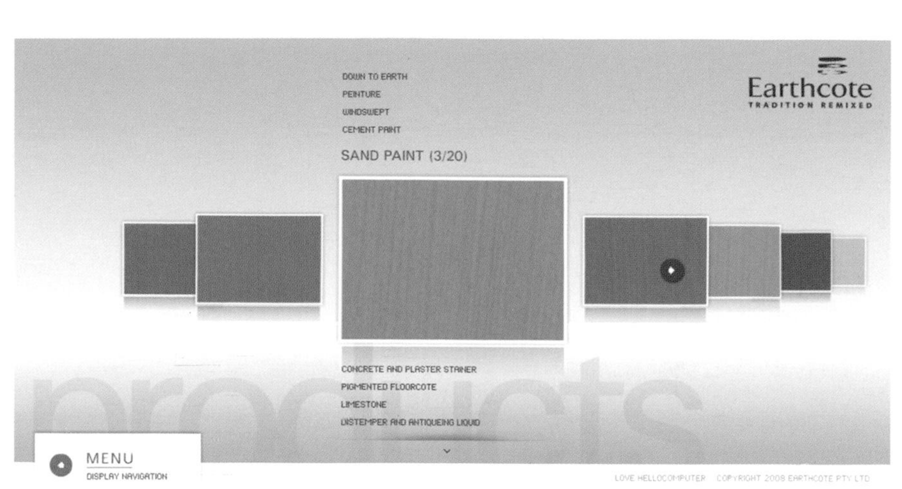
DOWN TO EARTH
PEINTURE
WINDSWEPT
CEMENT PAINT
SAND PAINT (3/20)
Earthcote
TRADITION REMIXED
CONCRETE AND PLASTER STAINER
PIGMENTED FLOORCOTE
LIMESTONE
DISTEMPER AND ANTIQUEING LIQUID
MENU
DISPLAY NAVIGATION
LOVE HELLOCOMPUTER   COPYRIGHT 2008 EARTHCOTE PTY LTD

Earthcote
MENU

Earthcote
MENU

Earthcote
MENU

MY FAVOURITES
Earthcote
MENU

ELAN WSTUDIO

SLOVENIA

http://wstudio.elanskis.com

2007

Concept

On this website, visitors must drag the slider to reveal the chosen content. /// Auf dieser Website ziehen die Besucher an einem Schieber, um den gewählten Content sehen zu können. /// **Dans ce site Web, les visiteurs doivent déplacer le curseur pour révéler le contenu sélectionné.**

Info

Design Studio: Webshocker <www.webshocker.net>. /// **Design:** Webshocker. /// **Programming:** Webshocker. /// **Client:** Elan Skis. /// **Tools:** Adobe Flash, Adobe Photoshop. /// **Awards:** FWA (Site of the Day), DOPE, E-creative, Website Design Awards, Fcukstar. /// **Cost:** 100 hours.

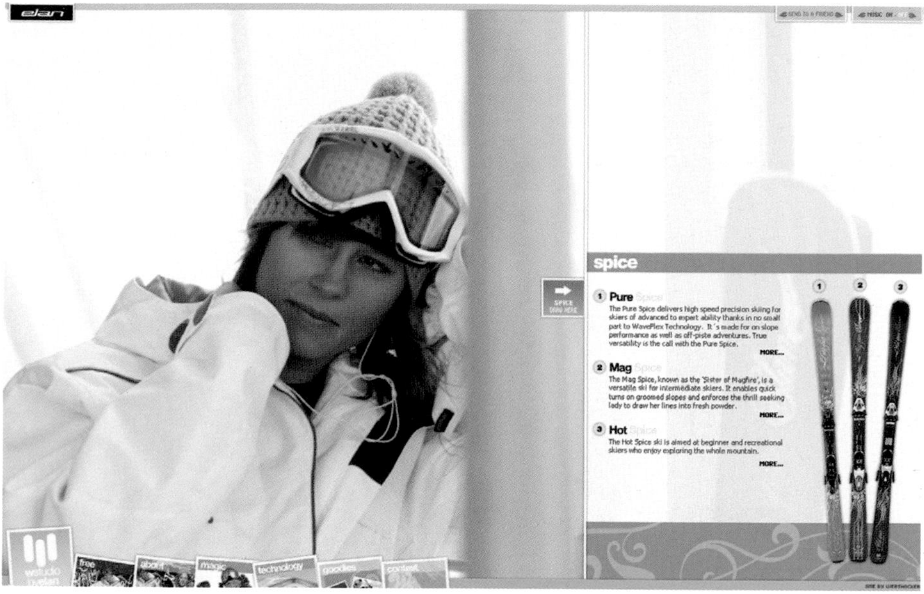
elan
SEND TO A FRIEND
MUSIC ON
SPICE
spice
1 Pure Spice
The Pure Spice delivers high speed precision skiing for skiers of advanced to expert ability thanks in no small part to WaveFlex Technology. It´s made for on slope performance as well as off-piste adventures. True versatility is the call with the Pure Spice.
MORE...
2 Mag Spice
The Mag Spice, known as the 'Sister of Magfire', is a versatile ski for intermediate skiers. It enables quick turns on groomed slopes and enforces the thrill seeking lady to draw her lines into fresh powder.
MORE...
3 Hot Spice
The Hot Spice ski is aimed at beginner and recreational skiers who enjoy exploring the whole mountain.
MORE...
free
about
magic
technology
goodies
contest

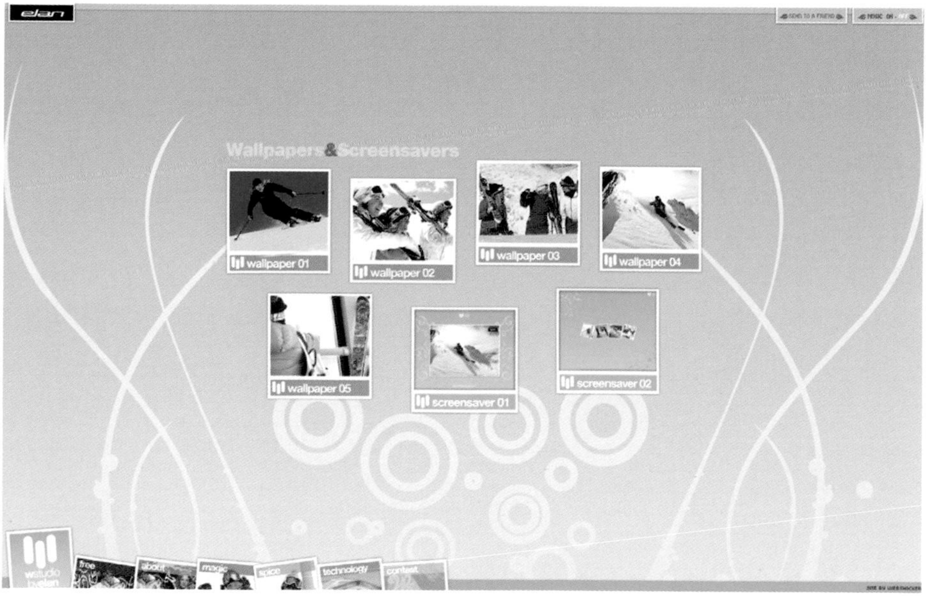
elan
SEND TO A FRIEND
MUSIC ON
Wallpapers&Screensavers
wallpaper 01
wallpaper 02
wallpaper 03
wallpaper 04
wallpaper 05
screensaver 01
screensaver 02
free
about
magic
spice
technology
contest

ETHNO PORT

POLAND

www.ethnoport.pl

2008

Concept

Website for the Ethno/World Music Festival, with all navigation based on a circle-shape which is common to all primitive cultures. /// Bei der Website für das Festival für Ethno- und Worldmusic beruht die gesamte Navigation auf Kreisformen, die bei allen primitiven Kulturen zu finden sind. /// **Site Web pour le festival de musique ethnique/world music, l'ensemble de la navigation reposant sur une forme circulaire commune à toutes les cultures primitives.**

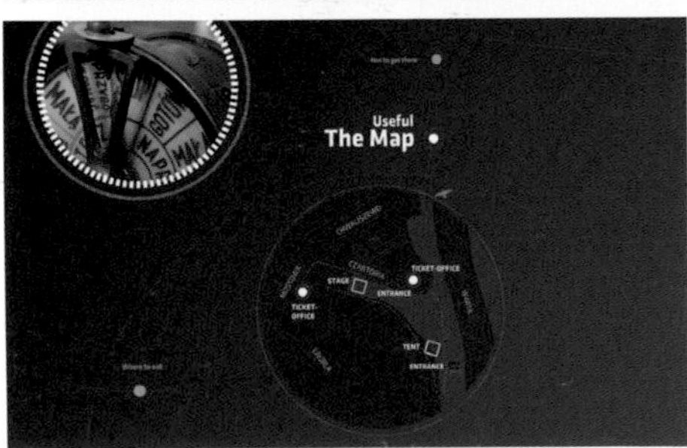

Info

Design Studio: Huncwot <www.huncwot.com>. /// **Design:** Arek Romanski, Lukasz Knasiecki. /// **Client:** Ethno Port Festival. /// **Tools:** FreeHand, Flash, SQL. /// **Awards:** FWA Site of the Day. /// **Cost:** 120 hours.

Tickets
ticket price for one day
15 zł
three day pass
30 zł
tickets on sale since May, the 15th:
Centrum Kultury Zamek /Poznań/
Acid Shop /Poznań/
Centrum Informacji Miejskiej /Poznań/
RockLong Luck /Poznań/
ticket-offices on the festival:
around entrances from Mostowa / Ewangelicka
and Czartoria streets

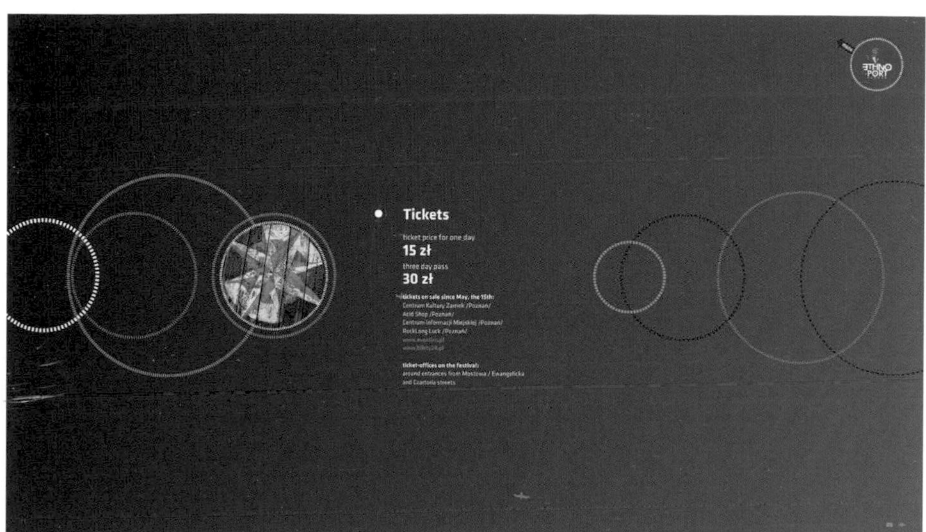

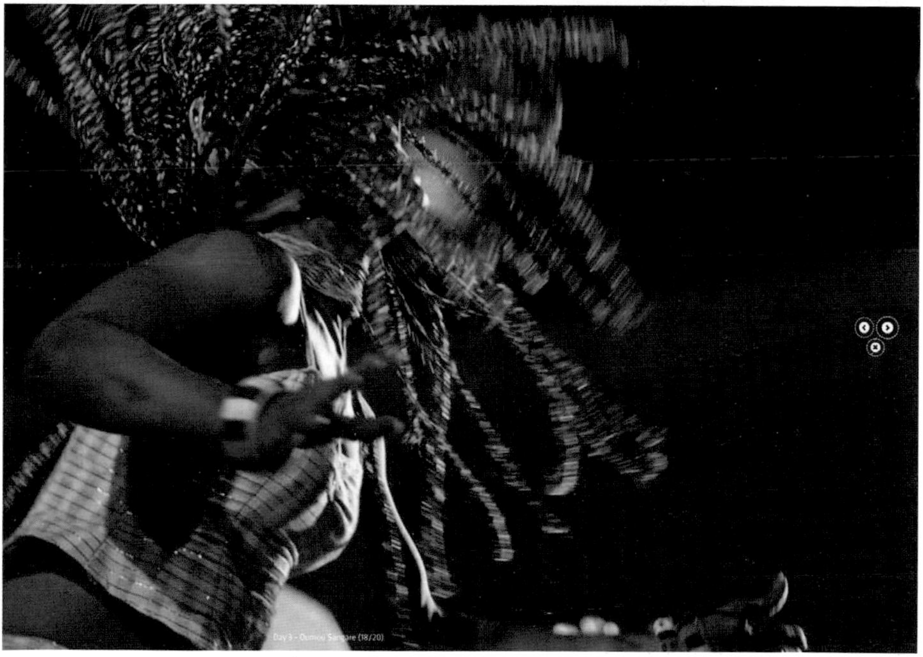

Day 3 - Oumou Sangare (18/20)

EXIT WITH ATTITUDE

UK

www.exitwithattitude.co.uk

2008

Concept

A bespoke street scene was created for this site, with a 'London' city vibe designed to appeal to 'more edgy' end-users. The street had specific shops created which are the face of each particular section of the site. /// Für diese Site wurde eine Straßenszene mit dem typischen Flair der Londoner City gestaltet, die trendigere User ansprechen soll. Auf der Straße bilden die verschiedenen Shops die Front für die jeweiligen Bereiche der Site. /// Une scène de rue sur mesure a été créée pour ce site, avec une ambiance londonienne conçue pour attirer les utilisateurs finaux les plus « tendance ». La rue compte des magasins pensés pour chaque section du site.

Info

Design Studio: RARE Design Associates <www.wearerare.com>. /// **Design:** Steve Simmonds, James Arnott. /// **Programming:** Steve Simmonds, Trevor Burton, James Arnott. /// **Others:** Working in-conjunction with Nexus-H agency. /// **Client:** Suzuki. /// **Tools:** Adobe Flash, Adobe Photoshop, Adobe Illustrator. /// **Cost:** 150 hours.

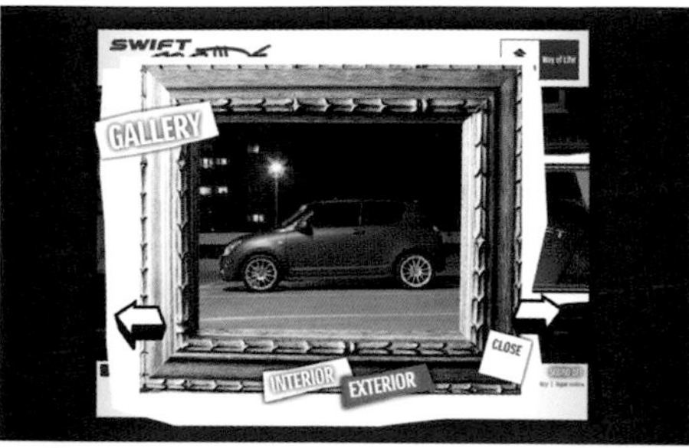

SWIFT
GALLERY
CLOSE
INTERIOR
EXTERIOR

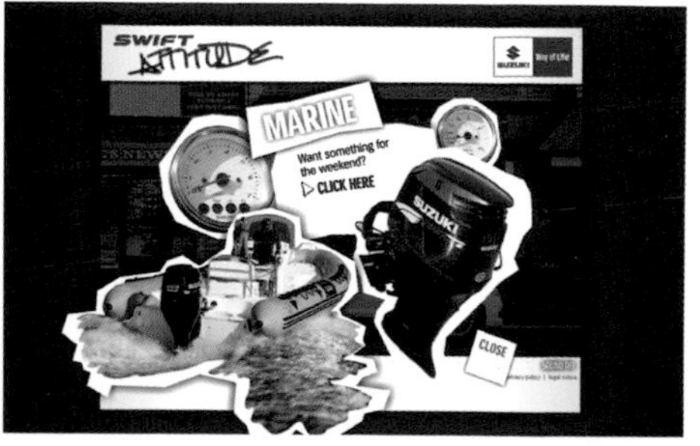

SWIFT ATTITUDE
SUZUKI
Way of Life!
MARINE
Want something for the weekend?
CLICK HERE
SUZUKI
CLOSE

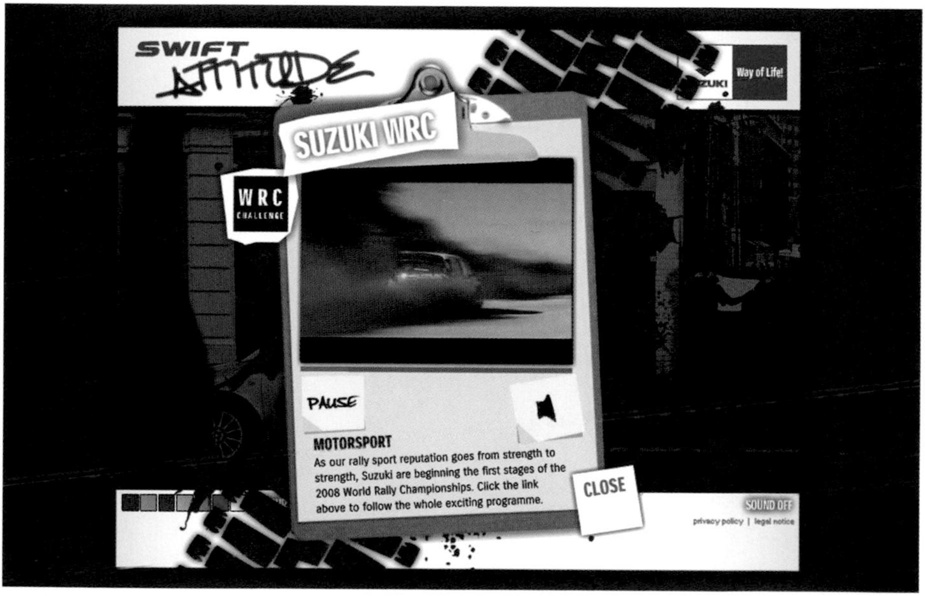

SWIFT ATTITUDE
SUZUKI
Way of Life!
SUZUKI WRC
WRC CHALLENGE
PAUSE
MOTORSPORT
As our rally sport reputation goes from strength to strength, Suzuki are beginning the first stages of the 2008 World Rally Championships. Click the link above to follow the whole exciting programme.
CLOSE
SOUND OFF
privacy policy | legal notice

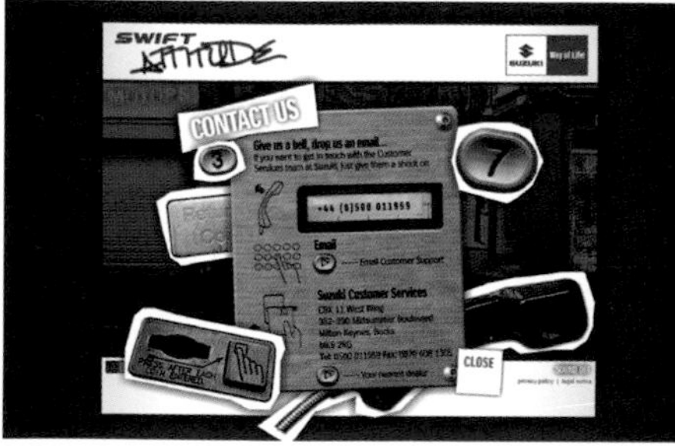

SWIFT ATTITUDE
SUZUKI
Way of Life!
CONTACT US
Give us a bell, drop us an email...
+44 (0)500 011959
Email
Suzuki Customer Services
CLOSE

SWIFT ATTITUDE
SUZUKI
Way of Life!
MONSTER MOTORS

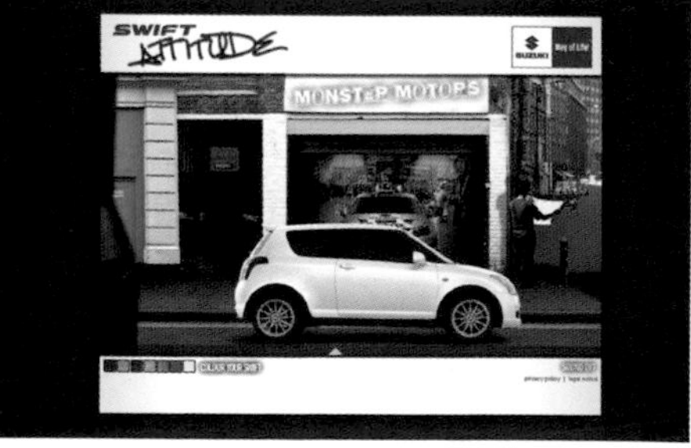

ENVIRON AVST

SOUTH AFRICA

www.advancedvitaminskintherapy.com

2008

Concept

The design team for this site aimed to create a navigation system that was simple, sexy and easy to use while still being 100 % aligned with the Environ brand. /// Das Designteam schuf für diese Site ein Navigationssystem, das schlicht, sexy und einfach zu bedienen ist, sich aber trotzdem hundertprozentig an der Marke Environ ausrichtet. /// **L'équipe de design de ce site souhaitait créer un système de navigation dépouillé, agréable et simple d'emploi, tout en collant à 100 % à l'image de la marque Environ.**

Info

Design Studio: Glasshouse <www.glasshouse.co.za>. /// **Design:** Franky van der Elst. /// **Programming:** Franky van der Elst, Cara Truter. /// **Client:** Environ Skin Care (Pty) Ltd. /// **Tools:** Adobe Photoshop, Adobe Flash, ActionScript, XML, Adobe After Effects. /// **Cost:** 94 hours.

FOLGEN SIE DER RUBINSCHWARZEN SPUR

GERMANY

2008

www.folgen-sie-der-rubinschwarzen-spur.de

Concept

To promote a flat-screen TV, the mouse scroll-over and the menu produce a neon-like visual trace. The video-rich site is very direct and the bottom-left menu allows quick access to information. /// Als Werbung für einen Flachbildfernseher produzieren Maus-Scrollover und Menü eine neonähnliche visuelle Spur. Die Site arbeitet hauptsächlich mit Videosequenzen, und über das Menü unten links kann schnell auf Informationen zugegriffen werden. /// Pour la promotion d'une télévision à écran plat, le déplacement de la souris et le menu laissent une trace visuelle évoquant un néon. Le site riche en vidéos est très explicite et le menu en bas à gauche permet d'accéder rapidement aux informations.

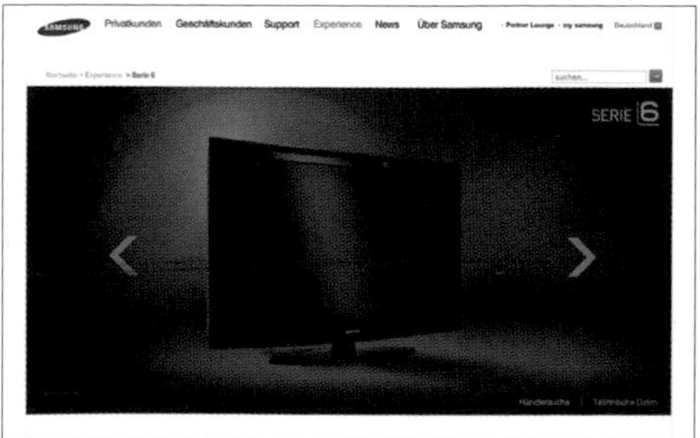

Info

DESIGN STUDIO: Scholz & Volkmer GmbH <www.s-v.de>. /// **DESIGN:** John Grøtting (Creative Direction); Vanessa Mikoleit (Art Direction). /// **PROGRAMMING:** Kerem Gülensoy (Flash). /// **OTHERS:** Christoph Kehren (Account Management); Rainer Eidemüller (Concept); Melanie Nürr (Copy); Jens Fischer (Sound Design); Marc Storch (Motion Design). /// **CLIENT:** Samsung (Cheil Communications Germany GmbH). /// **TOOLS:** HTML, Flash, ActionScript.

FACTORCITY RECORDS

SPAIN

www.factorcity.com

2006

Concept

The site navigation is inspired by a walk through Barcelona's city streets; it allows the user to move vertically in order to find the contents. It also displays an easy navigation tool on the right, inspired by a Macintosh applications menu. /// Die Site-Navigation wurde von Spaziergängen durch die Straßen von Barcelona inspiriert. Der User bewegt sich vertikal durch die Site und erforscht deren Inhalte. Auf der rechten Seite befindet sich eine einfache Navigationsleiste, die einem Macintosh-Menü nachempfunden ist. /// La navigation du site s'inspire d'une promenade dans les rues de Barcelone et permet à l'utilisateur de se déplacer verticalement pour consulter le contenu. Elle présente aussi un outil de navigation simple sur la droite, à l'image du menu d'applications sur Mac.

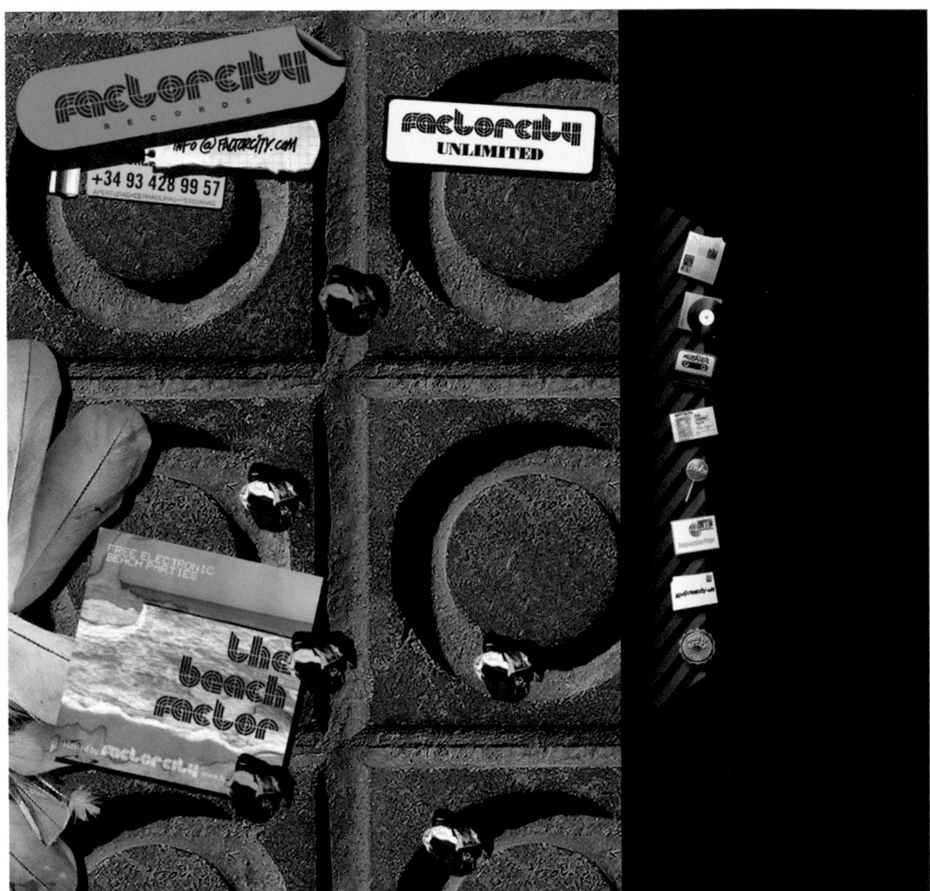

Info

Design Studio: area3 <www.area3.net>. /// **Design:** Sebastián Puiggrós, Chema Longobardo. /// **Programming:** Federico Joselevich, Sebastián Puiggrós. /// **Client:** Factorcity Records. /// **Tools:** Adobe Photoshop, Adobe Ilustrator, Adobe Flash. /// **Cost:** 400 hours.

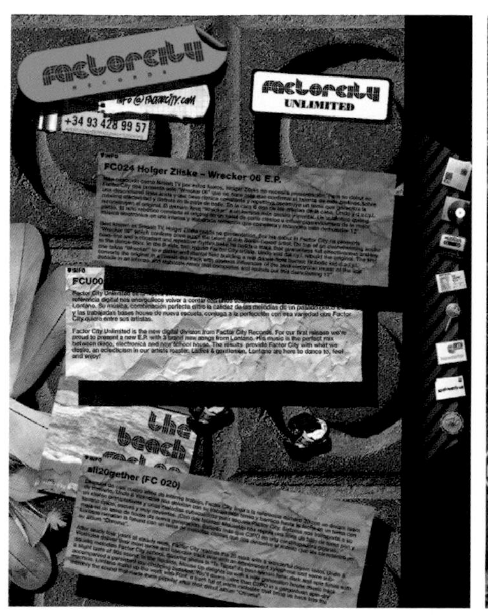
factorcity
info@factorcity.com
+34 93 428 99 57
factorcity UNLIMITED
FC024 Holger Zilske – Wrecker 06 E.P.
FCU00
Factor City Unlimited is the new digital division from Factor City Records. For our first release we're proud to present a new E.P. with 3 brand new songs from Lontano. His music is the perfect mix between disco, electronica and new school house. The results provide Factor City with what we desire, an eclecticism in our artists roster. Ladies & gentlemen, Lontano are here to dance to, feel and enjoy!
all20gether (FC 020)

up&
VIP
GANYAN AIR
Gabriel Berlanga
UNDO
Factorcity
Chic
SANT CUGAT
21 ESCARPAS
4 OZONES
VICKNOISE

Ellën
UNDO
vicKnoiSe

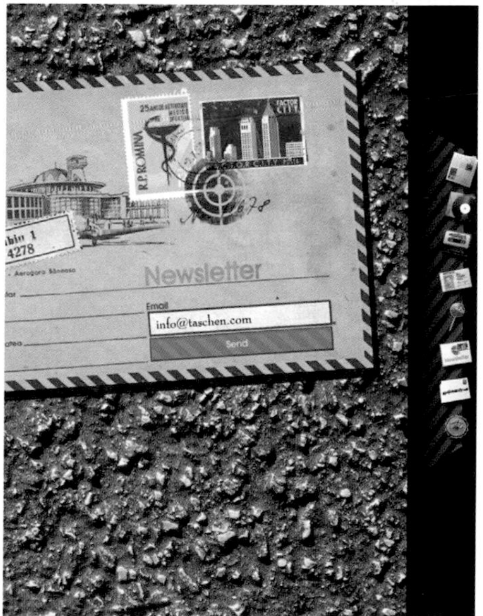
R.P.ROMINA
Newsletter
Email
info@taschen.com
Send

FIZZIX

USA

www.newfizzix.com

2007

Concept

The site promotes a new brand extension under the GoGurt line of yogurt, displaying two different games based on animation, sound, and humor. /// Die Site wirbt mittels zwei witziger Spiele mit Sound und Animationen für die Erweiterung des Joghurtangebots der Marke GoGurt. /// Le site vante une nouvelle extension de marque sous la ligne de yaourts *GoGurt*, en présentant deux jeux basés sur l'animation, des sons et de l'humour.

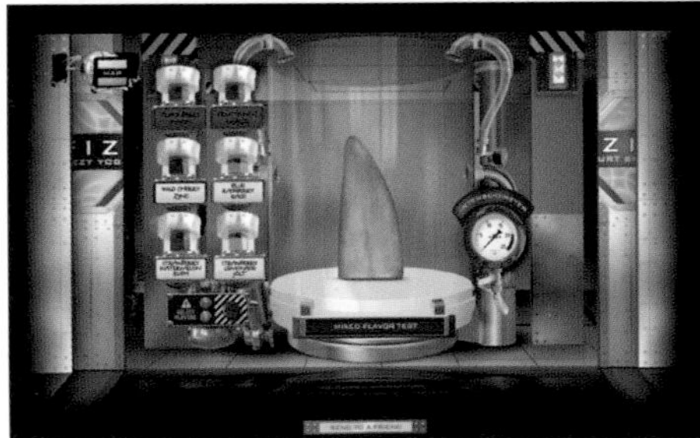

Info

Design Studio: JUXT Interactive <www.juxtinteractive.com>. /// **Design:** Todd Purgason, Jorge Fino, Justin Bernard, Alex Mustacich, Mike Tucker. /// **Programming:** Gary Stasiuk. /// **Others:** Mark Johnson (Project Manager). /// **Client:** General Mills. /// **Tools:** HTML, Adobe Photoshop, Adobe Flash, Adobe Illustrator. /// **Cost:** 3 months.

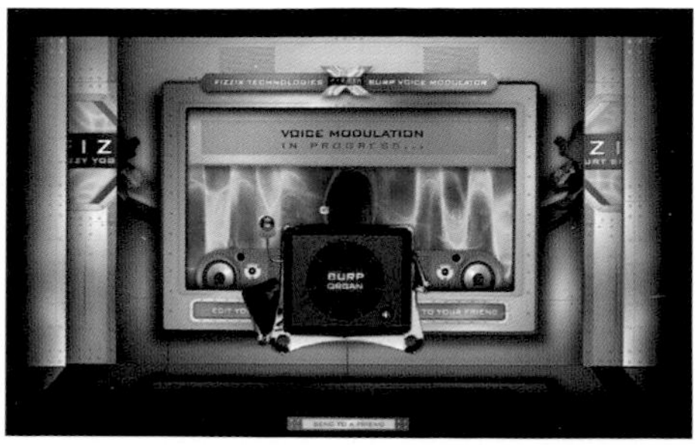

VOICE MODULATION
IN PROGRESS...
BURP
ORGAN

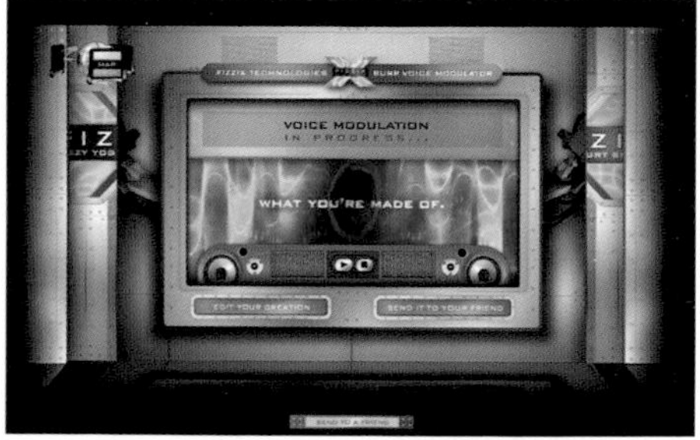

VOICE MODULATION
IN PROGRESS...
WHAT YOU'RE MADE OF.

MAP
SELECT
BEAT
28:14
SEND TO A FRIEND

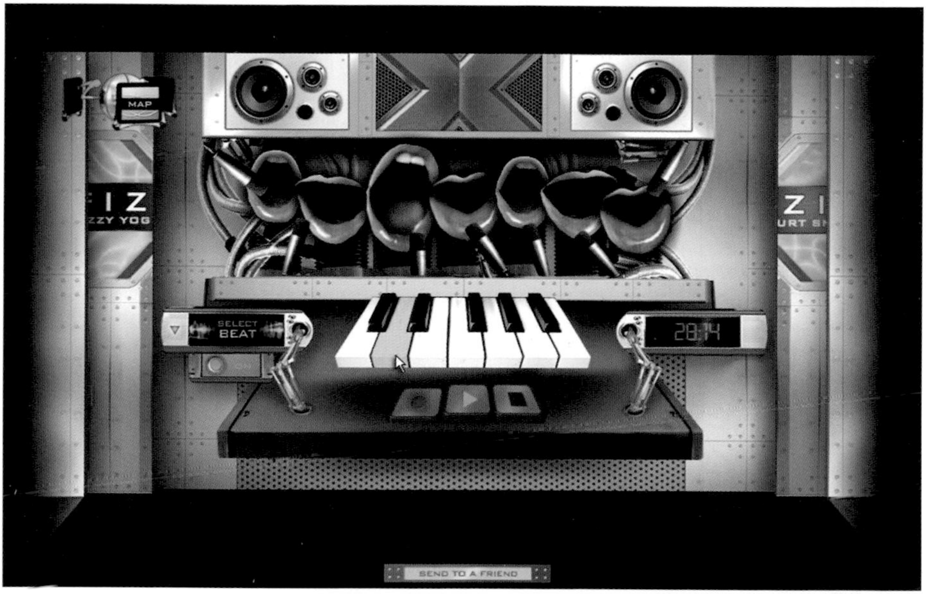

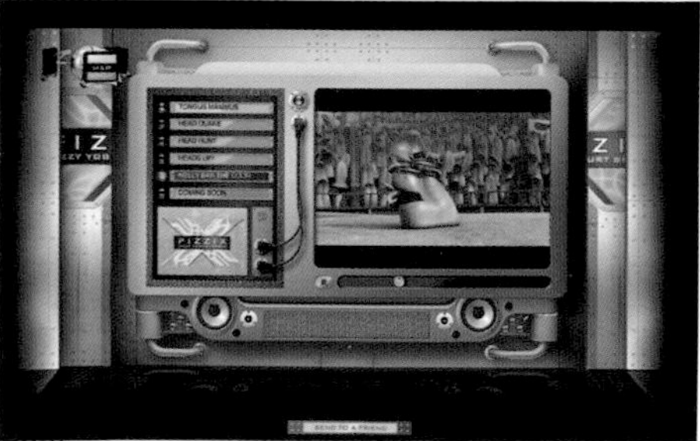

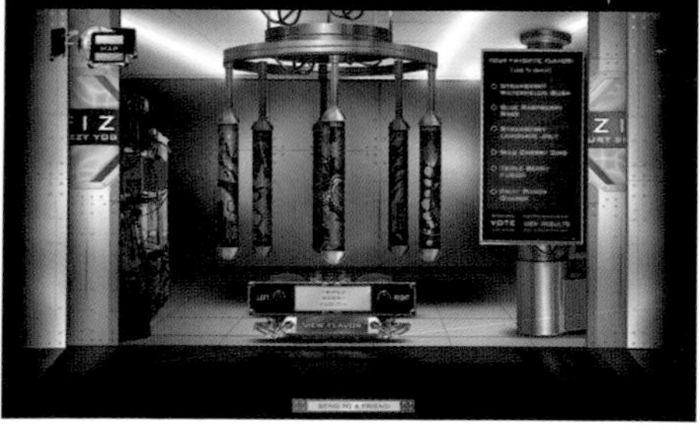

FURNITURES VAN AERDE

BELGIUM

www.meubelenvanaerde.be

2007

Concept

On this website, whenever the user clicks on a navigation button, the button reshapes itself. /// Sobald der User auf dieser Website eine Navigationsschaltfläche anklickt, verwandelt sie komplett ihre Form. /// **Sur ce site Web, chaque fois que l'utilisateur clique sur un bouton de navigation, la forme de ce bouton change.**

home catalogus over ons info contact

Welkom bij Van Aerde Meubelen

Philip en Myriam Van Aerde heten u van harte welkom in hun gezellige, sfeervolle toonzaal met vierduizend vierkante meter woonplezier in een uniek kader. Genoeg ideeën voor een smaakvol interieur.

Wij bieden u een ruim assortiment meubelen in de meest uiteenlopende stijlen voor elegant en stijlvol wonen. Vakmanschap en hoge kwaliteit zijn onze criteria. Levering en plaatsing van de aangekochte meubels behoren standaard tot onze service.

Het uitgesproken familiale karakter is kenmerkend voor ons bedrijf. Of u nu iets wil aankopen, iets wil weten over leveringen of beroep wil doen op onze service; u krijgt steeds te maken met een "Van Aerde".

Van Aerde
MEUBELEN

Info

Design Studio: Weblounge <www.weblounge.be>. /// **Design:** Kristof Van Rentergem. /// **Programming:** Maarten Bulckaen. /// **Client:** Meubelen Van Aerde. /// **Tools:** Adobe Flash, Adobe Photoshop, Adobe Dreamweaver. /// **Awards:** Dailyslurp (Site of the Day), Webcreme, Best Flash Website, TBD Best Design Award, American Design Award, Mowsnet (silver), Designlicks, Cool homepages, the dreamer. /// **Cost:** 40 hours.

Van Aerde

Van Aerde

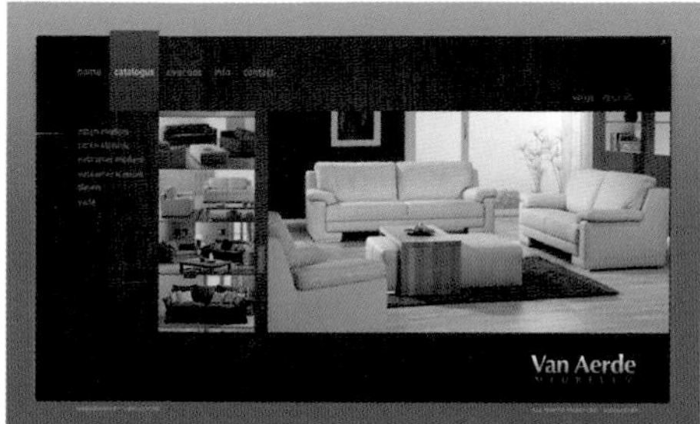

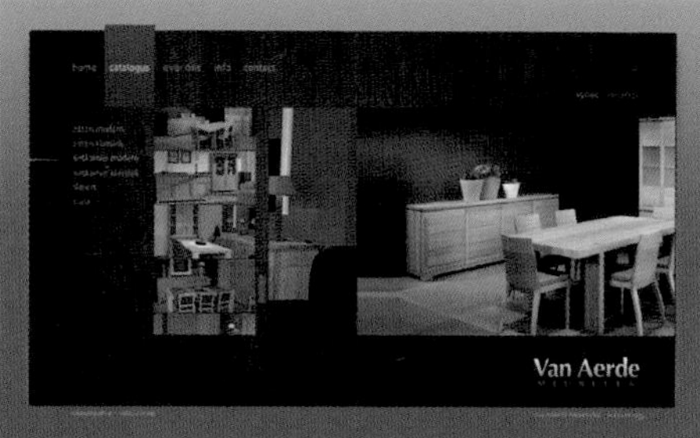

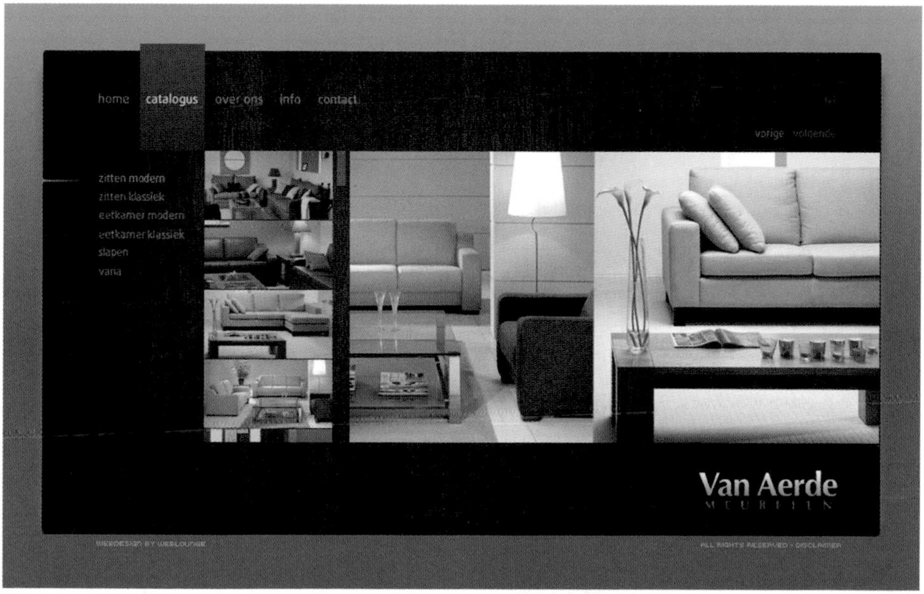

home
catalogus
over ons
info
contact
vorige
volgende
zitten modern
zitten klassiek
eetkamer modern
eetkamer klassiek
slapen
varia
Van Aerde
MEUBELEN
WEBDESIGN BY WEBLOUNGE
ALL RIGHTS RESERVED - DISCLAIMER

Van Aerde

Van Aerde

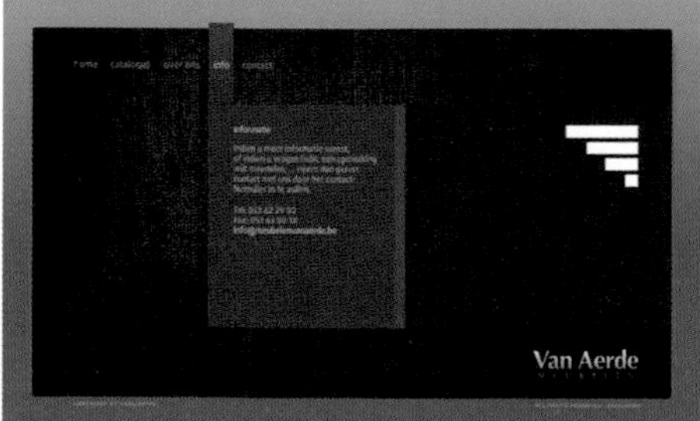

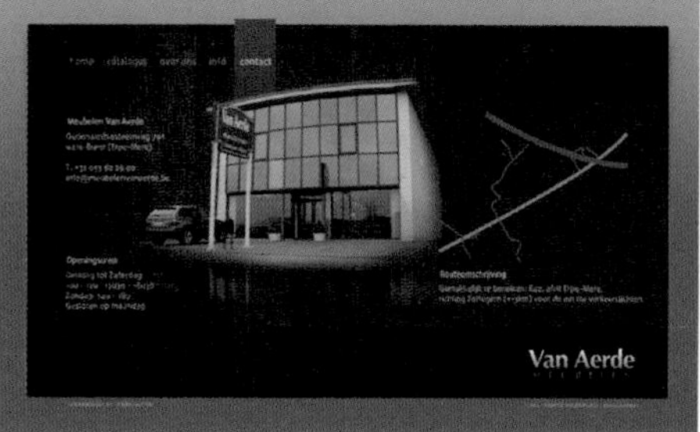

FUTURE READY PROTECTION

BRAZIL

www.futurereadyprotection.com

2008

Concept

Rexona is here presented as the anti-perspirant of the future in 3 interactive games and a web card that extended the offline campaign. /// Rexona wird hier in drei interaktiven Spielen und einer Web-Card in Ergänzung der Offline-Kampagne als das Deo der Zukunft präsentiert. /// Rexona présente ici le déodorant du futur dans 3 jeux interactifs et une carte Web comme extension de la campagne hors ligne.

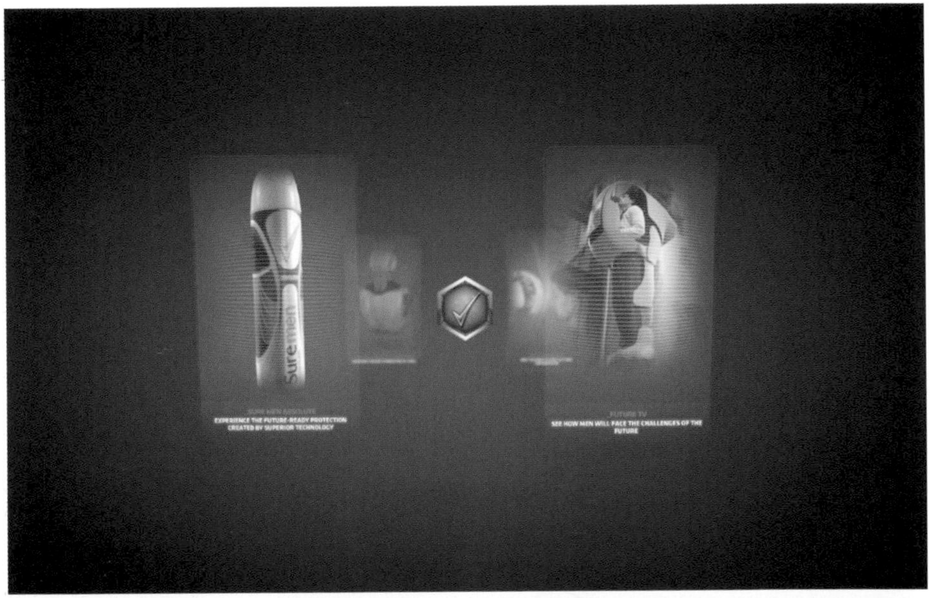

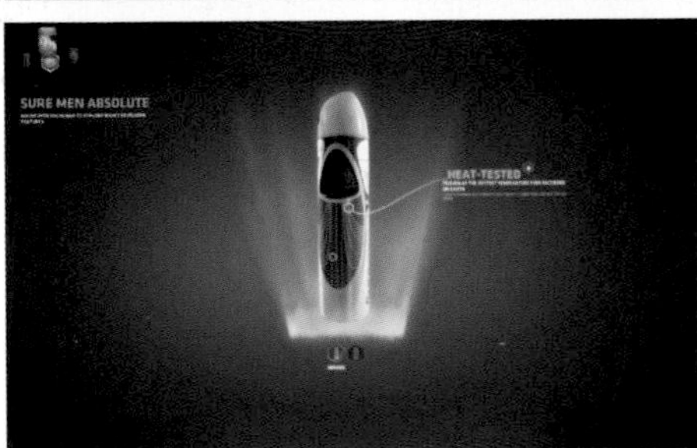

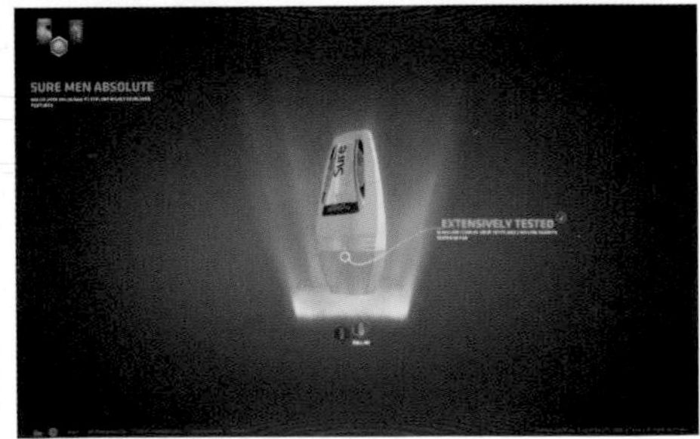

Info

Design Studio: Gringo <www.gringo.nu>. /// **Design:** Gringo. /// **Programming:** Gringo. /// **Others:** Danilo Almeida (3D); Gaia (Sound Design). /// **Client:** Rexona. /// **Tools:** Adobe Creative Suite, 3D Studio Max. /// **Cost:** 3,5 months.

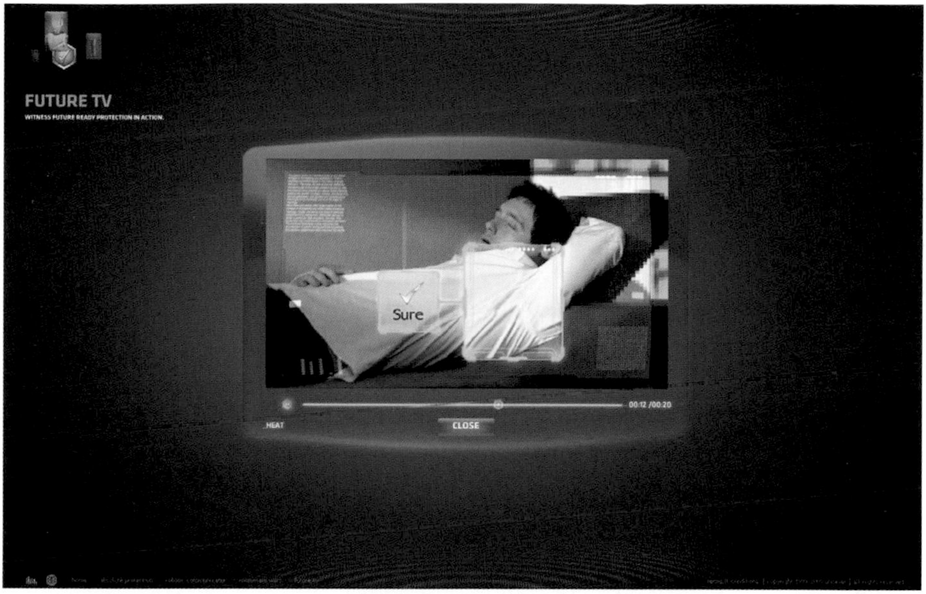

FUTURE TV

WITNESS FUTURE READY PROTECTION IN ACTION.

Sure

00:12 /00:20

HEAT

CLOSE

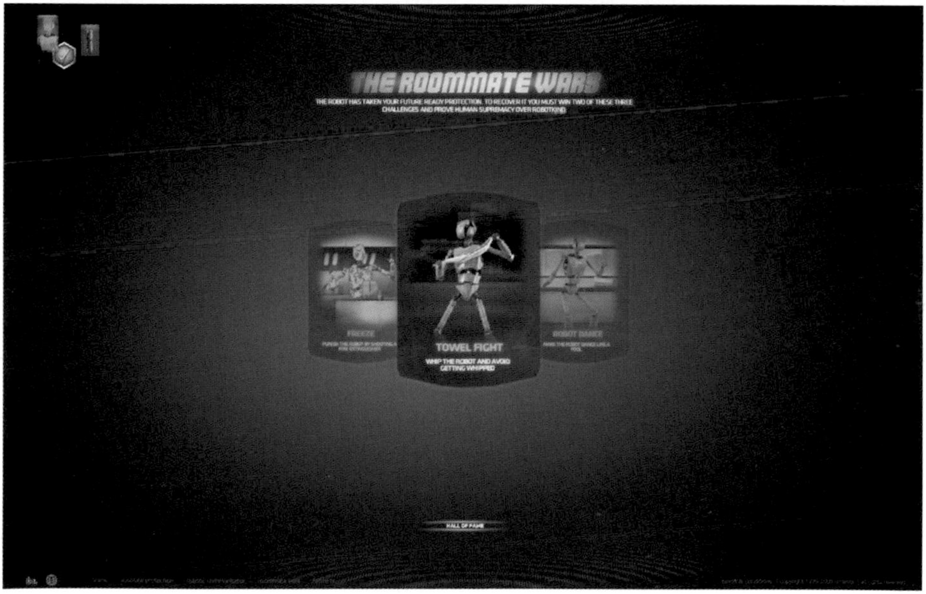

THE ROOMMATE WARS

THE ROBOT HAS TAKEN YOUR FUTURE READY PROTECTION. TO RECOVER IT YOU MUST WIN TWO OF THESE THREE CHALLENGES AND PROVE HUMAN SUPREMACY OVER ROBOTKIND.

FREEZE

TOWEL FIGHT

WHIP THE ROBOT AND AVOID GETTING WHIPPED

ROBOT DANCE

HALL OF FAME

GONDRY'S DREAM

BRAZIL

http://direct.motorola.com/hellomoto/razr2/razr2makingof

2008

Concept

Check out all the behind-the-scenes to Motorola's new ad by Michel Gondry. /// Ein umfassender Blick hinter die Kulissen des neuen Werbefilms von Michel Gondry für Motorola. /// **Découvrez toutes les coulisses du nouveau spot de Michel Gondry pour Motorola.**

Info

Design Studio: Gringo <www.gringo.nu>. /// **Design:** Gringo. /// **Programming:** Gringo. /// **Others:** Gaia (Sound Design). /// **Client:** Motorola. /// **Tools:** Adobe Creative Suite. /// **Cost:** 2,5 months.

01
Laura walks
SKETCHES
BUY PHONE
REGISTER FOR UPDATES
ABOUT MOTOROLA • HELLOMOTO.COM • PRIVACY STATEMENT • TERMS OF USE • CONTACT MOTOROLA
COPYRIGHT 1994 - 2007 MOTOROLA, INC. ALL RIGHTS RESERVED

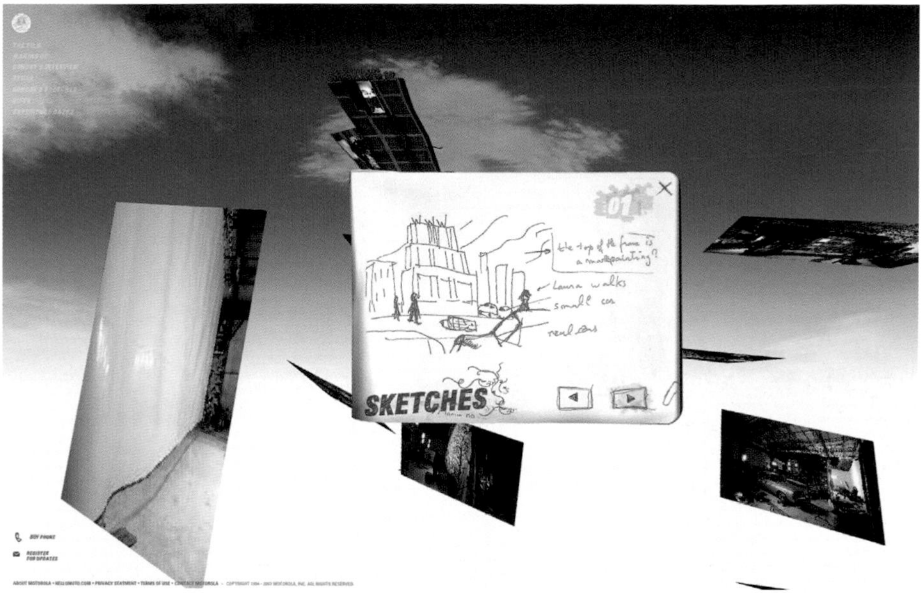

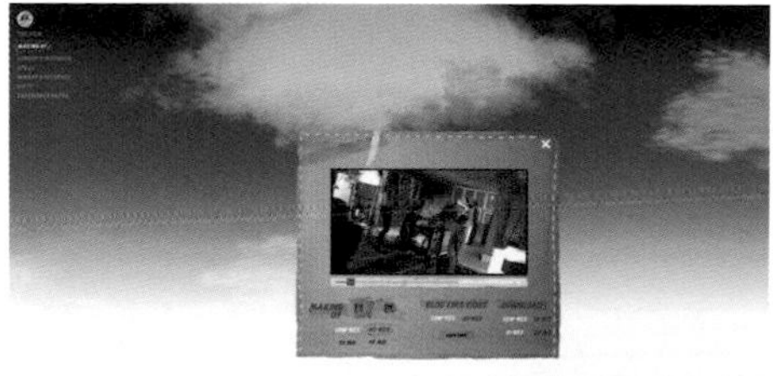

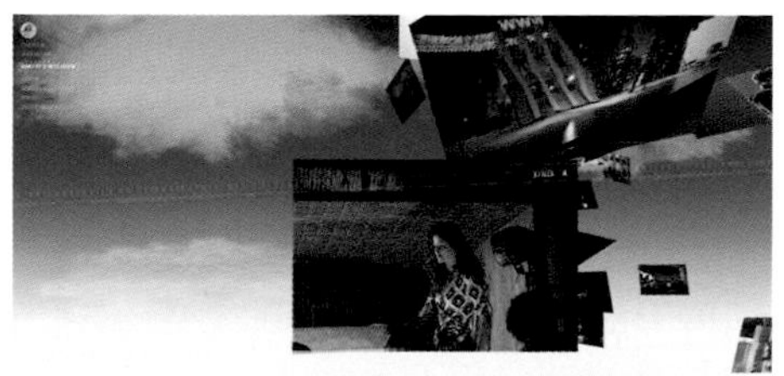

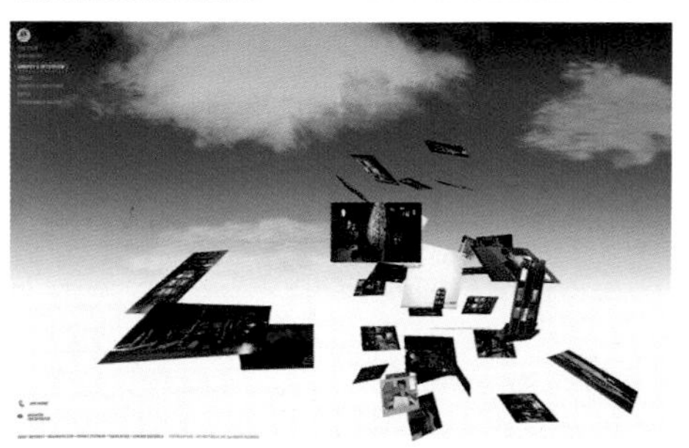

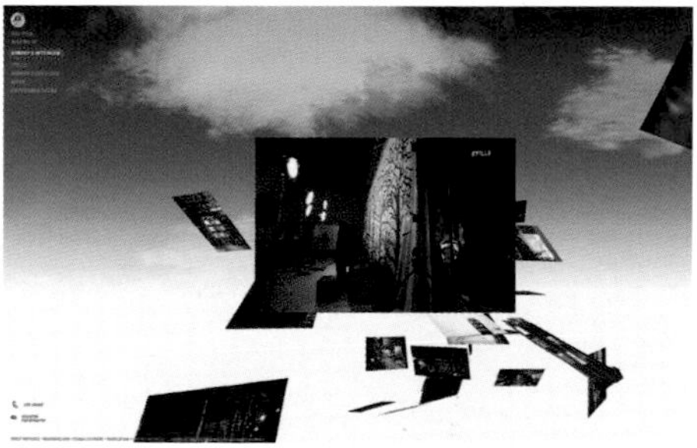

GEORGE RICHMOND

UK

www.georgerichmond.com

2008

Concept

A fully horizontal menu allows the user to choose from the content specified at the bottom of the page. It works fast and effectively to display both images and films. /// User aus den Inhalten am unteren Rand der Seite. So werden Bilder und Filme schnell und effektiv dargestellt. /// Un menu complètement horizontal permet à l'utilisateur de sélectionner du contenu figurant au bas de la page. Il est rapide et permet d'afficher des images et des vidéos.

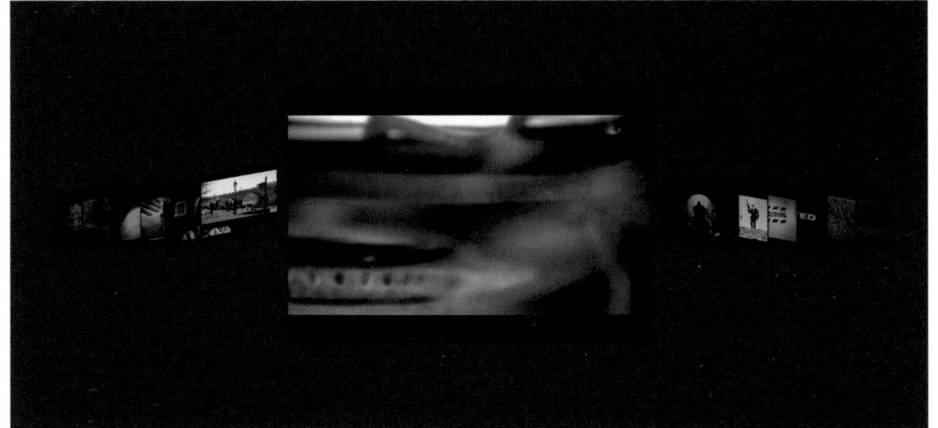

Info

Design Studio: Knowawall, Inc. <www.knowawall.com>. /// **Design:** Noah Wall. /// **Programming:** Benjamin Mace, Andrea Stein. /// **Client:** George Richmond. /// **Tools:** Adobe Photoshop, Flash, PHP. /// **Awards:** Communication Arts, NewWebPick. /// **Cost:** 20 Days.

GUDRUN & GUDRUN

DENMARK

www.gudrungudrun.com

2008

Concept

The website lets its users embark on a navigational journey inside the full-screen video. The more you click, the deeper you get and a double-click at the very end zooms you into the furthest reaches of the website. /// Auf dieser Website tauchen die User über die Navigation förmlich in das formatfüllende Video ein. Je mehr man klickt, desto tiefer kommt man, und per Doppelklick zoomt man schließlich bis zur tiefsten Ebene der Website. /// Le site Web permet à l'utilisateur d'entamer un voyage dans la vidéo plein écran. Plus vous cliquez, plus vous avancez et un double clic à la fin vous entraîne aux confins du site Web.

Info

Design Studio: Hello Monday <www.hellomonday.com>. /// **Design:** Sebastian Gram. /// **Programming:** Anders Jessen, Charlie Whitney. /// **Client:** Gudrun & Gudrun. /// **Tools:** Adobe Flash, Adobe Photoshop, Adobe Flex. /// **Awards:** FWA (Site of the Day). /// **Cost:** 150 hours.

HELLO SOUR SALLY

SINGAPORE

www.hellosoursally.com

2008

Concept

The 'platform game' style balloon navigation is both intuitive and at the same time adds a level of tactility, missing in most conventional websites. /// Die Ballon-Navigation im Stil eines Plattformspiels ist nicht nur intuitiv, sondern verleiht der Site auch einen gewissen taktilen Anklang, der den meisten konventionellen Websites fehlt. /// La navigation avec un ballon, qui fait penser à un « jeu de plate-forme », est intuitive et ajoute un niveau d'interaction tactile absent de la plupart des sites Web conventionnels.

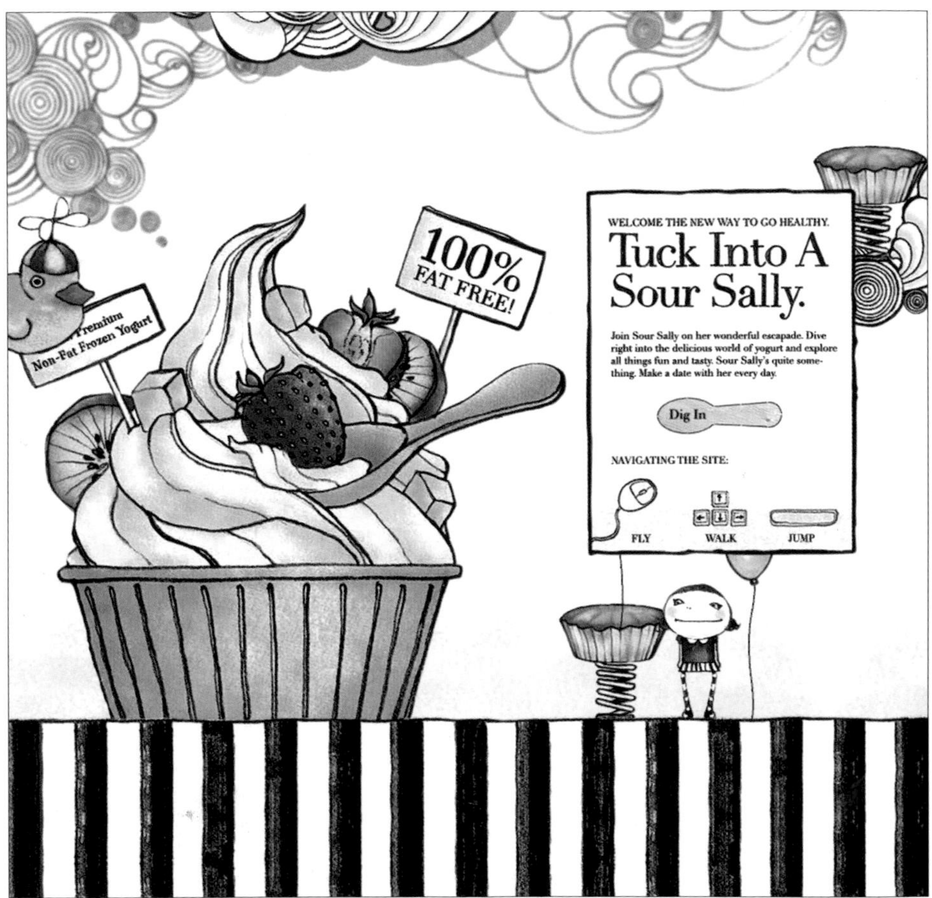

Info

DESIGN STUDIO: Kinetic Singapore <www.kinetic.com.sg>. /// **DESIGN:** Sean Lam (Creative Direction/Flash/Animation/Illustration/Sound Design), Leng Soh (Art Direction/Illustrator/Typographie). /// **PROGRAMMING:** JZ Wee. /// **OTHERS:** Victor Low (Music Composer); Eugene Tan (Copywriter). /// **CLIENT:** Sour Sally. /// **TOOLS:** Adobe Flash, Adobe Photoshop, Adobe Audition, Adobe Dreamweaver. /// **AWARDS:** FWA (Site of the Month). /// **COST:** ca. 180 hours.

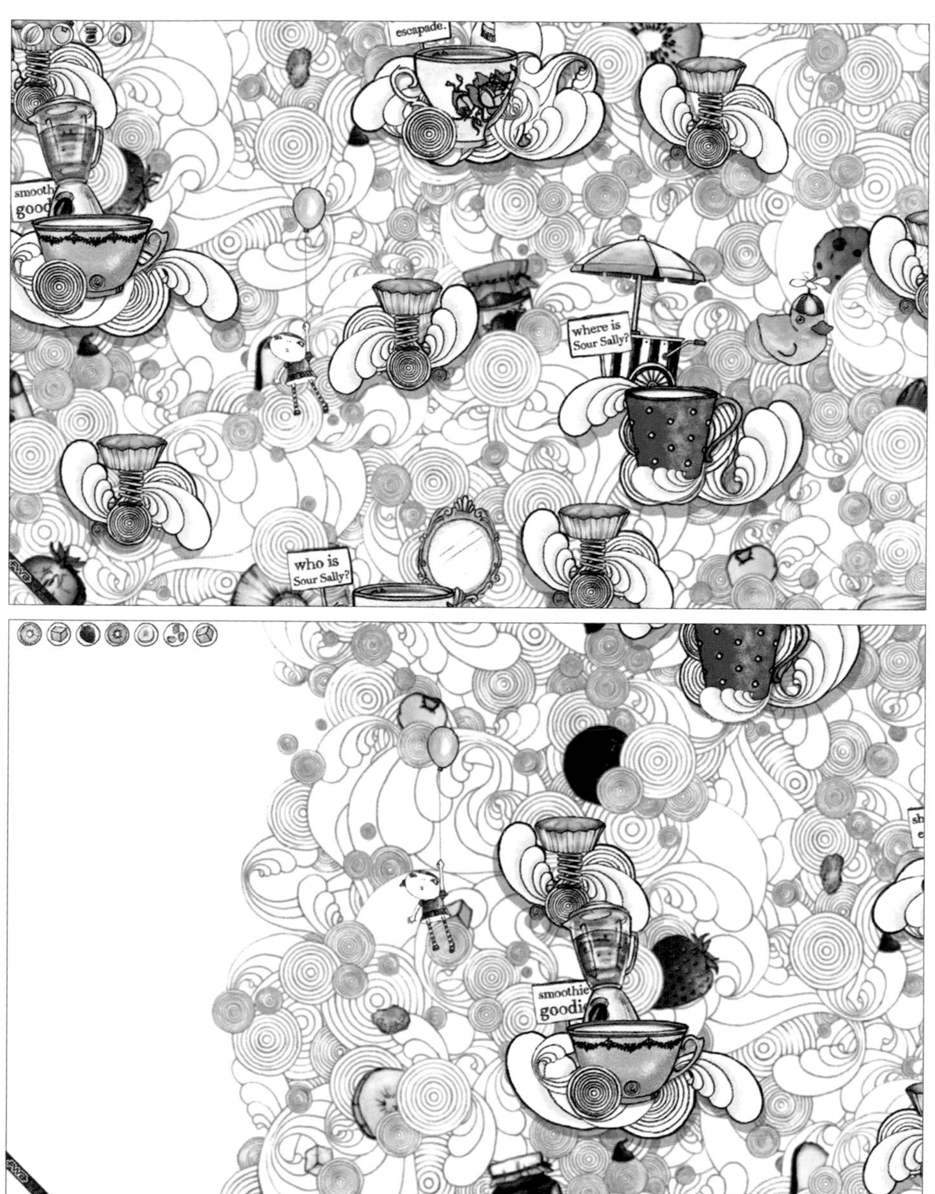

escapade.
where is
Sour Sally?
who is
Sour Sally?

HERMAN MILLER THOUGHTPILE

USA

www.thoughtpile.org

2008

Concept

ThoughtPile is Herman Miller's open invitation to people to share their ideas with the world. People submit ideas based on a weekly question, and can vote on other ideas. The ideas grow visually in real time and the biggest idea in the ThoughtPile receives the new Embody chair. /// Mit ThoughtPile lädt Herman Miller alle ein, der ganzen Welt die eigenen Vorstellungen mitzuteilen. Ausgehend von einer wöchentlichen Frage übermitteln die Menschen ihre Anregungen und können über die Ideen anderer abstimmen. Die Ideen werden im Laufe der Zeit optisch immer größer, und die größte Idee des ThoughtPiles erhält den neuen Embody-Stuhl. /// ThoughtPile est l'invitation d'Herman Miller pour que les gens partagent leurs idées avec le reste du monde. Les gens soumettent leurs idées à partir d'une question hebdomadaire et peuvent voter pour d'autres. Les idées grandissent visuellement en temps réel et la plus grosse dans la ThoughtPile est récompensée par la nouvelle chaise Embody.

Info

Design Studio: Freedom + Partners <www.FreedomandPartners.com>. /// **Design:** Freedom + Partners: Vas Sloutchevsky (Chief Creative Officer); mono: Travis Olson (Design Director). /// **Programming:** Freedom + Partners: Robert Forras (Chief Technology Officer); Iain Lawson, Oubi Sharon. /// **Others:** Freedom + Partners: Mark Ferdman (Chief Executive Officer), Craig Elimeliah (Senior Executive Producer); mono: Riley Kane (Creative Director/Writer). /// **Client:** mono & Herman Miller. /// **Tools:** Adobe Flash, Papervision 3D, MySQL. /// **Cost:** 360 hours.

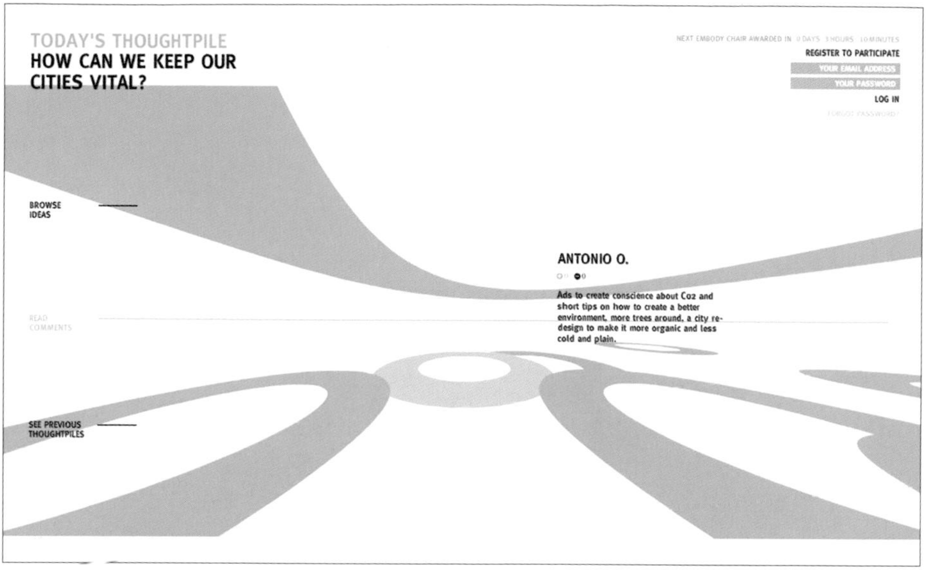

TODAY'S THOUGHTPILE
HOW CAN WE KEEP OUR CITIES VITAL?

NEXT EMBODY CHAIR AWARDED IN 0 DAYS 3 HOURS 10 MINUTES
REGISTER TO PARTICIPATE
YOUR EMAIL ADDRESS
YOUR PASSWORD
LOG IN
FORGOT PASSWORD?

BROWSE IDEAS

READ COMMENTS

SEE PREVIOUS THOUGHTPILES

ANTONIO O.

Ads to create conscience about Co2 and short tips on how to create a better environment, more trees around, a city re-design to make it more organic and less cold and plain.

TODAY'S THOUGHTPILE
HOW CAN WE KEEP OUR CITIES VITAL?

NEXT EMBODY CHAIR AWARDED IN 0 DAYS 3 HOURS 10 MINUTES
REGISTER TO PARTICIPATE
YOUR EMAIL ADDRESS
YOUR PASSWORD
LOG IN

BROWSE IDEAS

IDEAS NEXT
VISITED IDEAS

FAVORITE

MATTHEW C.

More Communal Space, More places where people can meet up and work together. Empowering Individuals through interaction between individuals would keep any population vital and alive.

PILE ON YOUR IDEA

READ COMMENTS

SEE PREVIOUS THOUGHTPILES

SOUND OFF

THOUGHTPILE IS SPONSORED BY HERMAN MILLER'S NEW CHAIR, EMBODY.

HMX20C

www.samsung.com/fr/microsite/hmx20c

FRANCE

2008

Concept

The user can navigate through a high-definition video and click on the key points or the timeline to discover the camera through animated features. /// Der User navigiert durch ein hochauflösendes Video und klickt auf die zentralen Punkte oder die Zeitleiste, um die Kamera anhand von Animationen zu erforschen. /// L'utilisateur peut naviguer dans une vidéo haute définition et cliquer sur les points clés ou la chronologie pour découvrir la caméra dans des animations.

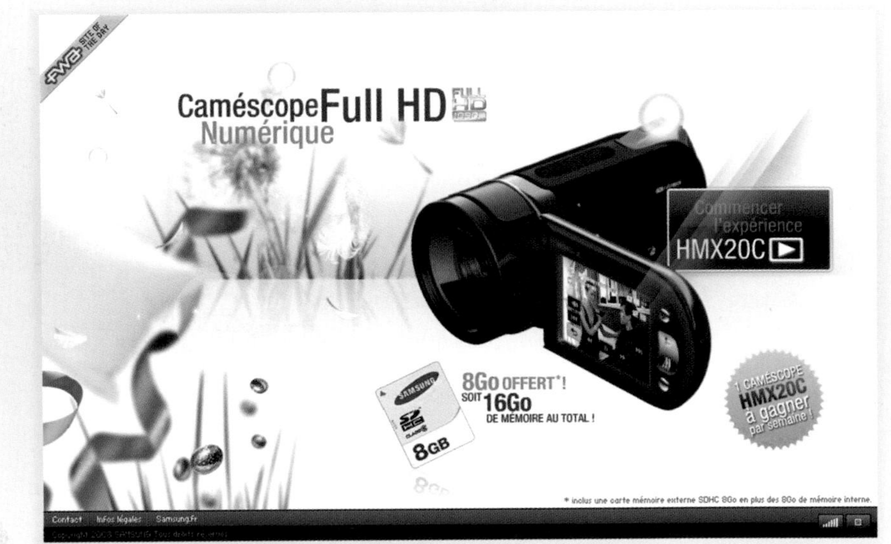

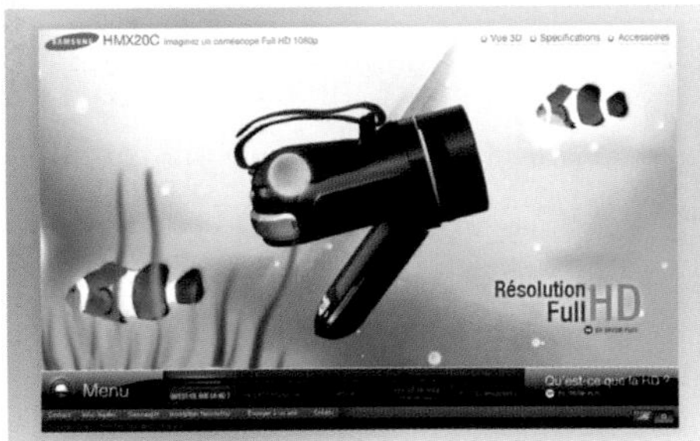

Info

Design Studio: Soleil Noir <www.soleilnoir.net>. /// **Design:** Antoine Menard, Sylvain Theyssens. /// **Programming:** Mathieu Vignau. /// **Others:** Olivier Marchand (Project Manager). /// **Client:** Cheil communication france. /// **Tools:** Adobe Flash, Adobe Photoshop, Adobe After Effects, Maya, XML. /// **Awards:** FWA (Site of the Day). /// **Cost:** 1 month.

HMX20C
Ecran
tactile
Menu
Facilité d'utilisation

Fonction Photo
jusqu' à 8 Mpx
Menu
Capteur

HMX20C
Mode ultra
ralenti
Menu
Plus technologiques

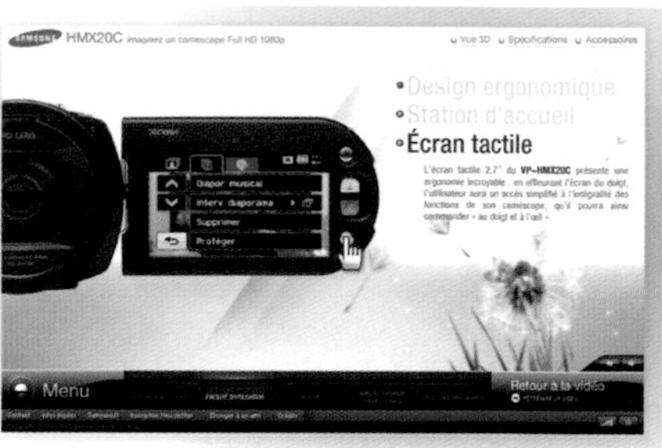
HMX20C
Design ergonomique
Station d'accueil
Écran tactile
Menu
Retour à la vidéo

SAMSUNG HMX20C imaginez un caméscope Full HD 1080p
Vue 3D
Spécifications
Accessoires
Capteur CMOS 6,4Mpx
Photo jusqu'à 8Mpx
Résolution photo de 4M pixels
Jusqu'à 8M pixels par interpolation
Impression A5
2304x1728 4M pixel
Impression A4
3264x2448 8M pixel
Menu
QU'EST-CE QUE LA HD ?
FACILITÉ D'UTILISATION
CAPTEUR
CAPACITÉ MÉMOIRE & PERFORMANCE
PLUS TECHNOLOGIQUES
Retour à la vidéo
REPRENDRE LA VIDÉO
Contact
Infos légales
Samsung.fr
Inscription Newsletter
Envoyer à un ami
Crédits

HOME INVEST

NORWAY

www.homeinvest.no

2008

Concept

The Monopoly board features environmental projects, art exhibitions, and business ventures giving an overview of investor Petter A. Stordalen's taste, drive and character. /// Auf einem Monopoly-Brett werden Öko-Projekte, Kunstausstellungen und Firmenprojekte dargestellt, die einen Eindruck vom Geschmack, der Dynamik und dem Charakter des Investors Petter A. Stordalen vermitteln. /// **Le plateau de Monopoly présente des projets sur l'environnement, des expositions artistiques et des entreprises, ce qui offre un aperçu du goût, de l'énergie et de la personnalité de l'investisseur Petter A. Stordalen.**

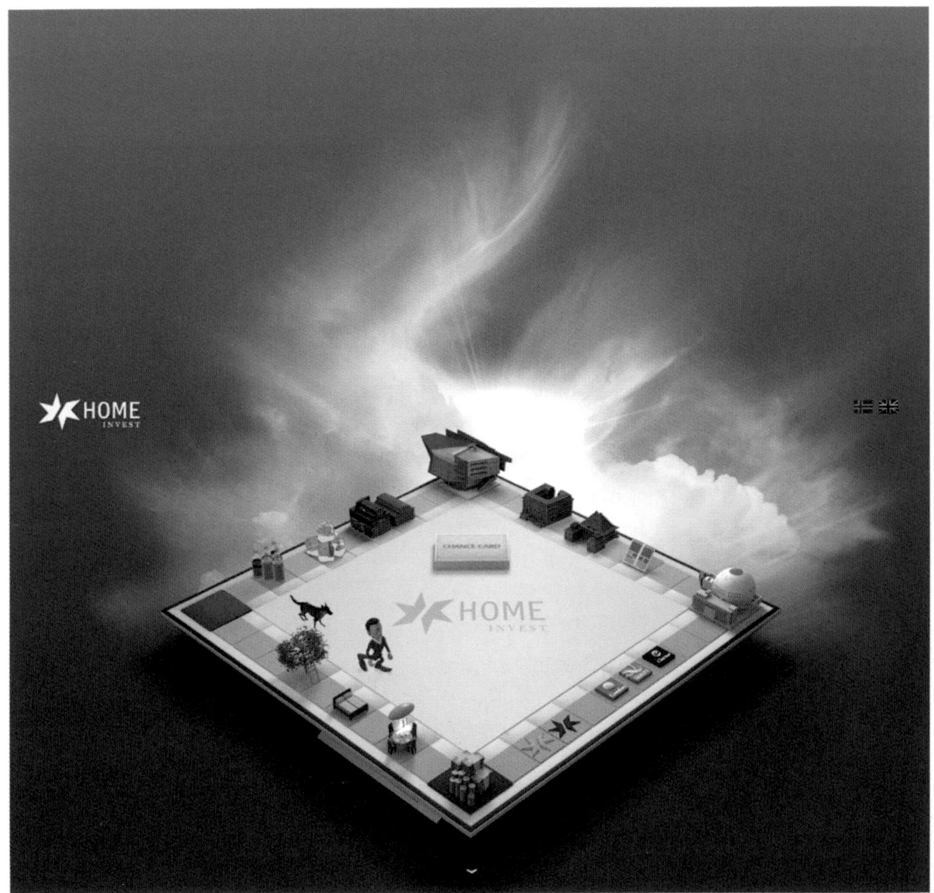

Info

Design Studio: Apt <www.apt.no>. /// **Design:** Morten Iveland (Design), Daniel Butler (Concept Developer), Roy Kristoffersen (3D/Motion). /// **Programming:** Paal Smith-Amundsen (Flash), Erland Wiencke. /// **Others:** Elin Johannson (Project Manager); Harald Gramnes (Project Manager); Thomas Karlsen (Consultant). /// **Client:** Home Invest. /// **Tools:** Adobe Photoshop, Adobe Illustrator, XML, Adobe After Effects, Maya, Realflow, Maxwell Render. /// **Cost:** ca. 1000 hours.

HOME

HOME

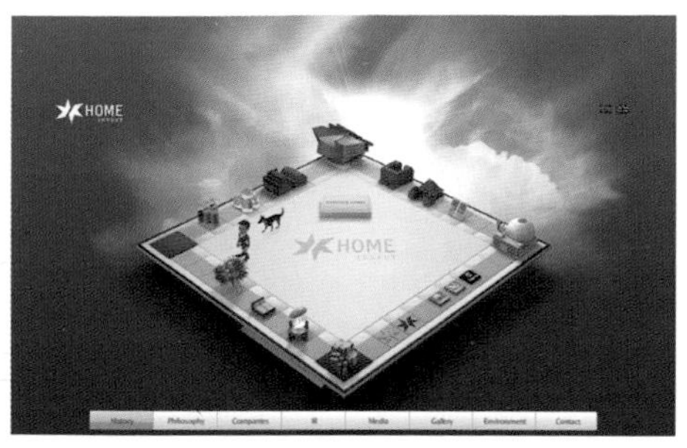

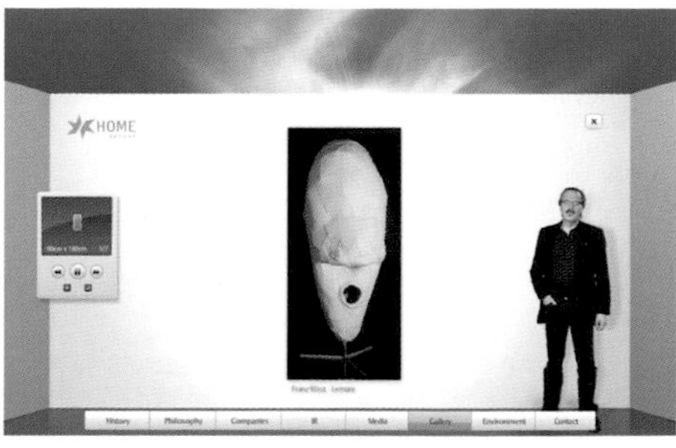

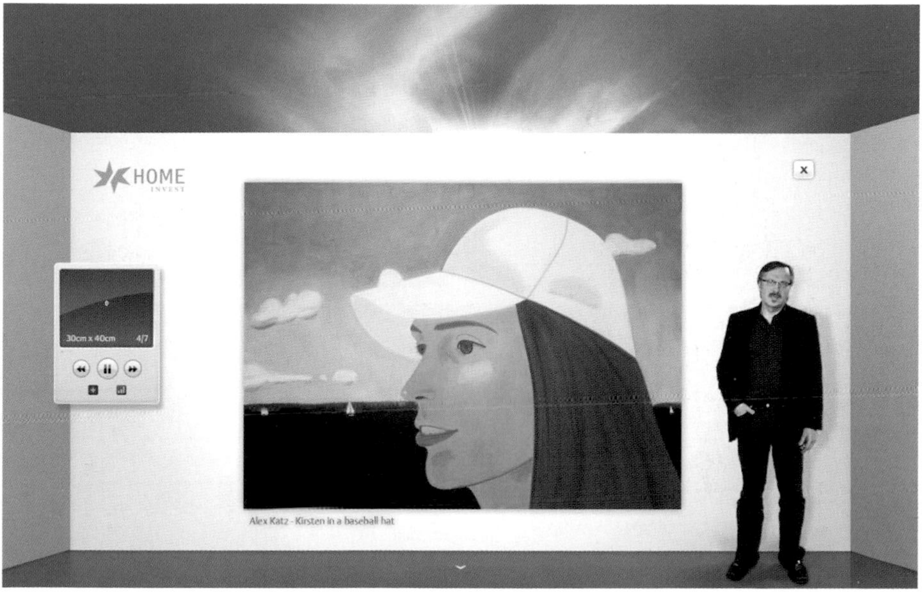

HOME
INVEST
30cm x 40cm
4/7
Alex Katz - Kirsten in a baseball hat

HOME
Companies
History
Philosophy
Companies
IR
Media
Gallery
Environment
Contact

HOME
Long-Term View and Potential
STORDALEN's
marked
History
Philosophy
Companies
IR
Media
Gallery
Environment
Contact

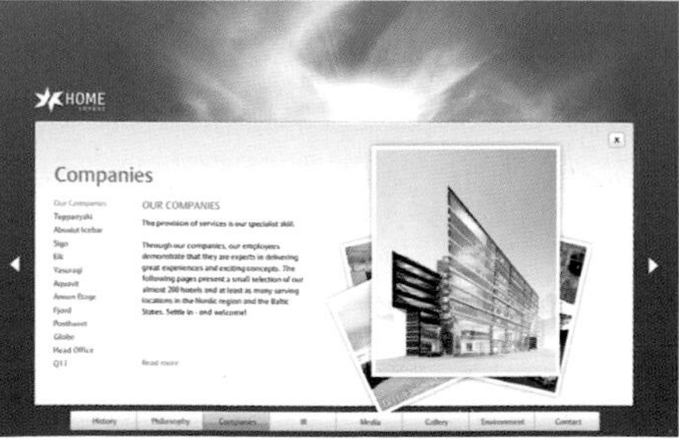

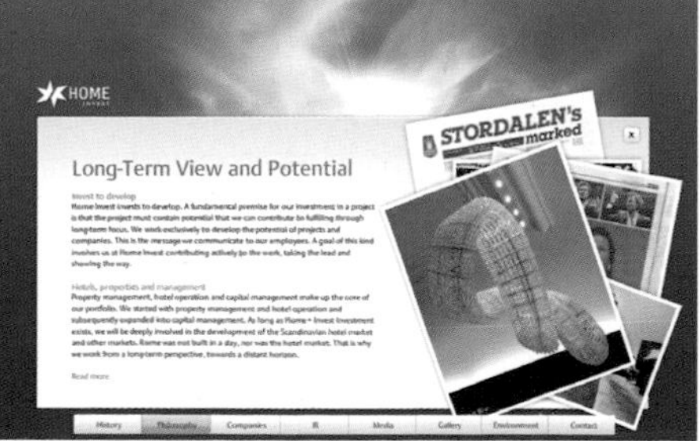

IDOHM

SPAIN

www.idohm.com

2008

Concept

Minimalistic website of music videos where the menu is integrated into a gadget that lets you browse all the web content. /// Minimalistische Website für Musikvideos, bei der das Menü in ein iPhone-ähnliches Gerät integriert ist, mit der man im gesamten Web-Content browsen kann. /// **Site Web minimaliste de vidéos musicales dans lequel le menu est intégré à un gadget permettant de naviguer dans l'ensemble du contenu.**

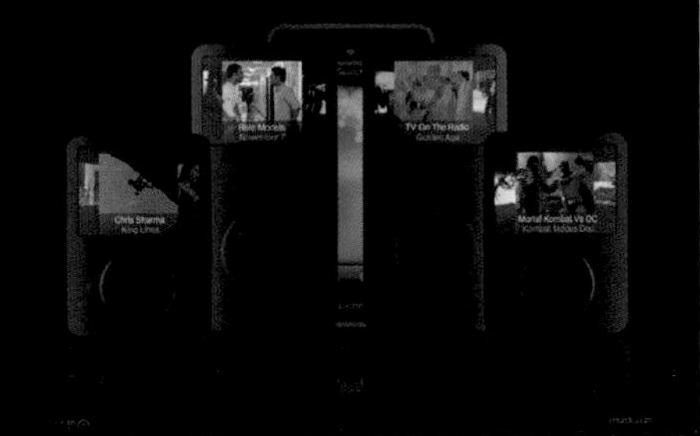

Info

Design Studio: Medusateam <www.medusateam.com>. /// **Design:** Medusateam. /// **Programming:** Medusateam. /// **Client:** Idohm. /// **Tools:** Adobe Flash, Adobe Photoshop. /// **Cost:** 400 hours.

JAN KNOFF PHOTOGRAPHY

GERMANY

www.janknoff.de

2007

Concept

The navigation changes according to the amount of pictures that are shown. /// Die Navigation ändert sich abhängig von der Anzahl der gezeigten Bilder. /// La navigation change en fonction de la quantité d'images à l'écran.

Info

Design Studio: Jan Knoff <www.janknoff.de>. /// **Design:** Jan Knoff. /// **Programming:** Wolfgang Kohlert. /// **Client:** Jan Knoff Photography. /// **Tools:** Adobe Flash. /// **Cost:** 40 hours.

JOHN ST.

CANADA

www.johnst.com

2005

Concept

The site presents a friendly hostess who welcomes and guides users through it, making use of video for the experience and for the company's online image, particularly in the "People" section. /// Auf dieser Site wird der User von einer freundlichen Dame begrüßt, die ihn durch die Site geleitet und dabei das Online-Image der Firma über Videos vermittelt, vor allem im „People"-Bereich. /// **Le site montre une aimable hôtesse qui accueille et guide l'utilisateur. La vidéo est employée pour l'expérience et pour l'image en ligne de l'entreprise, notamment dans la section « People ».**

Info

Design Studio: HELLOHELLO!! <www.HelloHello.BZ>. /// **Design:** Thierry Loa. /// **Programming:** Thierry Loa (Flash/Front-end); Nolan Dubeau (CMS/Back-end). /// **Others:** Production/Creation: Thierry Loa (Dr. Hello), Stephen Jurisic (john st.); Video/Sound: Thierry Loa; Project Coordination: Cheryl Kyte (john st.). /// **Client:** john st. /// **Tools:** Adobe Flash, ActionScript, Adobe ColdFusion, Flash Forms, Adobe Premiere, Adobe After Effects, Sound Forge. /// **Awards:** FWA (Site of the Day), Gold Awards at the 56th Advertising and Design Club of Canada. /// **Cost:** 3,5 months.

john st.
People
Shuffle Images
About us
Featured work
Portfolio
John st. mission
Book of john
Jobs

john st.
Portfolio
Browse TV
Browse Print
Browse Misc
Browse Clients

john st.
Book of john
be unignorable

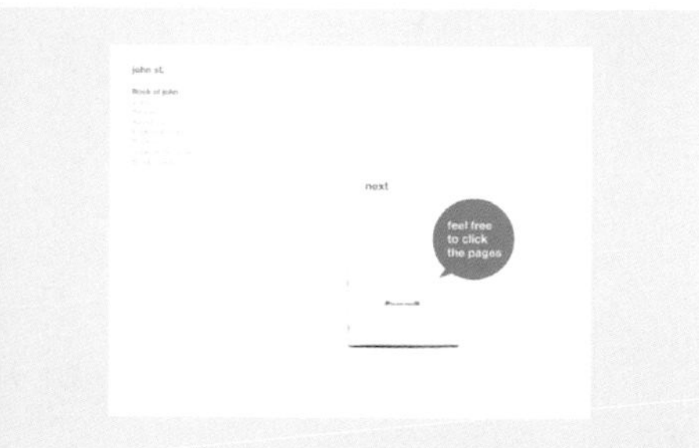
john st.
Book of john
next
feel free to click the pages

john st.
Book of john
prev
next

JOTUN LADY NOW

NORWAY

http://kampanjeweb.apt.no/jotun/ladynow/uk

2008

Concept

Site for Norway's largest producer of paint and decorative products which shows the latest trends in color of the Jotun Lady Now collection from the professionals' perspective, with the focus on how color can transform a space. /// Auf dieser Site für den größten norwegischen Hersteller von Farben und dekorativen Produkten werden die neuesten Farbtrends der Collection Jotun Lady Now aus Profiperspektive vorgestellt. Der Schwerpunkt liegt darauf, wie Farben einen Raum verwandeln können. /// Site pour le plus grand fabricant de peintures et de produits décoratifs de Norvège, qui présente les dernières tendances en matière de couleurs de la collection Jotun Lady Now d'un point de vue professionnel, en montrant comme la couleur peut transformer un espace.

Select a colour
Colours are fashion. Lady presents the new colour collection from the Lady NOW 08-09 colour chart. Find inspiration and suggestions for harmonious colour combinations which suit your interior.

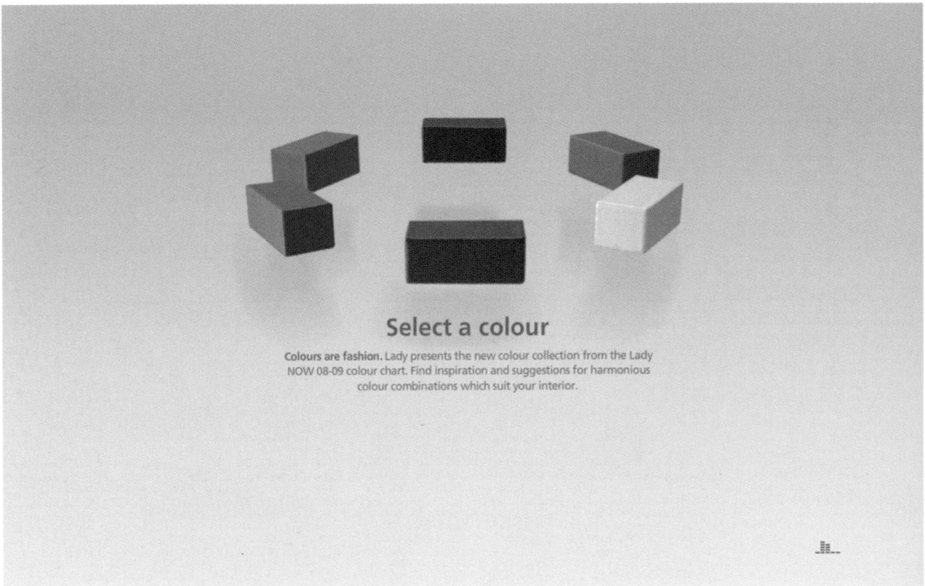

Info

Design Studio: Apt <www.apt.no>. /// **Design:** Morten Iveland (Design), Daniel Butler (Concept Developer), Roy Kristoffersen (3D/Motion). /// **Programming:** Paal Smith-Amundsen (Flash), Anders Stalheim Oefsdahl. /// **Others:** Christian Pettersen (Producer), Lukas Szachanski (Project Manager), Monica Rosengren (Project Manager), Joachim Levin (Consultant). /// **Client:** Jotun. /// **Tools:** Adobe Photoshop, Adobe Illustrator, XML, Adobe After Effects, Shake, Maya, Realflow, Maxwell Render. /// **Cost:** ca. 1000 hours.

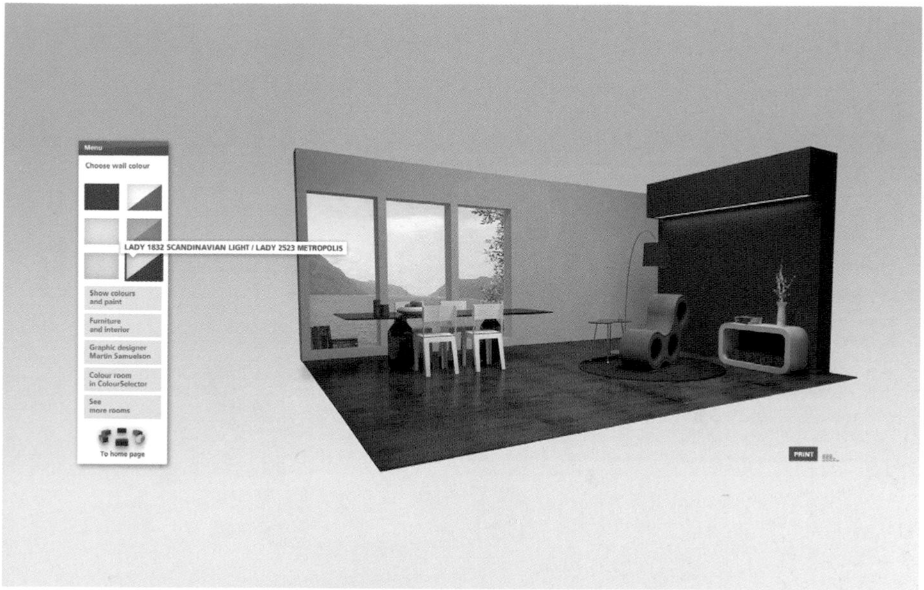

Menu
Choose wall colour
LADY 1832 SCANDINAVIAN LIGHT / LADY 2523 METROPOLIS
Show colours and paint
Furniture and interior
Graphic designer Martin Samuelson
Colour room in ColourSelector
See more rooms
To home page
PRINT

LADY 3211 EYELINER
LADY 9904 TWILIGHT
LADY 1001 EGG WHITE

INFO ABOUT ROOM
X
2008
MAY 25 TUE
PREVIOUS
NEXT

PRINT
X
INFO ABOUT ROOM
Paint and colours
Main section
2452 SALSA
LADY Wall Easy Clean
White surrounding wall
7236 CHI
LADY Wall Soft
Furniture and interior
Rug: Ikea »
Chair, wall clock and articles: R.O.O.M »
Desk: Ikea »

JULIE BAYARD

FRANCE

www.juliebayard.fr

2006

Concept

The main navigation is the zoom of the camera view over a thumbnail graphic grid. /// Die Hauptnavigation ist der Zoom der Kameraansicht über einen Raster mit Vorschaubildern. /// **La navigation principale est un zoom de la caméra sur une grille de vignettes.**

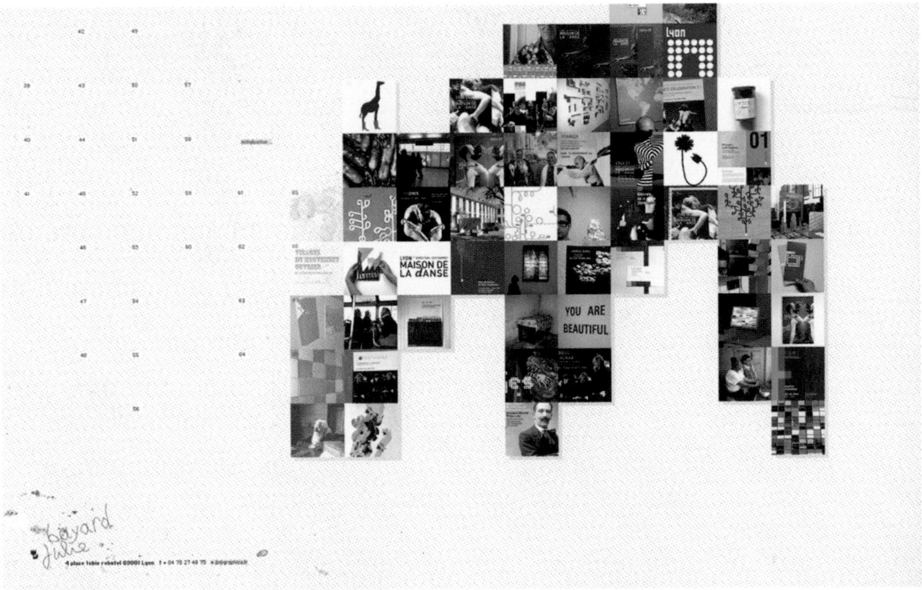

Info

Design Studio: Danka Studio <www.dankastudio.fr>. /// **Design:** Guillaume Bonnecase, Grégoire Gérardin. /// **Programming:** Grégoire Gerardin. /// **Others:** João Cabral (Project Manager). /// **Client:** Julie Bayard. /// **Tools:** Adobe Photoshop, Flash, XML. /// **Cost:** 150–200 hours.

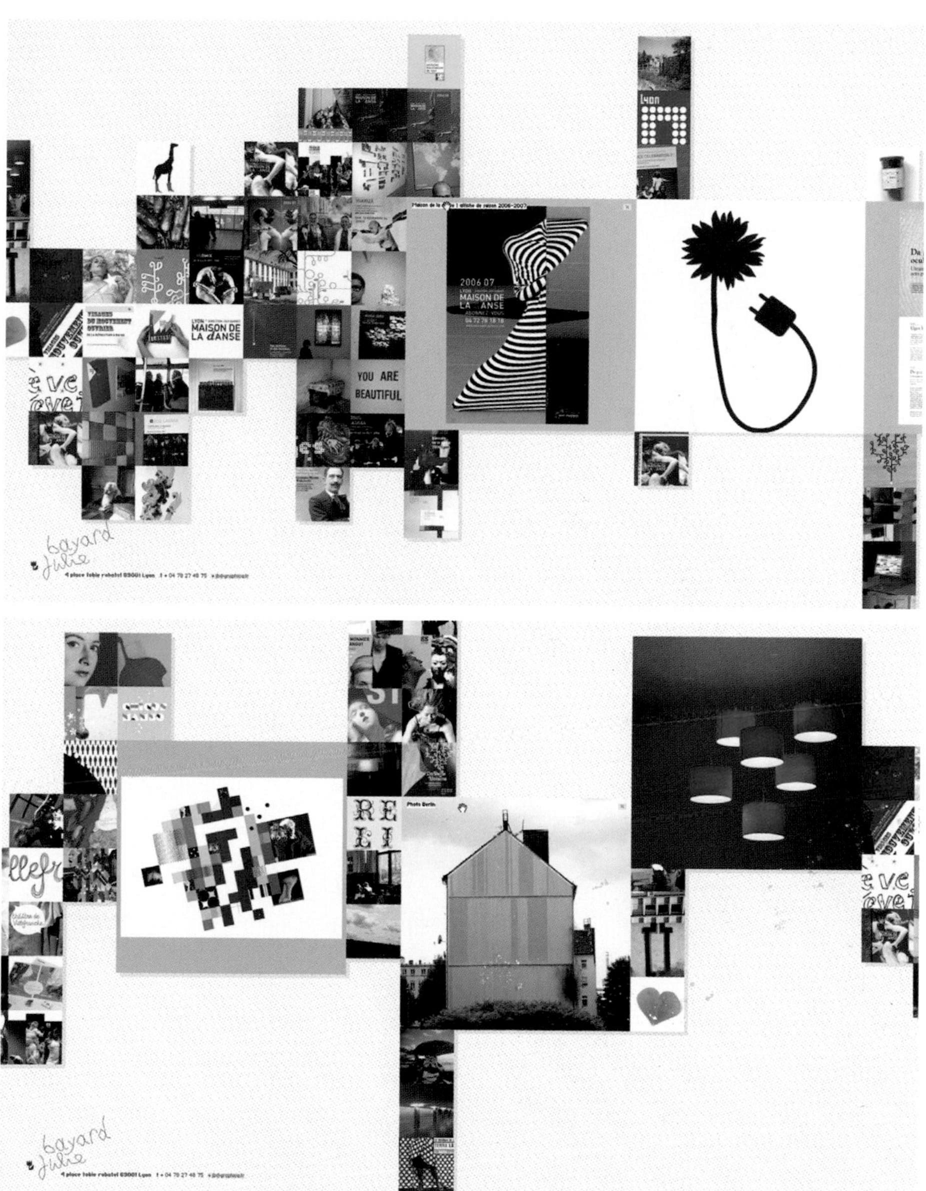

KONTAIN

WORLDWIDE

www.kontain.com

2008

Concept

Kontain is a free website for users to blog and share photos, videos and audio with friends, family, even beautiful strangers. /// Auf der Website von Kontain bloggen User kostenlos und geben Fotos, Videos und Audiodateien an Freunde, Familie und sogar schöne Unbekannte weiter. /// Kontain est un site Web gratuit pour que les utilisateurs échangent des messages, des photos, des vidéos et de l'audio avec des amis, des membres de leur famille ou de parfaits inconnus.

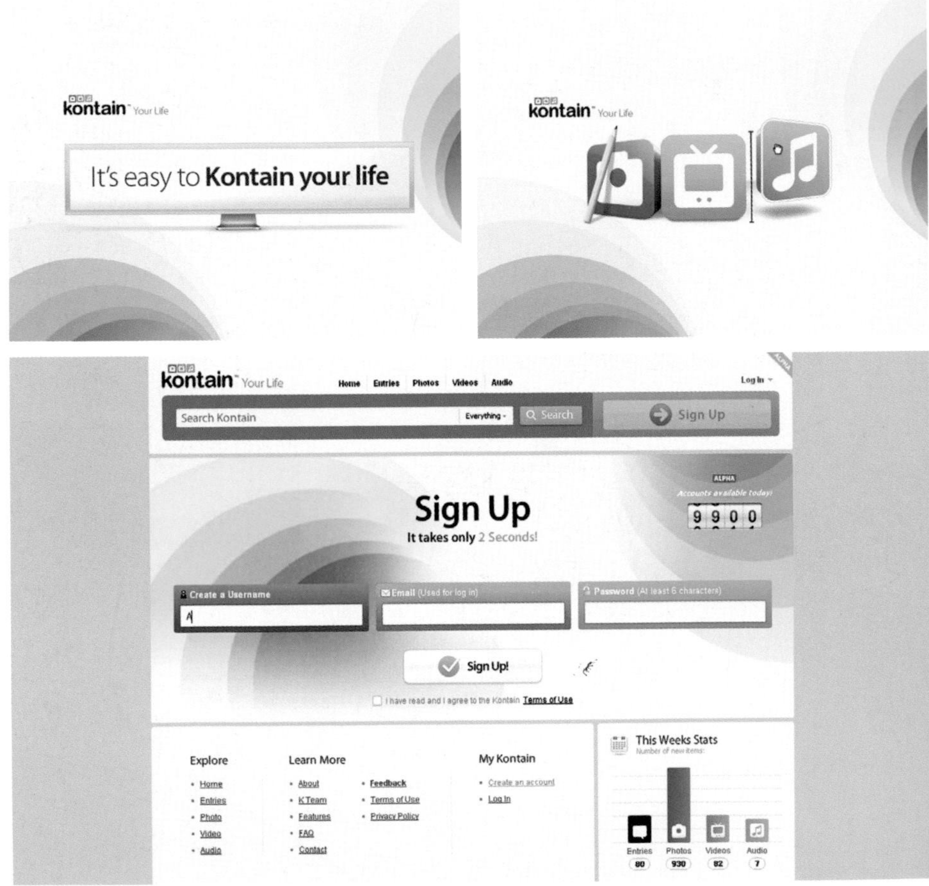

Info

DESIGN STUDIO: Fi <www.f-i.com>. /// **DESIGN:** David Hugh Martin (Creative Direction); David Engzell, Anton Repponen (Senior Designer); Yaron Schoen (Designer). /// **PROGRAMMING:** Stephen Martin (Executive Producer); Fi development team (Front-end/Back-end). /// **CLIENT:** Product of Fi. /// **TOOLS:** HTML, Flash, Java, Web services.

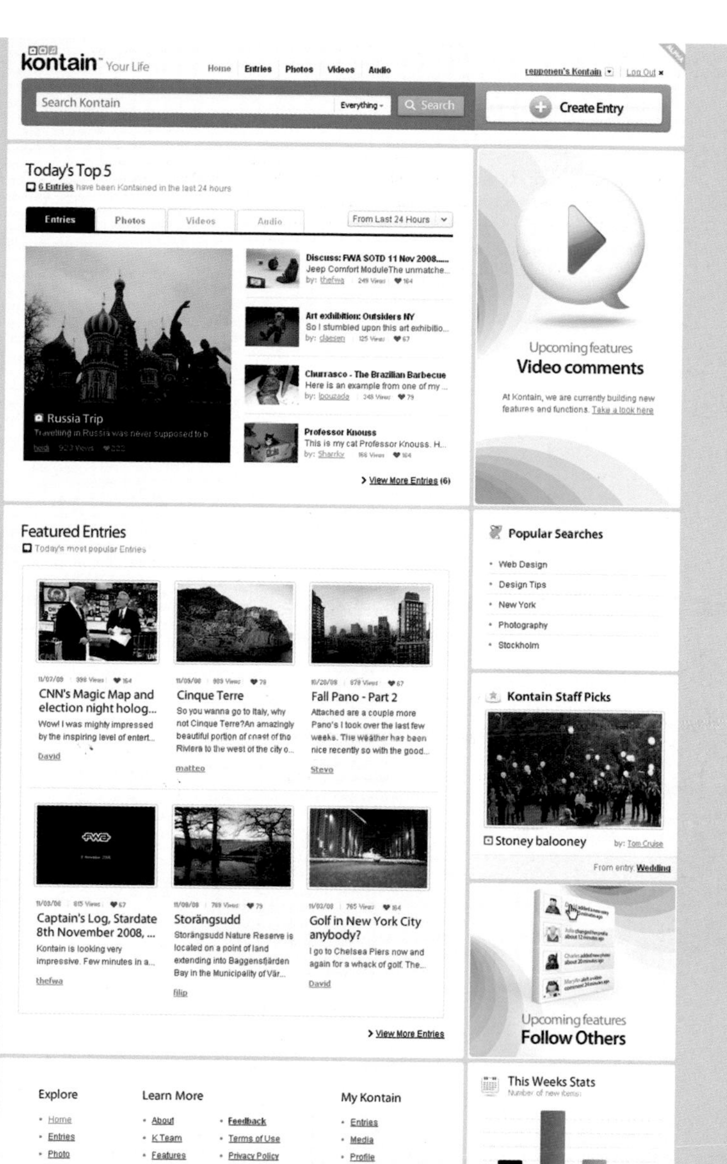
kontain Your Life
Home
Entries
Photos
Videos
Audio
Log Out
Search Kontain
Everything
Search
Create Entry
Today's Top 5
6 Entries have been Kontained in the last 24 hours
Entries
Photos
Videos
Audio
From Last 24 Hours
Discuss: FWA SOTD 11 Nov 2008......
Jeep Comfort ModuleThe unmatche...
Art exhibition: Outsiders NY
So I stumbled upon this art exhibitio...
Churrasco - The Brazilian Barbecue
Here is an example from one of my ...
Professor Knouss
This is my cat Professor Knouss. H...
Russia Trip
View More Entries (6)
Upcoming features
Video comments
At Kontain, we are currently building new features and functions. Take a look here
Featured Entries
Today's most popular Entries
CNN's Magic Map and election night holog...
Wow! I was mighty impressed by the inspiring level of entert...
David
Cinque Terre
So you wanna go to Italy, why not Cinque Terre?An amazingly beautiful portion of coast of the Riviera to the west of the city o...
matteo
Fall Pano - Part 2
Attached are a couple more Pano's I took over the last few weeks. The weather has been nice recently so with the good...
Stevo
Captain's Log, Stardate 8th November 2008, ...
Kontain is looking very impressive. Few minutes in a...
thefwa
Storängsudd
Storängsudd Nature Reserve is located on a point of land extending into Baggensfjärden Bay in the Municipality of Vär...
filip
Golf in New York City anybody?
I go to Chelsea Piers now and again for a whack of golf. The...
David
View More Entries
Popular Searches
Web Design
Design Tips
New York
Photography
Stockholm
Kontain Staff Picks
Stoney balooney
by: Tom Cruise
From entry: Wedding
Upcoming features
Follow Others
Explore
Home
Entries
Photo
Video
Audio
Learn More
About
K Team
Features
FAQ
Contact
Feedback
Terms of Use
Privacy Policy
My Kontain
Entries
Media
Profile
Dashboard
This Weeks Stats
Number of new items
Entries
823
Photos
7332
Videos
3993
Audio
373

LA CHANGA WEAR

MEXICO

www.lachangawear.com

2008

Concept

Easy to navigate site with motion, sound and graphic details, as well as animated actions for every command on the menu. /// Leicht zu navigierende Site mit Animationen, Sounds und grafischen Details sowie animierten Aktionen für jeden Menübefehl. /// **Site de navigation simple avec des éléments d'animation, audio et graphiques, ainsi que des actions animées pour chaque commande du menu.**

Info

Design Studio: WeEatDesign <www.weeatdesign.com>. /// **Design:** Carlos Alonzo. /// **Programming:** Alfredo Bolio. /// **Client:** La Changa Wear. /// **Tools:** Adobe Photoshop, Adobe Flash, HMTL. /// **Cost:** 80 hours.

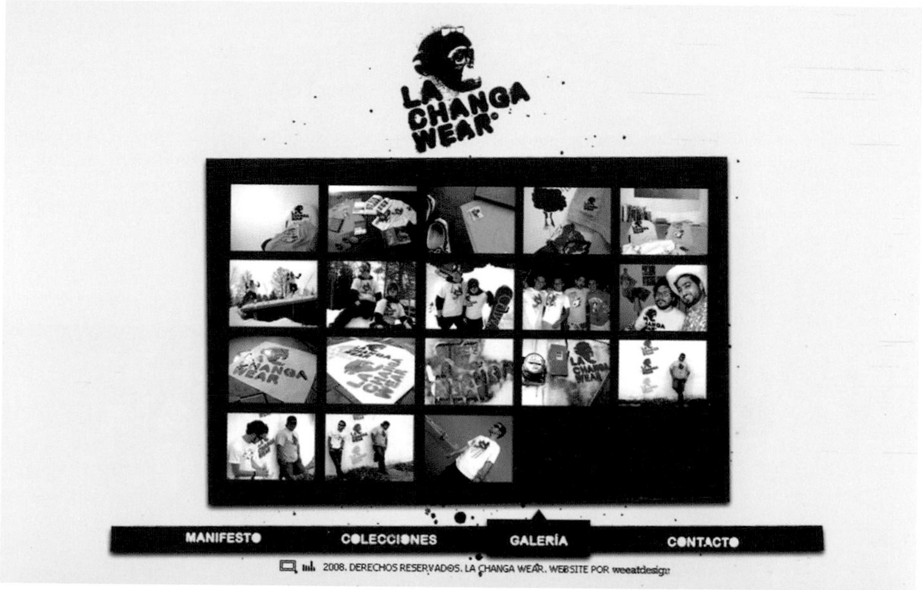
LA CHANGA WEAR
MANIFESTO
COLECCIONES
GALERÍA
CONTACTO
2008. DERECHOS RESERVADOS. LA CHANGA WEAR. WEBSITE POR weeatdesign

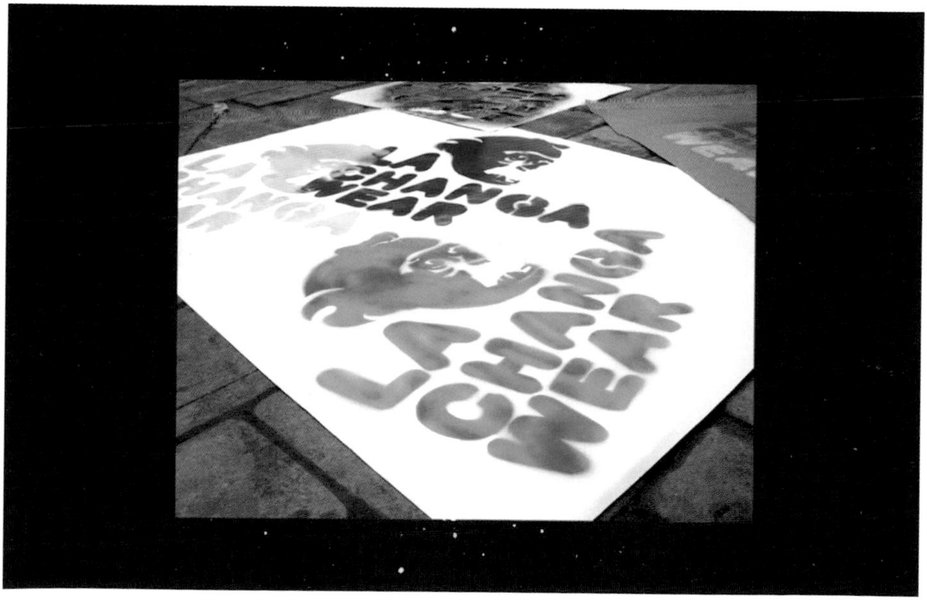
LA CHANGA WEAR
LA CHANGA WEAR

LEE TOWNDROW PHOTOGRAPHY

CANADA

www.towndrow.ca

2008

Concept

The first idea here was to make viewers forget that they were looking at a website, as such, but rather an interactive gallery of photos using intuitive user interface and interaction and full-screen. /// Hier war die Grundidee, über ein intuitives Interface und Interaktionen sowie die Vollbildansicht die Betrachter vergessen zu lassen, dass sie eine Website anschauen, sondern es vielmehr mit einer interaktiven Fotogalerie zu tun haben. /// **L'idée de départ était que les visiteurs oublient qu'ils étaient face à un site Web en tant que tel, et qu'ils consultent plutôt une galerie interactive de photos grâce à une interface intuitive, de l'interaction et un affichage plein écran.**

Info

Design Studio: HELLOHELLO!! <www.HelloHello.BZ>. /// **Design:** Thierry Loa. /// **Programming:** Thierry Loa (Front-end/FlashAS); Clayton Partridge (Back-end/CMS). /// **Others:** Production/Creation: Thierry Loa. /// **Client:** Lee Towndrow. /// **Tools:** Adobe Flash, ActionScript, Adobe ColdFusion, Flash Remoting. /// **Awards:** FWA Site of the Day. /// **Cost:** 6 weeks.

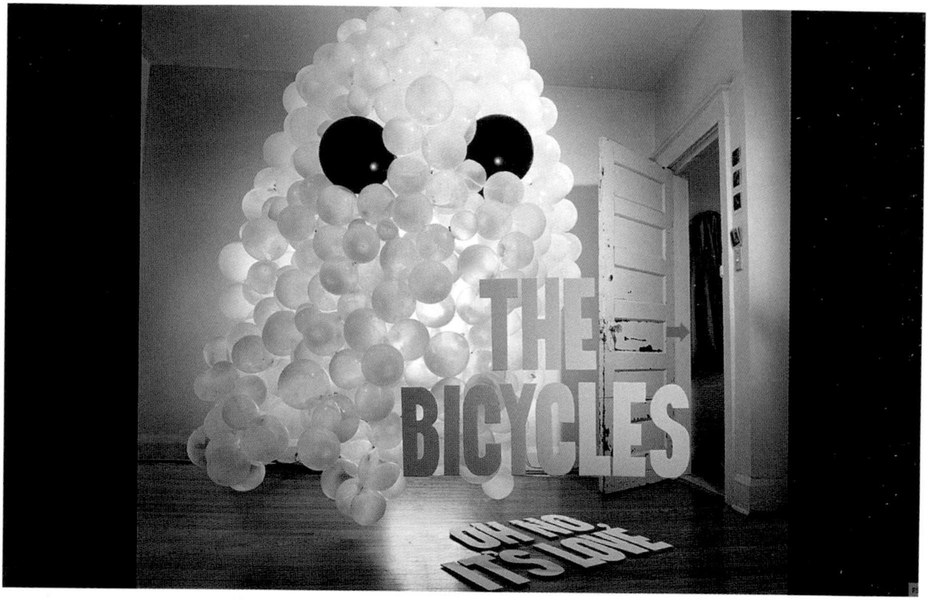
THE
BICYCLES
OH NO
IT'S LOVE

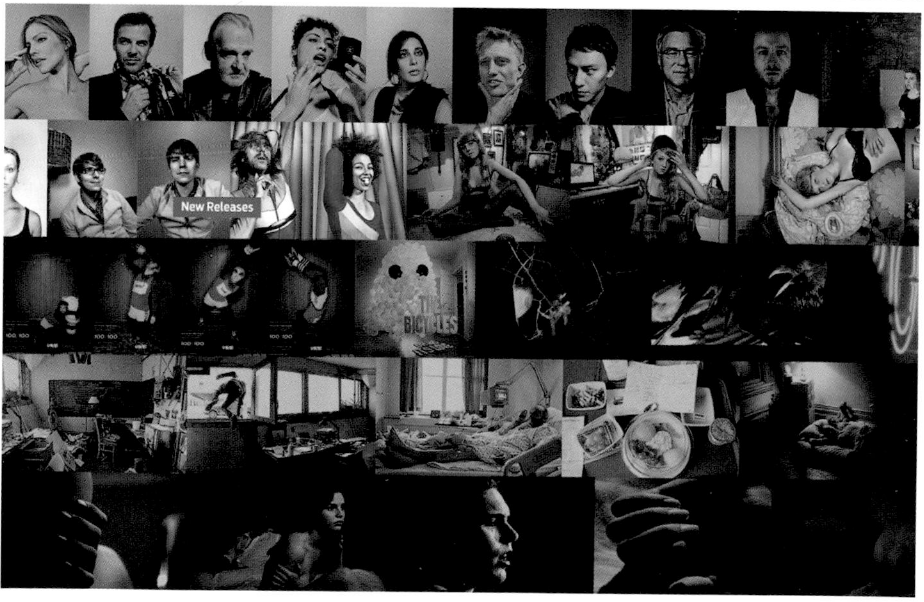
New Releases
THE
BICYCLES

LIKATEK

www.likatek.net

KOSOVO

2007

Concept

One-page horizontal menu, with clear and quickly displayed options for every bar featured on the screen. /// Horizontales Menü mit nur einer Seite und klaren, flott dargestellten Optionen für jede auf dem Bildschirm dargestellten Säule. /// Menu horizontal sur une page, avec des options qui s'affichent clairement et rapidement pour chaque barre visible à l'écran.

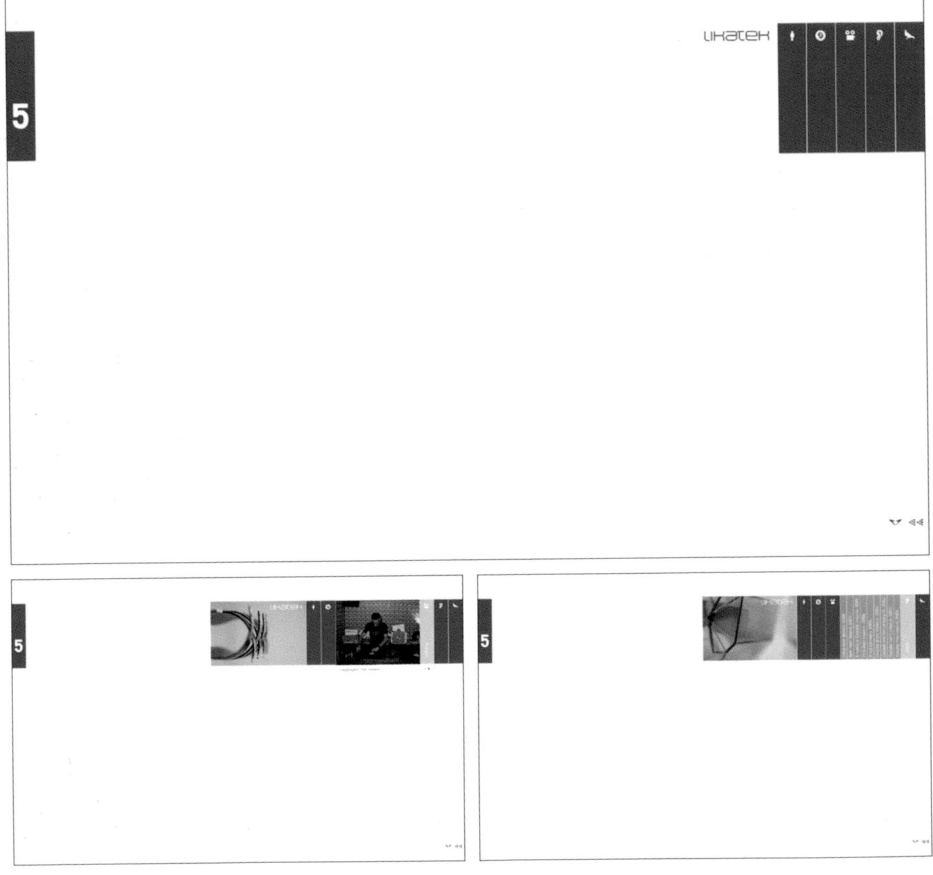

Info

Design Studio: Project Graphics <www.projectgraphics.eu>; Frakton <www.frakton.com>. /// **Design:** Agon Çeta. /// **Programming:** Mentor Paçarada. /// **Others:** Lirak Hamiti (Concept), Agon Çeta (Photos). /// **Client:** DJ Likatek. /// **Tools:** Corel Draw, Adobe Photoshop, Flash, html. /// **Cost:** 85 hours.

LOS TROMPOS

MEXICO

www.lostrompos.com.mx

2008

Concept

Easy to navigate site for this food retail chain, displaying quickly and clearly the information needed, from addresses and contact information to gallery images. /// Auf der Site für diese Lebensmitteleinzelhandelskette kann man leicht navigieren. Die gewünschten Informationen (Adressen, Kontaktdaten, Bildergalerien) werden schnell gefunden und klar dargestellt. /// Site de navigation simple pour cette chaîne de supermarchés, qui présente rapidement et clairement les informations utiles (adresse, données de contact, galerie d'images).

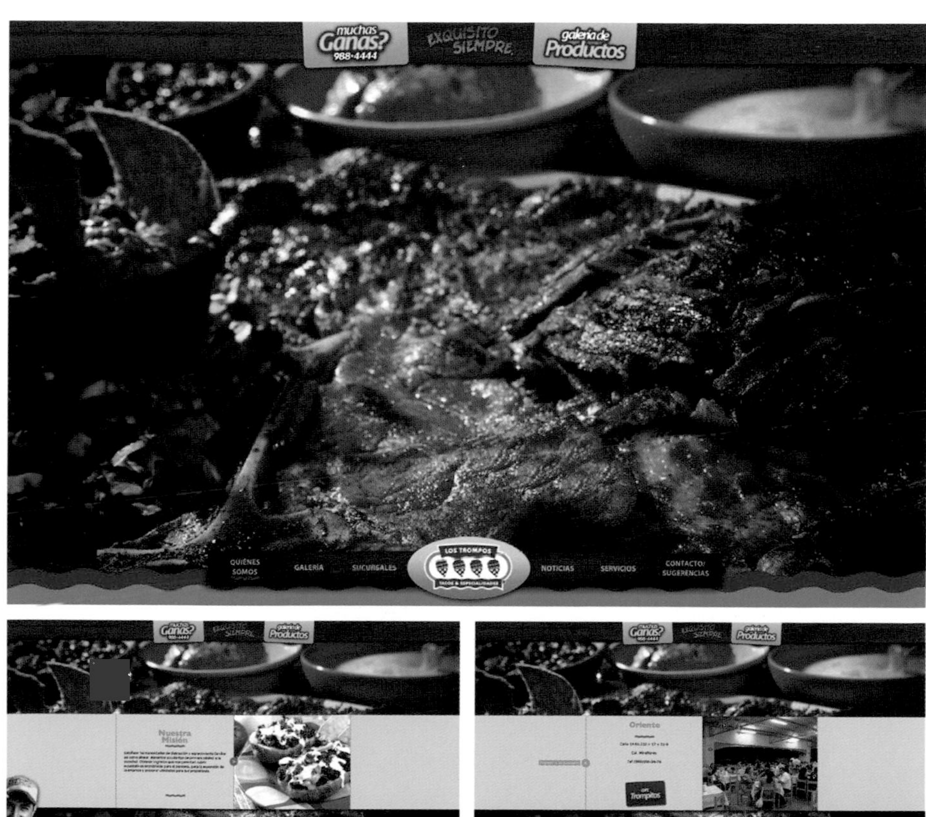

Info

DESIGN STUDIO: WeEatDesign <www.weeatdesign.com>. /// **DESIGN:** Carlos Alonzo. /// **PROGRAMMING:** Alfredo Bolio. /// **CLIENT:** Los Trompos. /// **TOOLS:** Adobe Photoshop, Flash, PHP, HTML. /// **COST:** 160 hours.

MADE IN ITALY

ITALY

www.valore-italia.it

2007

Concept

All the contents are available simultaneously on a flat plan that is further extended every time a part of the menu is clicked. /// Alle Inhalte stehen simultan auf einem flachen Plan zur Verfügung, der sich erweitert, sobald ein Teil des Menüs angeklickt wird. /// **L'ensemble du contenu est disponible sur une surface plane qui s'étend chaque fois que l'utilisateur clique dans le menu.**

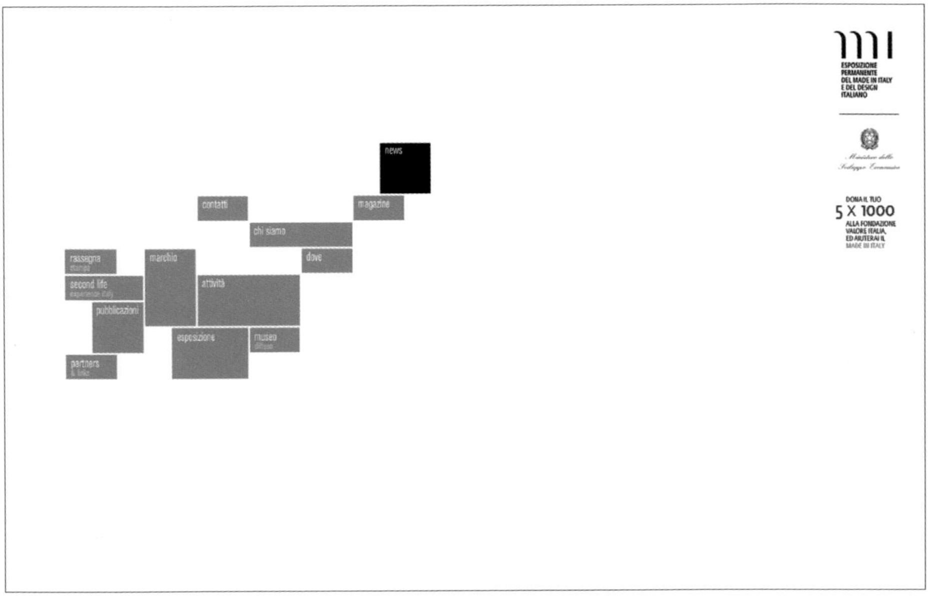

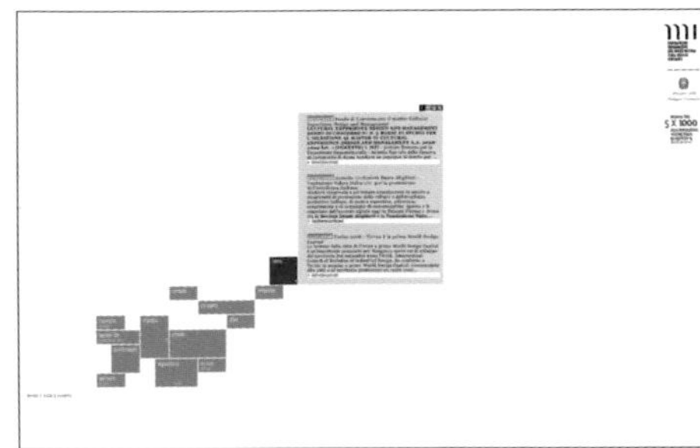

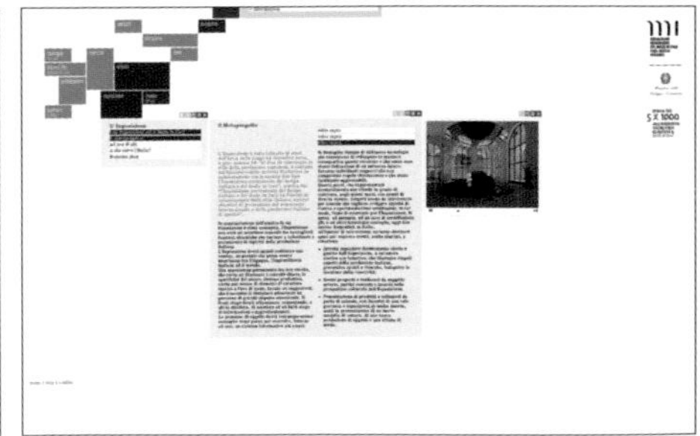

Info

Design Studio: studio FM milano <www.studiofmmilano.it>. /// **Design:** studio FM milano. /// **Programming:** studio FM milano. /// **Client:** Fondazione Valore Italia. /// **Tools:** Adobe Flash, prototype+Script.aculo.us. /// **Awards:** European Design Awards – Stockholm 08 (Merit).

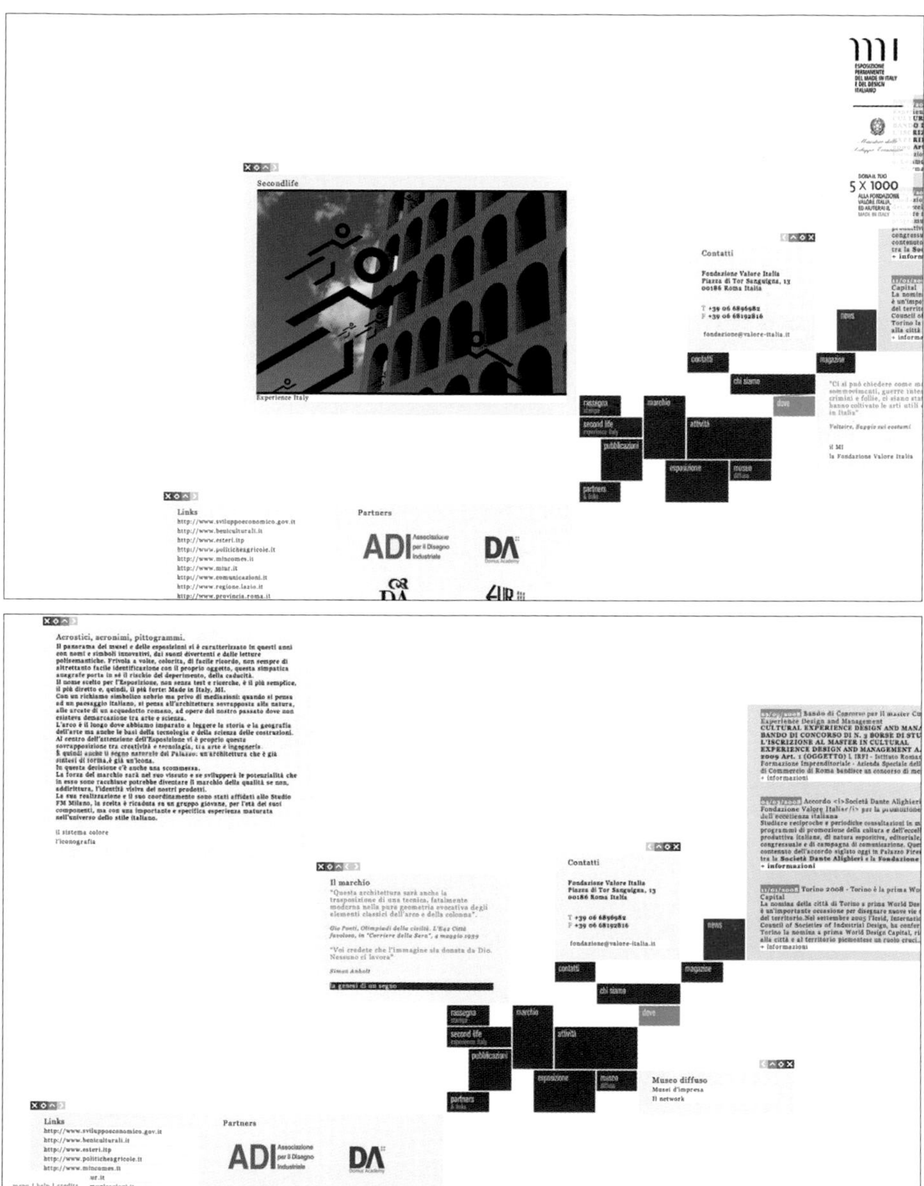

MARK HOLTHUSEN PHOTOGRAPHY

USA

www.markholthusen.com

2008

Concept

With a hidden menu at the bottom, the site displays well compressed images in full-screen, allowing the user to see the photographer's work in detail. /// Über ein verstecktes Menü am unteren Rand zeigt die Site gut komprimierte Bilder in Vollansicht, sodass der User die Arbeit des Fotografen im Detail studieren kann. /// Avec un menu caché au bas, le site affiche des images bien compressées en plein écran, ce qui permet à l'utilisateur de voir en détail le travail du photographe.

Info

DESIGN STUDIO: Ever Growing Studio <www.evergrowing.net>. /// **DESIGN:** Arron Bleasdale. /// **PROGRAMMING:** Arron Bleasdale. /// **CLIENT:** Mark Holthusen Photography. /// **TOOLS:** Adobe Flash, Adobe Photoshop, Adobe Illustrator. /// **COST:** 160 hours.

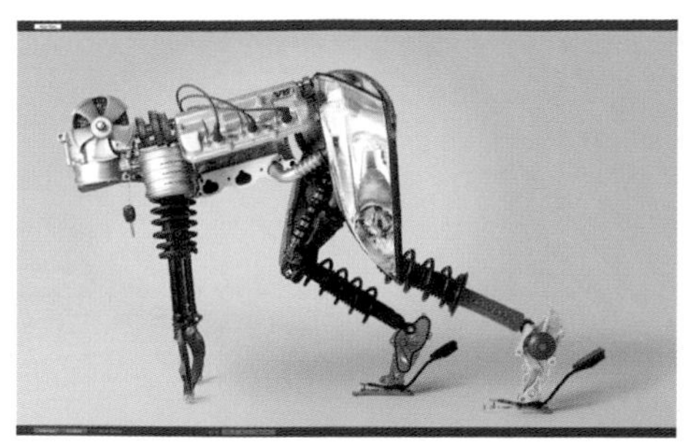

Mark Holthusen
Photography

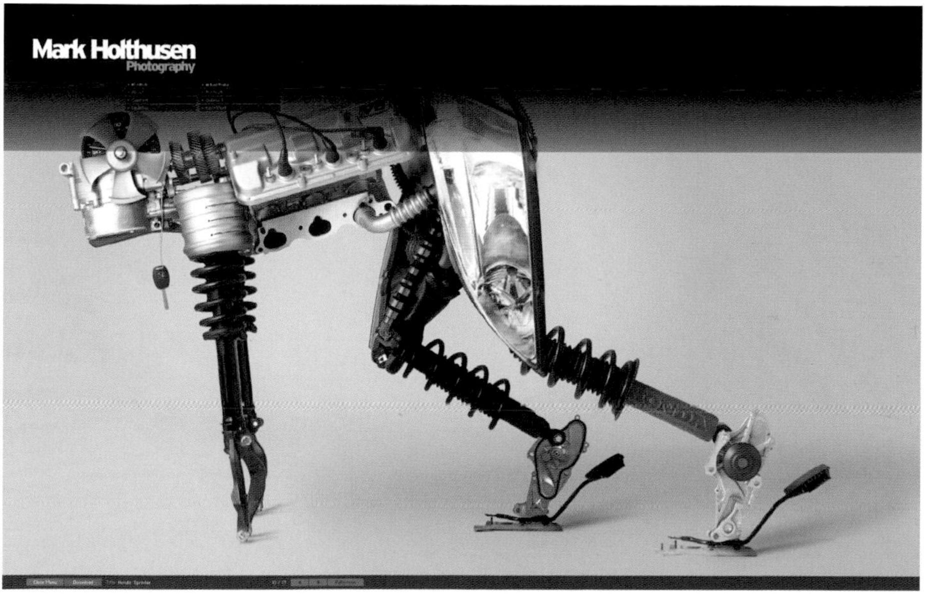

Mark Holthusen
Photography

Mark Holthusen
Photography

MAVERICKS

SOUTH AFRICA

www.mavericks.co.za

2008

Concept

Very interactive navigation to drive all the attention to the models of this escort services company. There is also the option of removing some of the clothes if the user is registered. /// Sehr interaktive Navigation, die die gesamte Aufmerksamkeit auf die Models dieses Escort-Services lenkt. Wenn der User registriert ist, kann er auch Teile ihrer Kleider entfernen. /// Navigation très interactive pour attirer l'attention sur les modèles de cette entreprise de services d'accompagnement. Une option permet aussi de retirer les vêtements si l'utilisateur est enregistré.

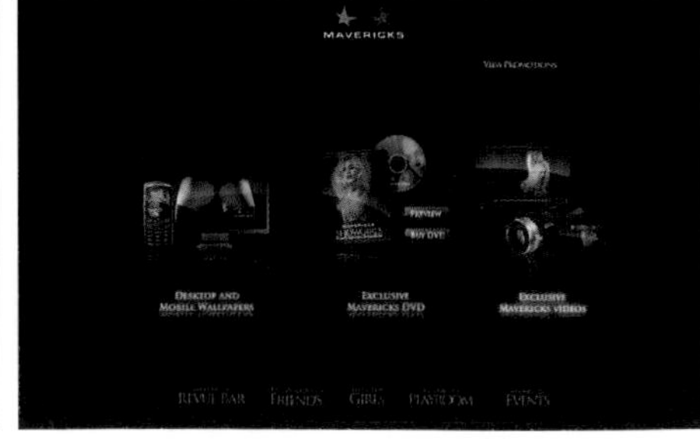

Info

Design Studio: HelloComputer <www.hellocomputer.net>. /// **Design:** Mark Tomlinson, Simon Spreckley. /// **Programming:** Kyle Ward. /// **Client:** Mavericks Review Bar. /// **Tools:** Adobe Flash, Adobe Photoshop, Adobe Illustrator, Maya, HTML, JSP, XML. /// **Awards:** Loerie Award (Experiential/Digital – Bronze). /// **Cost:** 320 hours.

MIA SABLE

USA

www.miasable.com

2007

Concept

Website for singer Mia Sable, constructed like a theatre set, with the menu hidden around the place, and also featuring animated surprises. /// Die Website der Sängerin Mia Sable ist wie eine Theaterbühne gestaltet. Das Menü ist versteckt über den ganzen Bildschirm verteilt und überrascht mit kleinen Animationen. /// **Site Web de la chanteuse Mia Sable, construit comme une scène de théâtre, avec les options du menu un peu partout et des surprises animées.**

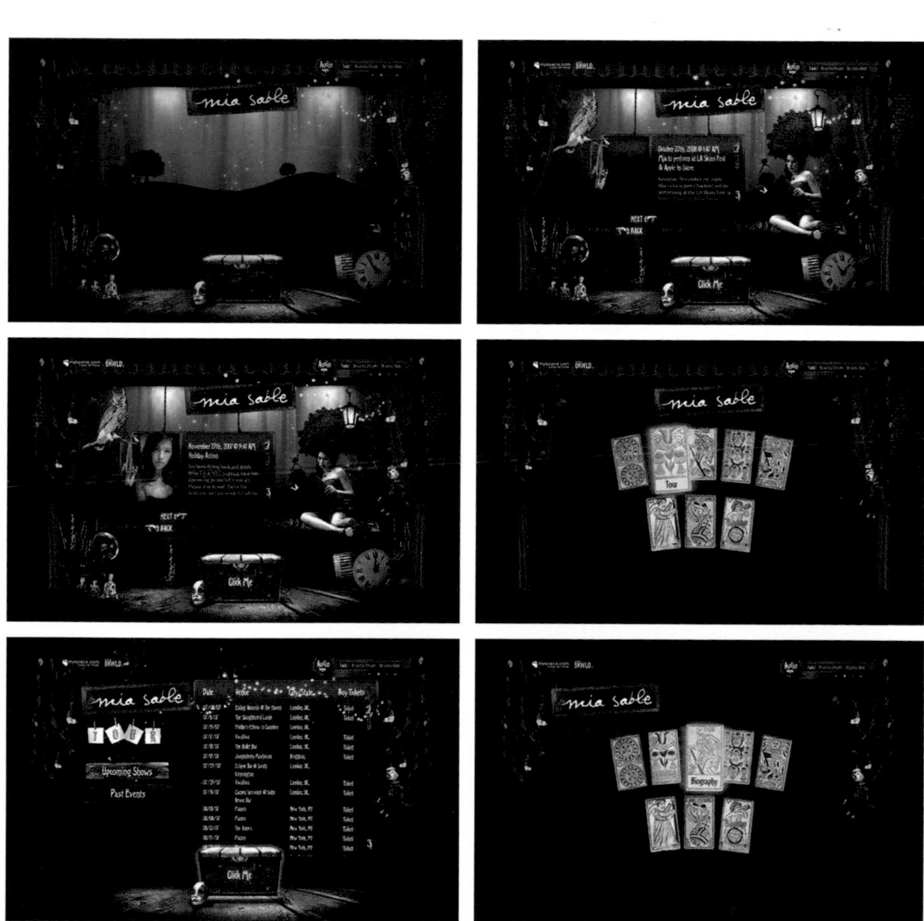

Info

Design Studio: BKWLD <www.bkwld.com>. /// **Design:** Jeff Toll. /// **Programming:** Ben Borowski. /// **Client:** J Records. /// **Tools:** XML, HTML, Adobe Photoshop, Adobe Flash, PHP. /// **Awards:** e-Creative.net.

MEDIATIONS BIENNALE

POLAND

www.mediations.pl

2008

Concept

This is a website combining HTML functionality (deep linking, tags) and free Flash-driven navigation based on vector 3-D space with mouse-wheel used as the main arranging tool. /// Diese Website kombiniert HTML-Funktionalität (Deep Linking, Tags) mit einer offenen Flash-Navigation, die auf Vektoren im 3-D-Raum beruht und über das Mausrad arrangiert wird. /// **Ce site Web combine la fonctionnalité HTML (liens en profondeur, balises) et une navigation Flash basée sur un espace 3D vectoriel, la molette de la souris servant d'outil principal.**

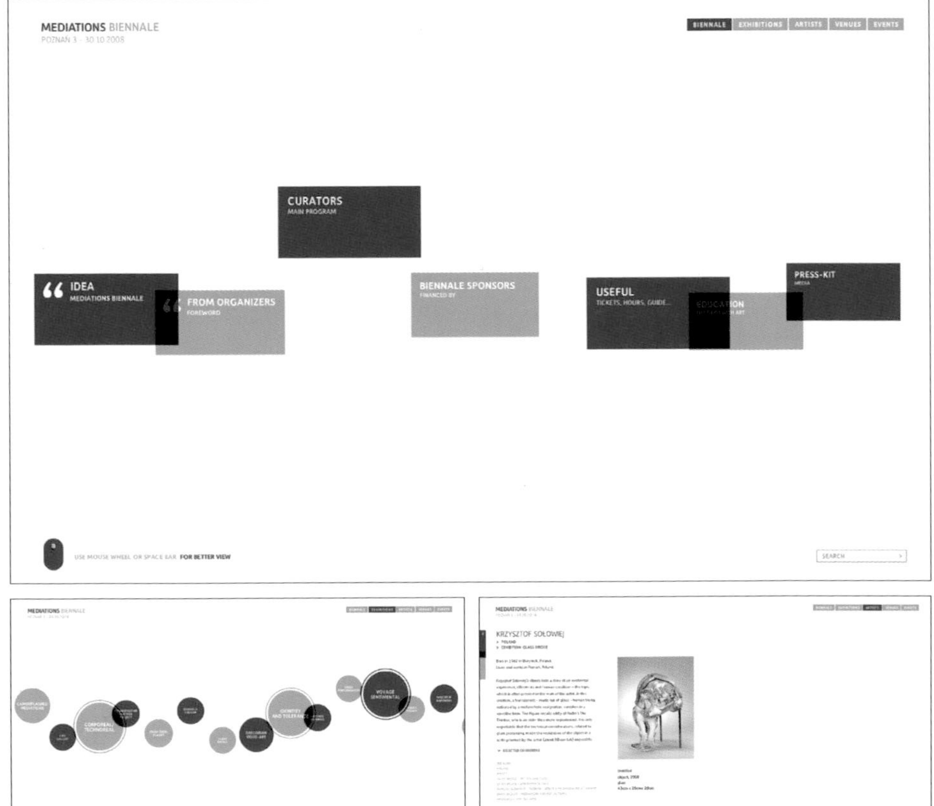

Info

DESIGN STUDIO: Huncwot <www.huncwot.com>. /// **DESIGN:** Arek Romanski, Lukasz Knasiecki. /// **CLIENT:** Mediations Biennale. /// **TOOLS:** Adobe Flash, Adobe Photoshop, Adobe Illustrator, SQL. /// **COST:** 160 hours.

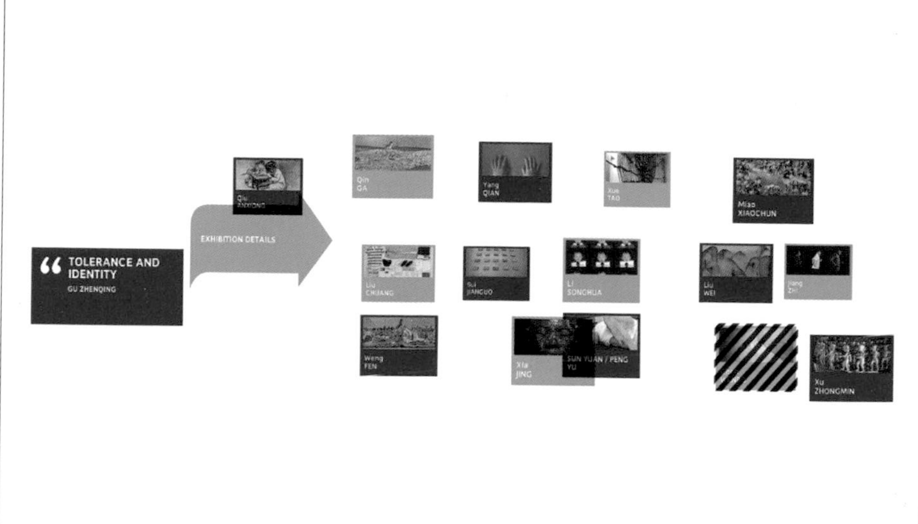

TOLERANCE AND IDENTITY
GU ZHENQING
EXHIBITION DETAILS
Qiu ANXIONG
Qin GA
Yang QIAN
Xue TAO
Miao XIAOCHUN
Liu CHUANG
Sui JIANGUO
Li SONGHUA
Liu WEI
Jiang ZHI
Weng FEN
Xia JING
SUN YUAN / PENG YU
Xu ZHONGMIN

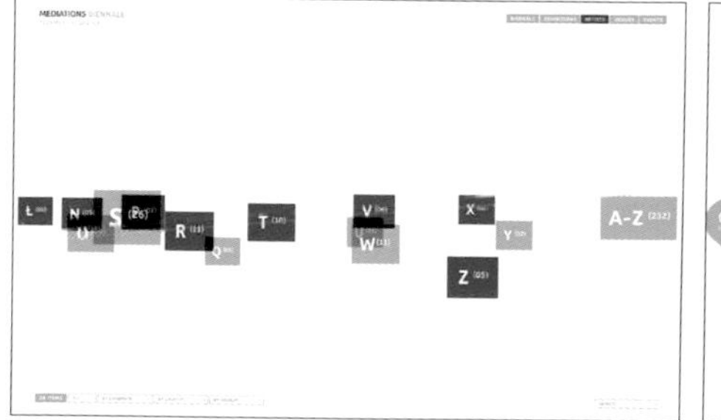

MEDIATIONS BIENNALE
A-Z (232)

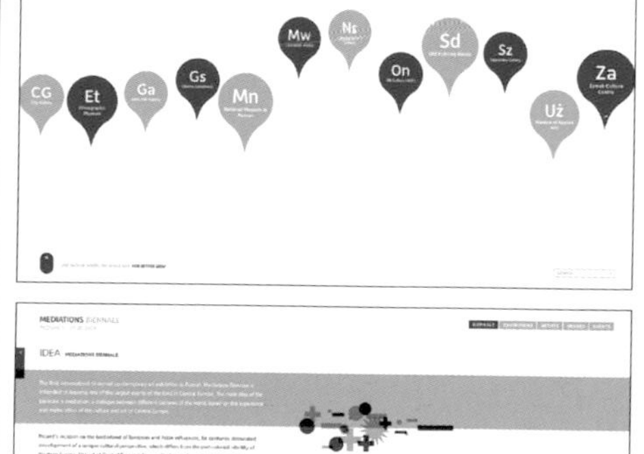

MEDIATIONS BIENNALE
CG
Et
Ga
Gs
Mn
Mw
Nt
On
Sd
Sz
Uż
Za

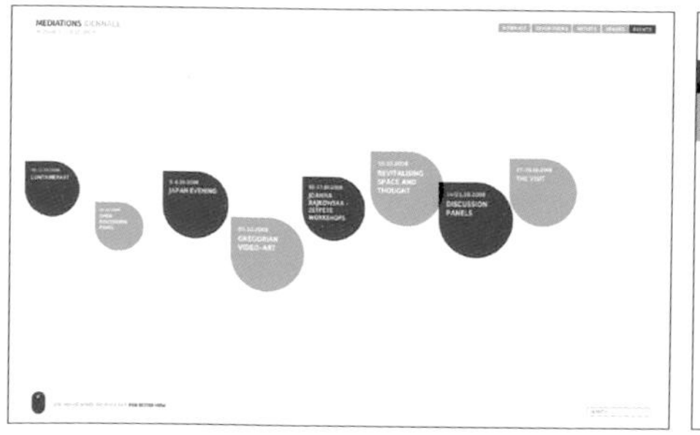

MEDIATIONS BIENNALE
JAPAN EVENING
GREGORIAN VIDEO-ART
REVITALISING SPACE AND THOUGHT
DISCUSSION PANELS
THE VISIT

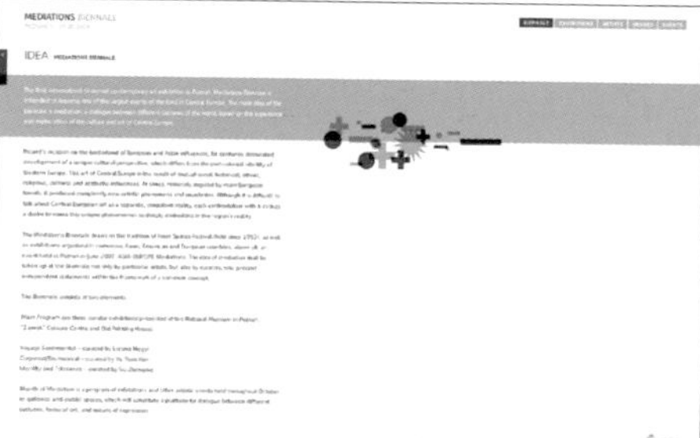

MEDIATIONS BIENNALE
IDEA

MIGLIORE+SERVETTO

ITALY

www.miglioreservetto.com

2007

Concept

The horizontal menu of the page constructs and deconstructs itself vertically (with the bub-options) in order to list the content to be displayed. /// Das horizontale Menü der Seite wird vertikal mit neuen Optionen konstruiert, um die darzustellenden Inhalte aufzulisten, und bei anderer Wahl wieder zerlegt. /// Le menu horizontal de la page se construit et se déconstruit verticalement (les options s'accumulant en dessous) pour répertorier le contenu à afficher.

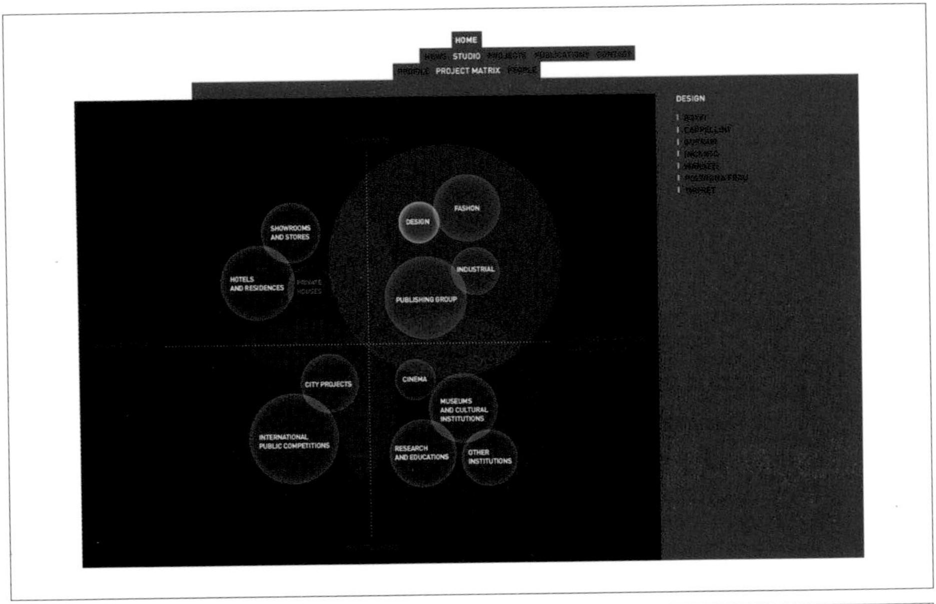

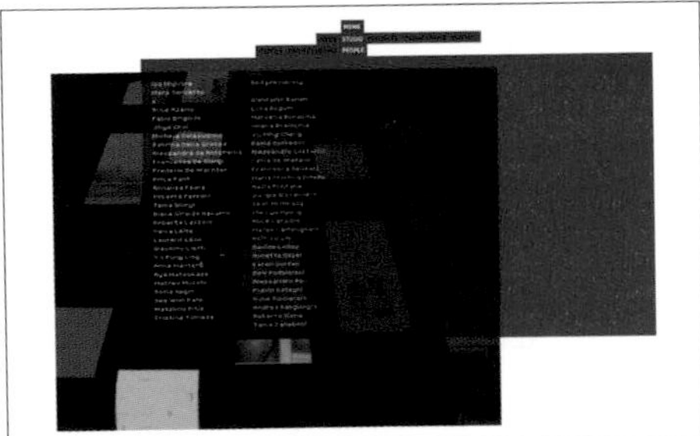

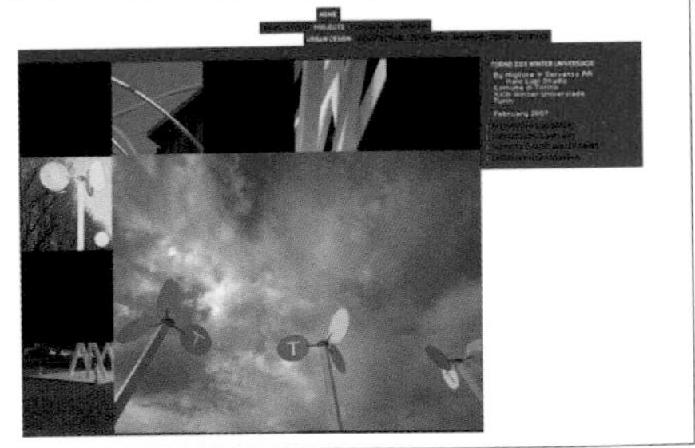

Info

DESIGN STUDIO: studio FM milano <www.studiofmmilano.it>. /// DESIGN: studio FM milano. /// PROGRAMMING: Park Media. /// CLIENT: Migliore+Servetto Architetti Associati. /// TOOLS: Adobe Flash. /// AWARDS: European Design Awards – Stockholm 08 (Merit).

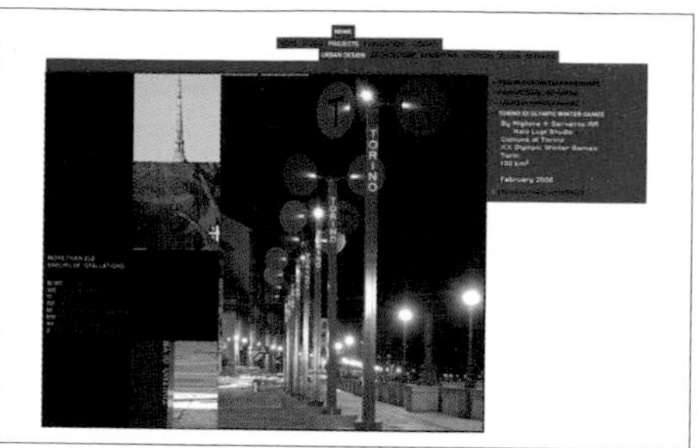

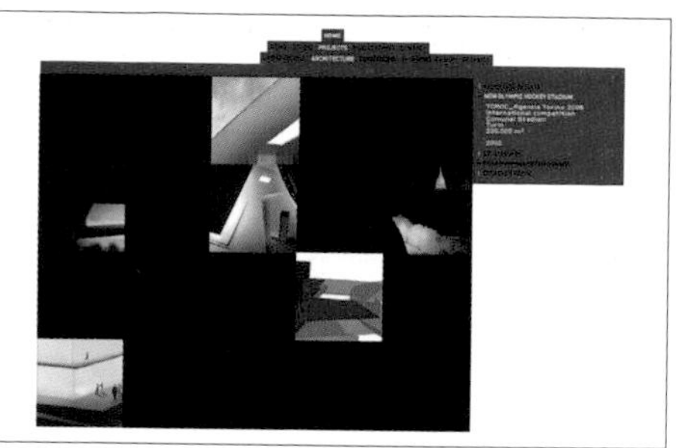

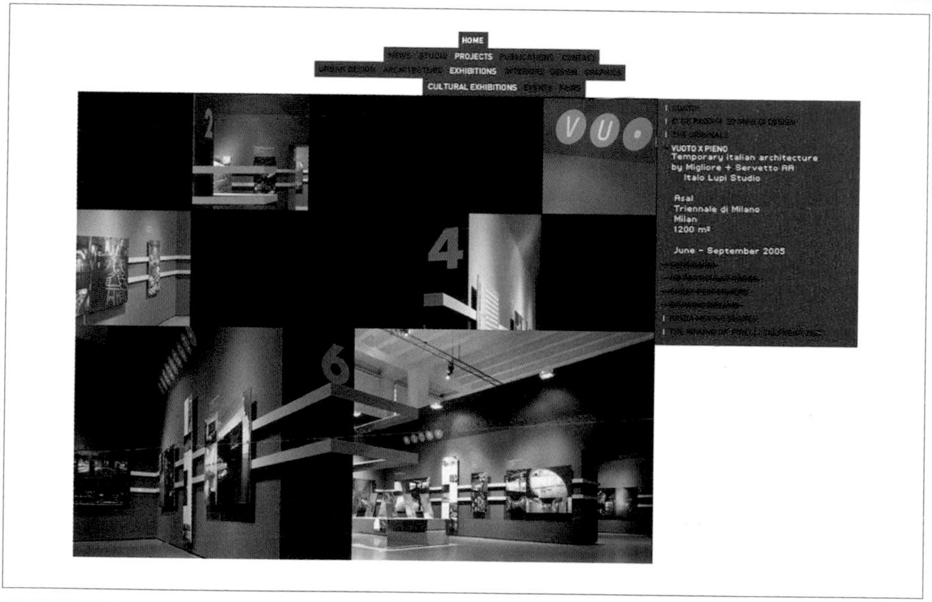

HOME

NEWS STUDIO PROJECTS PUBLICATIONS CONTACT

URBAN DESIGN ARCHITECTURE EXHIBITIONS INTERIORS DESIGN GRAPHICS

CULTURAL EXHIBITIONS EVENTS FAIRS

VUOTO X PIENO
Temporary italian architecture
by Migliore + Servetto AA
Italo Lupi Studio

Asal
Triennale di Milano
Milan
1200 m²

June – September 2005

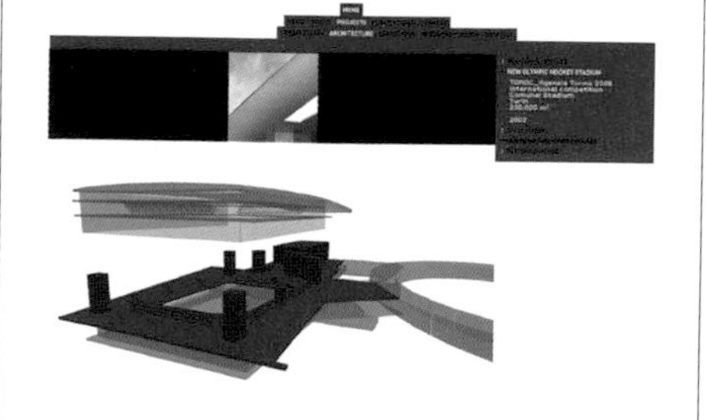

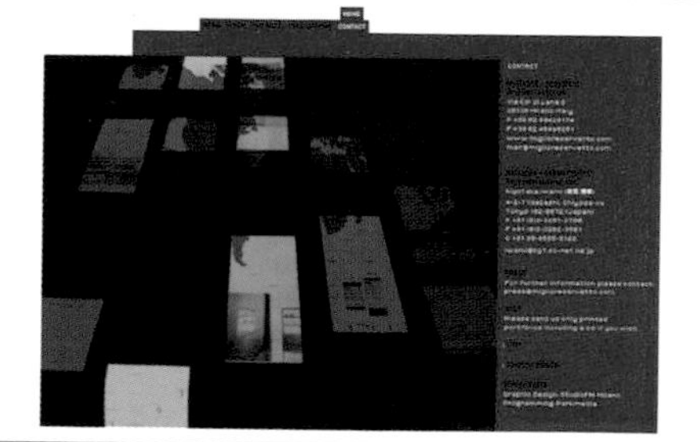

MIJO CORPORATION ONLINE

CANADA

www.mijo.ca

2006

Concept

The website uses the approach of storytelling while providing a stimulating audio, visual, and interactive experience. /// Die Website arbeitet mit Storytelling und bietet interessante akustische, visuelle und interaktive Erfahrungen. /// Le site Web opte pour la communication narrative, assortie d'une expérience audio, visuelle et interactive stimulante.

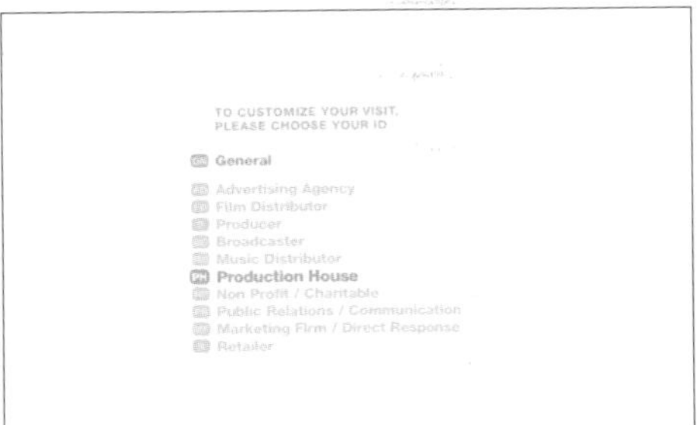

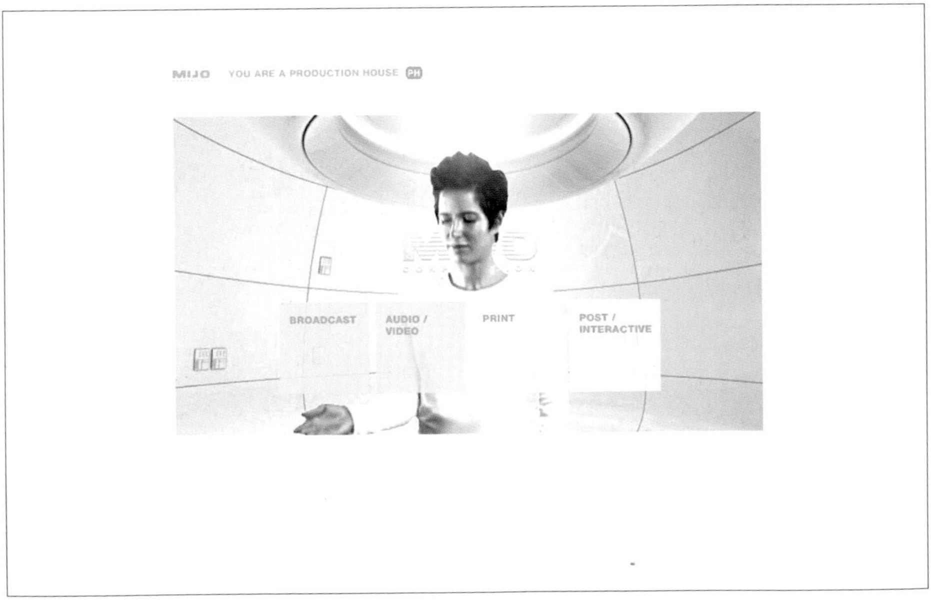

Info

Design Studio: HELLOHELLO!! <www.HelloHello.BZ>. /// **Design:** Thierry Loa. /// **Programming:** Thierry Loa (Flash/Front-end); Nolan Dubeau (CMS/Back-end); Lorraine Spiess (Additional Flash). /// **Others:** Production/Creation/Direction/Visual Effects: Thierry Loa; Jorge Weisz (Camera/DP); Richard Devine (Music/Sound); Gabe Lee (Voice-over Engineering). /// **Client:** MIJO Corporation. /// **Tools:** Adobe Flash, ActionScript, Adobe ColdFusion, Flash Forms, Premiere, Adobe After Effects, Sound Forge. /// **Awards:** Webby Awards (Honoree). /// **Cost:** 5 months.

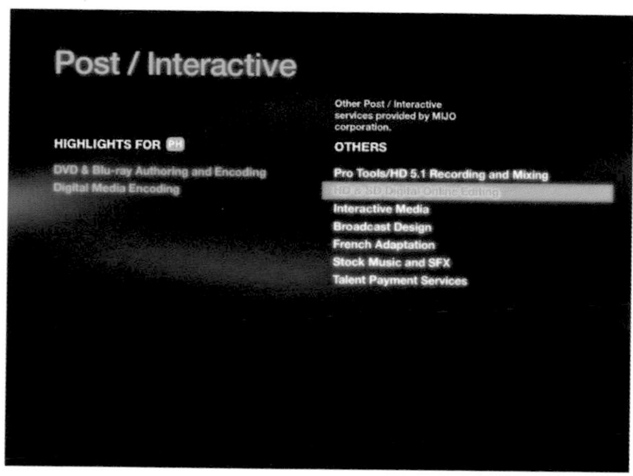
MIJO
YOU ARE A PRODUCTION HOUSE PH
BACK
Post / Interactive
Other Post / Interactive services provided by MIJO corporation.
HIGHLIGHTS FOR PH
DVD & Blu-ray Authoring and Encoding
Digital Media Encoding
OTHERS
Pro Tools/HD 5.1 Recording and Mixing
HD & SD Digital Online Editing
Interactive Media
Broadcast Design
French Adaptation
Stock Music and SFX
Talent Payment Services

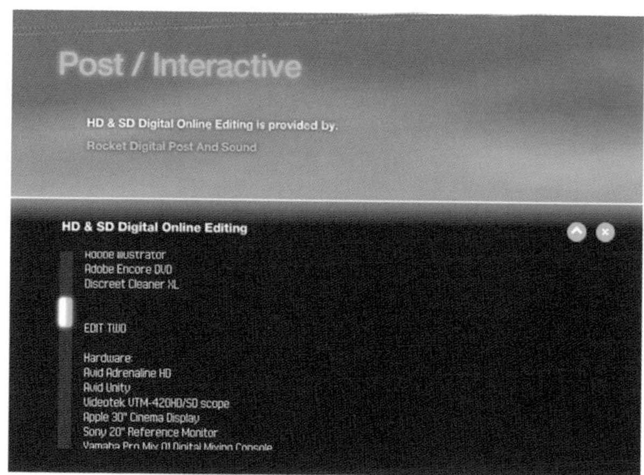
MIJO
YOU ARE A PRODUCTION HOUSE PH
Post / Interactive
HD & SD Digital Online Editing is provided by.
Rocket Digital Post And Sound
HD & SD Digital Online Editing
Adobe Encore DVD
Discreet Cleaner XL
EDIT TWO
Hardware:
Avid Adrenaline HD
Avid Unity
Videotek UTM-420HD/SD scope
Apple 30" Cinema Display
Sony 20" Reference Monitor

MOON

UK

www.unit9.com/moon

2004

Concept

The subtle underlying concept is that of reaching the moon (also the name of the company). Each director's section is decorated with a small diagram depicting a dreamy, childlike, fantastical idea of how this can be done. /// Das subtil umgesetzte Konzept dieser Site ist eine Fahrt zum Mond (Moon lautet auch der Name der Firma). Die Infobereiche über die Regisseure sind mit kleinen Diagrammen geschmückt, die anschaulich kindliche, fantastische oder träumerische Ideen darstellen, wie man zum Mond kommen könnte. /// **Le subtil concept sous-jacent est d'atteindre la lune (le nom de l'entreprise). La section de chaque réalisateur affiche un petit graphique illustrant une façon fantastique, onirique et enfantine de procéder.**

Info

DESIGN STUDIO: unit9 <www.unit9.com>. /// **DESIGN:** unit9. /// **PROGRAMMING:** unit9. /// **CLIENT:** Moon Productions. /// **TOOLS:** Adobe Creative Suite. /// **AWARDS:** LIAA, FWA, Design Week, CR Annual. /// **COST:** 8 weeks.

Moon Tv Commercials Production Company
Directors:
MIKE STEPHENSON
TIMEBANK
Turned Tables.
COI ARMY
Trust.
WARBURTONS
Dog Car.
McDONALDS
Everlasting Love.
FIRST DIRECT
Charge.
PERSIL
Young Winstons.
GROLSCH
Paper Plane.
TEACHER TRAINING
ASSOCIATION
Talking Heads.
> VIEW ARCHIVE

Moon Tv Commercials Production Company
Mike Stephenson
TIMEBANK
Turned Tables.
COI ARMY
Trust.
WARBURTONS
Dog Car.
McDONALDS
Everlasting Love.
FIRST DIRECT
Charge.
PERSIL
Young Winstons.
GROLSCH
Paper Plane.
TEACHER TRAINING
ASSOCIATION
Talking Heads.
> VIEW ARCHIVE
play
stop
McDONALDS
Everlasting Love

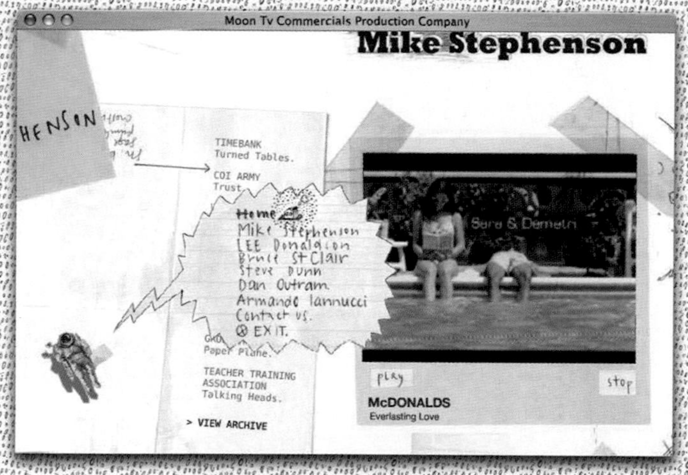

Moon Tv Commercials Production Company
Mike Stephenson
HENSON
TIMEBANK
Turned Tables.
COI ARMY
Trust.
Home
Mike Stephenson
LEE Donaldson
Bruce St Clair
Steve Dunn
Dan Outram.
Armando Iannucci
Contact us.
EXIT.
Paper Plane.
TEACHER TRAINING
ASSOCIATION
Talking Heads.
> VIEW ARCHIVE
Sara & Demetri
play
stop
McDONALDS
Everlasting Love

Moon Tv Commercials Production Company
ARMANDO
IANNUCCI
Director:
1. Ibiza Opera
2. Clown Teacher Stripper Fireman
3. Rodeo Funeral
4. Washing Machine
5. Suicide Note
6. The Making of Millionaire
DIRECTIR
MOON
DAN GOES TO THE MOON

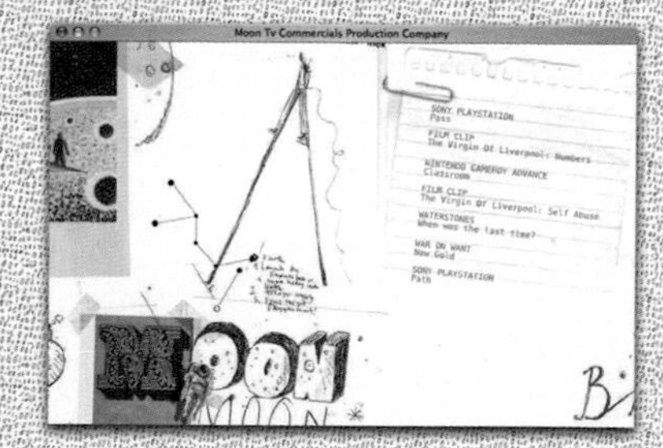

Moon Tv Commercials Production Company
SONY PLAYSTATION
Pass
FILM CLIP
The Virgin of Liverpool: Numbers
NINTENDO GAMEBOY ADVANCE
Classroom
FILM CLIP
The Virgin of Liverpool: Self Abuse
WATERSTONES
When was the last time?
WAR ON WANT
New Gold
SONY PLAYSTATION
Path
MOON

NALINDESIGN

GERMANY

www.nalindesign.com

2008

Concept

This site is a free and dynamic desktop with randomly placed cards the user can browse through and pick up to play with. The right-click menu works as a quick navigation to provide options like copying direct links and sorting/shuffling cards. /// Diese Site ist ein offener und dynamischer Desktop mit zufällig angeordneten Karten, die der User nach Belieben ansehen und aufnehmen kann, um damit zu spielen. Per Rechtsklick erreicht man ein Menü, um die direkten Links zu kopieren oder die Karten zu sortieren bzw. zu mischen. /// **Ce site est un bureau dynamique, sur lequel sont placées de façon aléatoire des cartes que l'utilisateur peut consulter et prendre pour jouer. Le menu qui s'ouvre d'un clic droit offre une navigation rapide et affiche des options comme la copie de liens directs et le tri/mélange des cartes.**

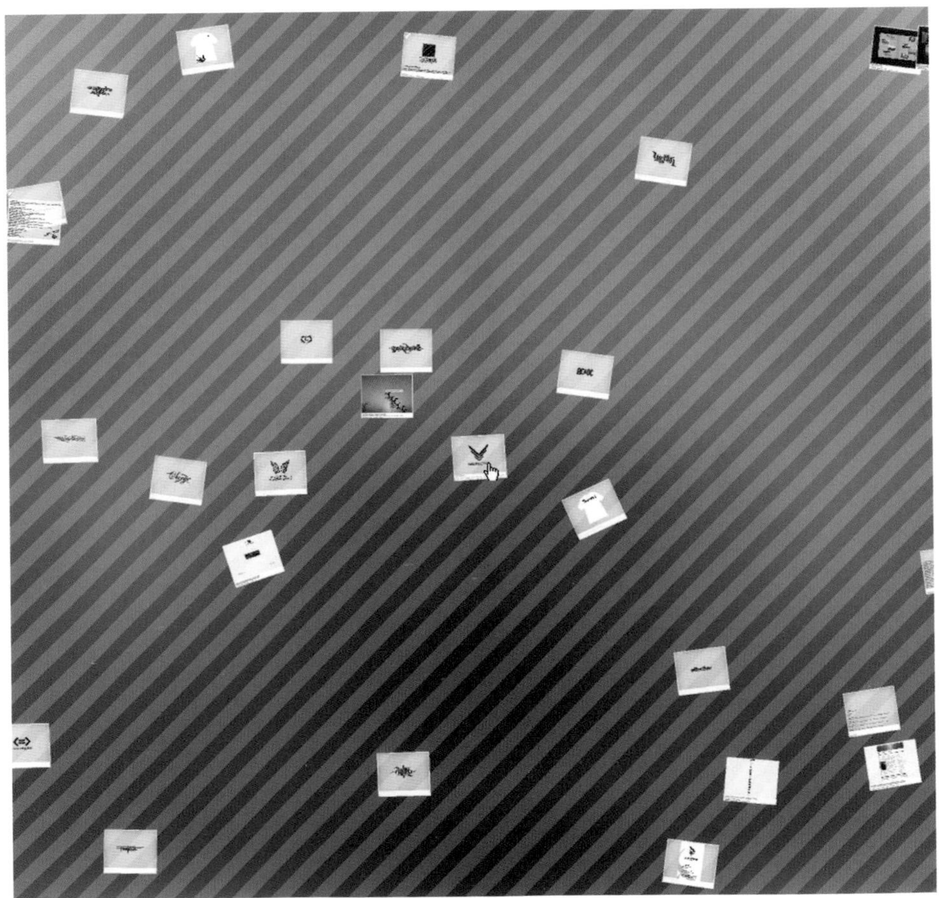

Info

Design Studio: NALINDESIGN <www.nalindesign.com>. /// **Design:** Andre Weier. /// **Programming:** Andre Weier. /// **Others:** Samuel Trebbin (Sound Design). /// **Tools:** Adobe Flash, Adobe Photoshop, text editor, XML, PHP, CSS, JavaScript, htaccess, effective CMS. /// **Cost:** 3 months.

NOWHERE

USA

www.nowherenyc.com

2006

Concept

The website was designed to frame the work of the design studio with no other distractions. White space was employed, and sound was eliminated to create a peaceful viewing experience. /// Das Design der Website bildet den Rahmen für die Arbeit des Designstudios, ohne ablenkend zu wirken. Durch die weißen Flächen und das Weglassen einer Hintergrundmusik wird eine friedliche Betrachtung der Site möglich. /// Le site Web a été conçu pour présenter le travail du studio de design sans autres distractions. L'espace blanc a été retenu et le son a été éliminé pour permettre une consultation dans le calme.

Info

Design Studio: Nowhere <www.nowherenyc.com>. /// **Design:** Michael Robinson. /// **Programming:** Multu Isik, Peggy Tan, Antonio Serna. /// **Tools:** Adobe Flash. /// **Cost:** 20 hours.

NRK ANNUAL REPORT 07

NORWAY

www.nrk.no/aarsrapport/2007

2008

Concept

NRK aims to inform, involve, and entertain by providing a wide and varied service. The website constructed in Flash takes users through NRK's wide range of programs and content. /// NRK will durch seinen breit gefächerten und vielfältigen Service informieren, Kunden einbinden und unterhalten. Die mit Flash konstruierte Website führt die User durch die große Bandbreite von Programmen und Inhalten von NRK. /// **NRK souhaite informer, impliquer et amuser en offrant un service complet et varié. Le site Web en Flash plonge les utilisateurs dans une large gamme de programmes et de contenus de NRK.**

Info

DESIGN STUDIO: Apt <www.apt.no>. /// **DESIGN:** Eric Lauritzen, Magnus Cederholm. /// **PROGRAMMING:** Alexander Pope (Flash). /// **OTHERS:** Lukas Szachanski (Project Manager), Joachim Levin (Consultant). /// **CLIENT:** NRK (Norwegian Broadcaster). /// **TOOLS:** Adobe Photoshop, Adobe Illustrator, XML, Adobe After Effects. /// **COST:** ca. 400 hours.

NRK

CHILDREN / DOWNLOAD CHAPTER / PDF

Separate Super channel for *Children*
«Children of all ages who like games and fun where music features heavily should watch this wonderful new series on children's TV»
Stavanger Aftenblad 31.03.2007 Elisabeth Bie om Skrimmel Skrammel

On Saturday 1 December 2007, NRK launched its new alternative for children and young people, NRK Super. This new children's channel is responsible for almost a six-fold increase in the choices being offered to children by NRK, i.e. up from 750 to 4,380 broadcasting hours per year. This channel provides children and young people with content, and it is an important part of NRK's public broadcasting mandate. Superuniverset (Super Universe) is an integrated radio, Internet and TV alternative for children.

Clips from NRK

Gaven 1:46

NRK Super åpning 1:09

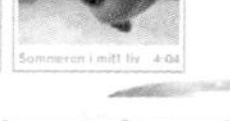
Sommeren i mitt liv 4:04

Children

NRK

CHANNELS / DOWNLOAD CHAPTER / PDF

NRK on all platforms

NRK's ambition is to be wherever people are to be found, both now and in the future. Here is a selection of programmes from each genre showing the extent and availability of this service to the public.

Entertainment

News
Music
Culture
Norwegian Drama
Nature
Facts/Science
Children/Youth
Religion
Sport

	NRK 1	NRK 2	NRK 3/NRK super	NRK P1	NRK P2	NRK P3	nrk.no	mobil	podcast
20 spørsmål	●			●			●	●	●
Balsam				●			●		●
Beat for beat	●	●					●	●	
Bollywoodsommer		●							
Drømmerollen	●	●					●	●	
Fra hjerte til hjerte	●	●					●	●	
Først & sist med Fredrik Skavlan	●	●					●	●	
Grosvold	●	●					●	●	
Halvseint	●		●				●	●	
Hallo i uken					●		●		
Herreavdelingen				●			●		●
Hjemme hos Bye og Rønning	●		●				●	●	
Ken eller Torkil						●	●		●
Kveldsmat				●			●		
Kveldsåpent				●			●		
Kvitt eller dobbelt	●	●					●	●	
Lyden av lørdag	●	●					●		
Løvebakken	●	●					●	●	
Nitimen				●			●		●
Nordkalotten 365	●	●					●	●	
Norsk attraksjon	●	●					●	●	
Nostalgia				●			●		
Nytt på nytt	●	●					●	●	
Osenbanden						●	●		●
Pepper og pasjon				●			●		●
Popquiz				●			●		
Reiseradioen				●			●		
Sommeråpent	●	●					●	●	
Topp 10	●	●					●		

Channels

NO EN

PORSCHE — I CAN

USA

www.porsche.com/all/usa/ican

2008

Concept

The navigation within the Flash site is entirely down to video transitions, from the initial carousel of a family of cars that lets the user guide the camera around them. The navigation allows users literally to create their own path within the video. /// Die Navigation dieser Flash-Site arbeitet komplett mit durch Videos gestalteten Übergängen. Das beginnt schon bei der ersten Palette einer Autofamilie, bei der man die Kamera herumführen kann. Mit der Navigation können sich die User buchstäblich einen eigenen Pfad innerhalb des Videos schaffen. /// **La navigation dans le site en Flash repose entièrement sur des transitions vidéo, à commencer par le cercle formé par des modèles et autour desquels l'utilisateur peut faire tourner la caméra. La navigation permet aux utilisateurs de créer leur propre parcours dans la vidéo.**

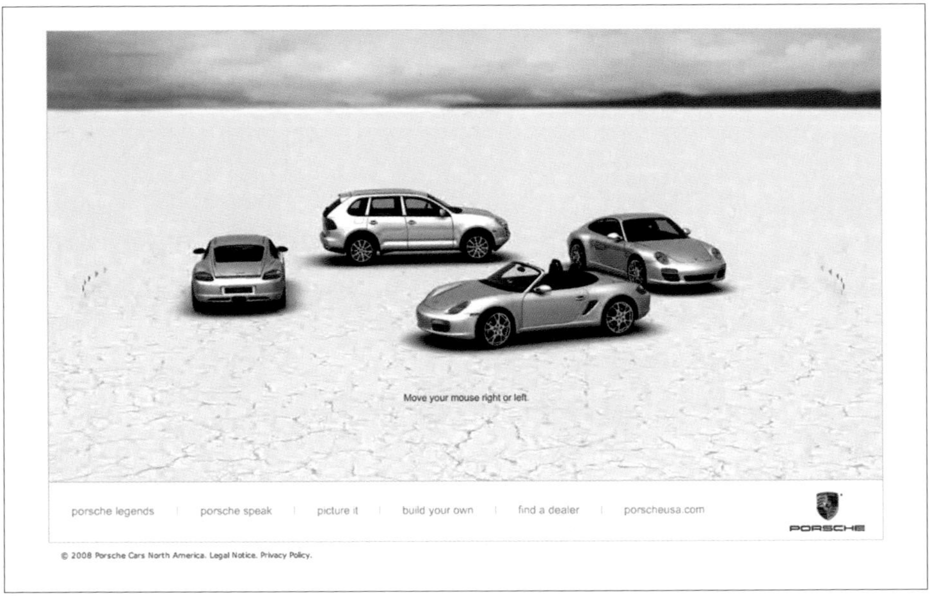

Move your mouse right or left.
porsche legends
porsche speak
picture it
build your own
find a dealer
porscheusa.com
PORSCHE
© 2008 Porsche Cars North America. Legal Notice. Privacy Policy.

The 911
The absolute definition of the term sports car.
$75,600

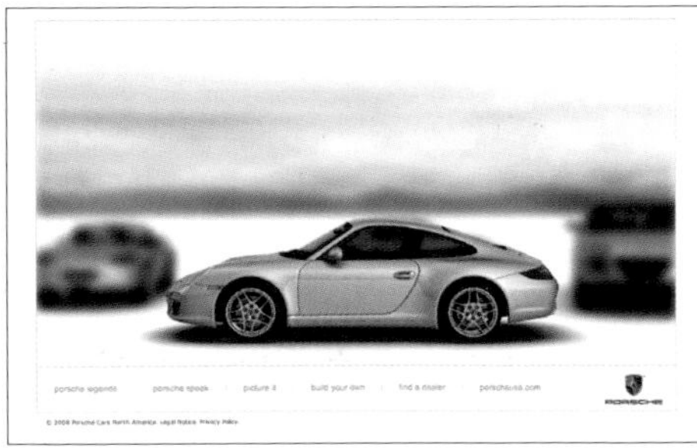

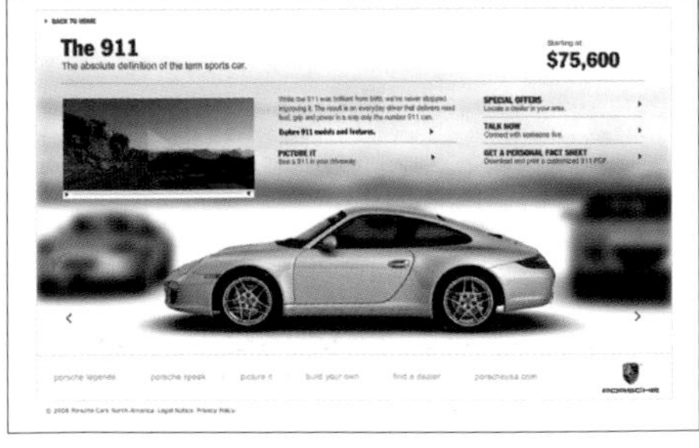

Info

DESIGN STUDIO: Cramer-Krasselt <www.c-k.com>; Domani Studios <www.domanistudios.com>. /// **DESIGN:** Cramer-Krasselt, Domani Studios. /// **PROGRAMMING:** Domani Studios. /// **CLIENT:** Porsche. /// **TOOLS:** Adobe Flash, Adobe Flex, ActioScript, XML, .Net, HTML, Maya. /// **AWARDS:** Creative Website Awards. /// **COST:** 2 months.

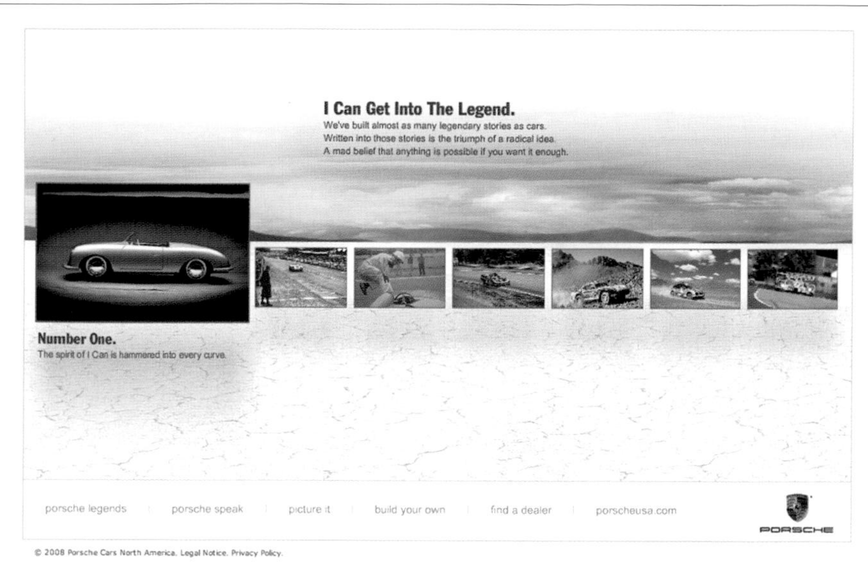
I Can Get Into The Legend.
We've built almost as many legendary stories as cars.
Written into those stories is the triumph of a radical idea.
A mad belief that anything is possible if you want it enough.
Number One.
The spirit of I Can is hammered into every curve.
porsche legends
porsche speak
picture it
build your own
find a dealer
porscheusa.com
PORSCHE
© 2008 Porsche Cars North America. Legal Notice. Privacy Policy.

I Can Get Into The Legend.
The Ignition Is On The Left.
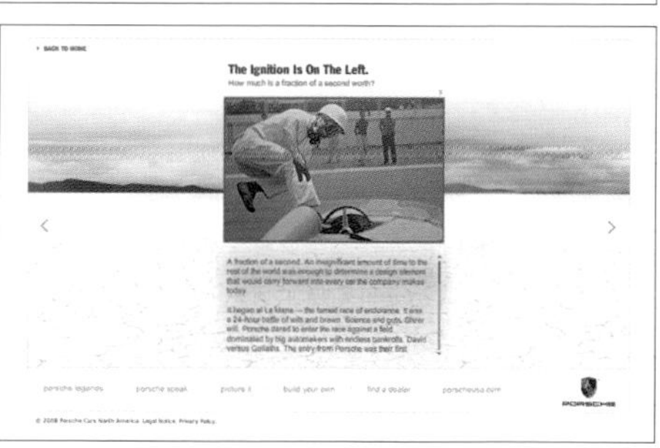
The Ignition Is On The Left.
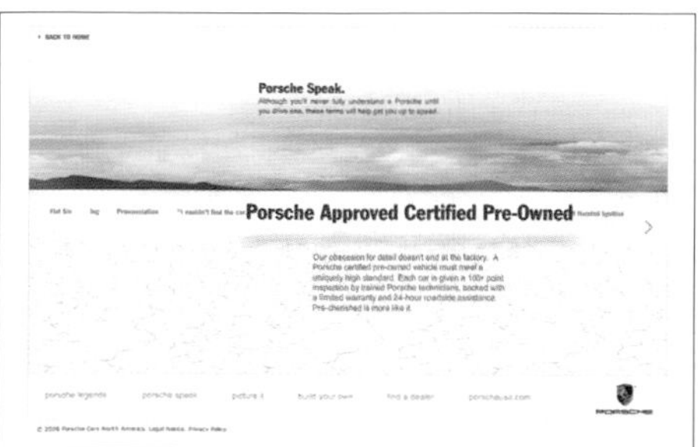
Porsche Speak.
Porsche Approved Certified Pre-Owned

Picture it.

PROTECCIÓN ES LA JUGADA

USA

www.proteccioneslajugada.com

2008

Concept

The site includes a unique navigation system, wherein users click and shoot a set of soccer balls at Memo, as he stands at the ready in front of goal. Each ball represents a section of the site and plays a full-screen video transition of a ball being shot at and subsequently deflected by Memo, thus leading the user to their chosen content area. /// Zu der Site gehört ein einzigartiges Navigationssystem, bei dem der User per Mausklick verschiedene Fußbälle auf Memo schießt, der als Abwehr vor einem Tor steht. Jeder Ball repräsentiert einen Bereich der Site und spielt das bildschirmfüllende Video eines Balls ab, der abgeschlagen und dann von Memo abgefälscht wird und somit den User zum gewünschten Content-Bereich führt. /// Le site comprend un système unique de navigation, dans lequel les utilisateurs cliquent et envoient une série de ballons de football à Memo, qui se trouve juste devant la cage du gardien. Chaque ballon correspond à une section du site et présente une transition vidéo plein écran d'un ballon lancé et dévié par Memo, ce qui mène l'utilisateur à la zone de contenu choisie.

Info

Design Studio: Domani Studios <www.domanistudios.com>. /// **Design:** Domani Studios. /// **Programming:** Domani Studios. /// **Others:** Film Production: Domani Studios. /// **Client:** Leo Burnett / Lapiz. /// **Tools:** Adobe Photoshop, Adobe Illustrator, Adobe After Affects, 3D Modeling, Flash, XML, PHP. /// **Cost:** 3 months.

PROTECCIÓN ES LA JUGADA | EL LOCKER DE MEMO | CREA TU BALÓN | LA TRIBUNA | GALERÍA DEL TRI | DIRIGE LA PORRA | VIDEOS | ENCUENTRA UN AGENTE | OBTÉN UNA COTIZACIÓN

MENÚ PRINCIPAL

Allstate. PATROCINADOR OFICIAL | MEXICO

PROTECCIÓN ES LA JUGADA | EL LOCKER DE MEMO | CREA TU BALÓN | LA TRIBUNA | GALERÍA DEL TRI | DIRIGE LA PORRA | VIDEOS | ENCUENTRA UN AGENTE | OBTÉN UNA COTIZACIÓN

MENÚ PRINCIPAL

1. Elige Una Porra
elige una de las dos porras de fondo

¡MEXICO!
CIELITO LINDO

2. Hazte Escuchar
usa las teclas para controlar a los fanáticos

A S D F G

3. Haz clic para grabar tu porra

Allstate. PATROCINADOR OFICIAL | MEXICO

x reinicia la porra

READER'S DIGEST

USA

www.rd.com

2008

Concept

The challenge was to bring the most widely read magazine in the world on to the Internet in a way that would be worthy of the Reader's Digest brand, while generating meaningful revenue opportunities. /// Die Herausforderung bestand darin, das weltweit am meisten gelesene Magazin ins Internet zu bringen, und zwar auf eine Weise, die der Marke Reader's Digest gerecht wird. Gleichzeitig sollen sinnvolle Einnahmequellen erschlossen werden. /// **L'objectif était de présenter sur Internet le magazine le plus lu dans le monde d'une façon digne de la marque Reader's Digest, tout en assurant des sources sérieuses de bénéfices.**

Info

Design Studio: HUGE <http://hugeinc.com>. /// **Design:** David Skokna, Matthew Abate, Meredith Bagerski, Michal Pasternak, Luis Cabezas, Sean Preston. /// **Programming:** Martin Olson, Michael Squashic, Rafael Mumme. /// **Others:** Lilie Chang, Tara McNulty, Lauren Rubin. /// **Client:** Reader's Digest. /// **Tools:** Adobe Flash, Adobe Photoshop. /// **Cost:** 5 months x 8 workers x 40 hours.

Sign In | Join Now | Customer Care

Search

Reader's Digest
rd.com

Best Deal: Save up to 73%!

Subscribe to RD | Renew
Give a Gift | Go to the RD Store

YOUR AMERICA | LIVING HEALTHY | ADVICE & KNOW-HOW | LAUGHS! | GAMES & MORE | In the Magazine | Make Your Mark

Today's Digest April 9, 2008, Brought to you by STAPLES

Latest Stories

Adrift in Antarctica

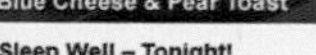

Blue Cheese & Pear Toast

Hot Drink Recipe
From The Best Cafe Au Lait we ever tasted to perfect Mocha-Cinnamon Hot Chocolate.

The Perfect Mother's Day
- Choose the Right Gift
- Treat Mom to Brunch
- Send Her an E-Card

Top Features

What's Your Fear Factor?

Sleep Well – Tonight!
- 5 Ways To Set Your Body's Clock
- 12 Tips to Create a Sleep Haven
- 20 Stress Fixers for Better Rest
- Plus: More Tips In Our Sleep Center

Funny Girl Tina Fey

Barbaro the Brave

Keeping It Light

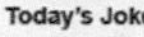

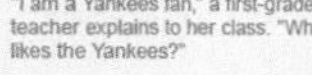

Cute Pet Photo Contest

Today's Joke
"I am a Yankees fan," a first-grade teacher explains to her class. "Who likes the Yankees?"
Read More

The Seven-Year-Old Doctor

The Daily 5

1. 10 Amazing Google Search Tips
A TECH LIST from techtracer.com
2. Prescription Drugs Found in Some U.S. Drinking Water
HEALTH NEWS from cnn.com
3. The Florida-Michigan Morass
PRIMARY ANALYSIS from blogs.nytimes.com
4. 1,000 Colorful Places to See Before You Die
TRAVEL PHOTOGRAPHY from colourlovers.com/blog
5. Extraordinary Uses for Ordinary Things
A USEFUL TOOL from rd.com

Yesterday | This Week

In the Magazine

MARCH 2008
Journey to Joy
Lorem ipsum dolor sit amet. Lorem ipsum dolor sit amet.

Dance to Life
Lorem ipsum dolor sit amet. Ipsum dolor sit amet.

Disturbing Trends Among America's Youth
Lorem ipsum dolor sit amet. Ipsum dolor sit ametamet.

To Catch an Identity Theif
Lorem ipsum dolor sit amet. Lorem ipsum dolor sit amet.

An Ode to Hamburgers
Lorem ipsum dolor sit amet. Lorem ipsum dolor sit amet.

More in This Issue | Other Issues

RD Store
Go to the Store

Lazy Day Slow Cookers
Lorem ipsum dolor sit amet.

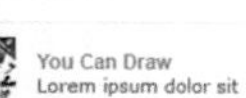

You Can Draw
Lorem ipsum dolor sit amet.

The Dig Game by C.F. Payne
Lorem ipsum dolor sit amet.

Contest & Sweeps
See All

$35000 Giveaway
Lorem ipsum dolor sit amet.

Funny Photos Contest
Lorem ipsum dolor sit amet.

Win a Panini Maker!
Lorem ipsum dolor sit amet.

Get Our Free Newsletter
Find out what's new on RD.com each week!

Enter Your Email Address | Sign Up

Dont' worry, we don't spam. See our privacy policy.

Get Our Best Deal!
Save up to 73% and be entertained and inspired with America's favorite magazine.

First Name

Helpful Links

RD.Com Topics
- YOUR AMERICA
Celebrities, Environment, Government
- LIVING HEALTHY
Nutrition, Marriage, Family, Exercise

Stay In Touch
- Newsletters
- RSS feeds
- Magazine subcriptions

More on RD.com
- In the Magazine
- Make It Matter
- Customer Care

RED ISSUE

www.red-issue.com

DENMARK

2008

Concept

Fashion brand Red Issue's strong focus on playful creativity and its hand-written logo lent itself to the creation of a new and more playful way of interacting with the website. The idea was to let users draw their way to where they wanted to be. /// Dass die Modemarke Red Issue besonderen Wert auf spielerische Kreativität und das handgeschriebene Logo legt, war der Anreiz, um eine neue und spielerische Art zu schaffen, mit der Website zu kommunizieren. Hier malt sich der User selbst den Weg, den er nehmen will. /// **La priorité donnée par la marque Red Issue à la créativité ludique, et son logo manuscrit, ont conduit à une façon plus amusante d'interagir avec le site Web. L'idée était de permettre aux utilisateurs de tracer le chemin les menant à ce qu'ils voulaient être.**

Info

Design Studio: Hello Monday <www.hellomonday.com>. /// **Design:** Sebastian Gram. /// **Programming:** Anders Jessen, Charlie Whitney. /// **Client:** Red Issue. /// **Tools:** Adobe Flash, Adobe Photoshop, Nintendo DS (playing with gestures), Adobe Flex. /// **Awards:** FWA (Site of the Day). /// **Cost:** 160 hours.

01-10

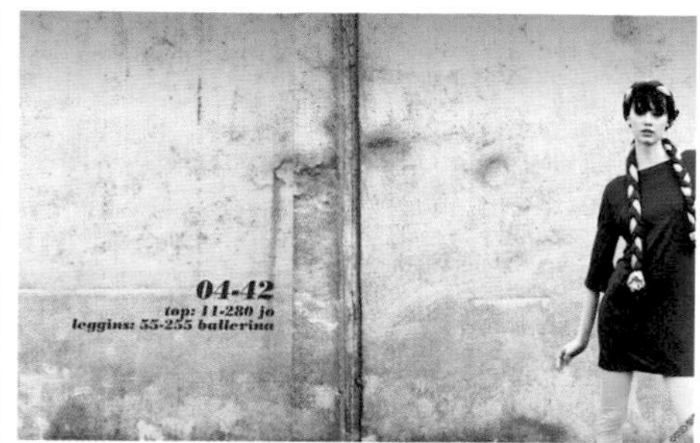
04-42
top: 11-280 jo
leggins: 55-255 ballerina

04-10

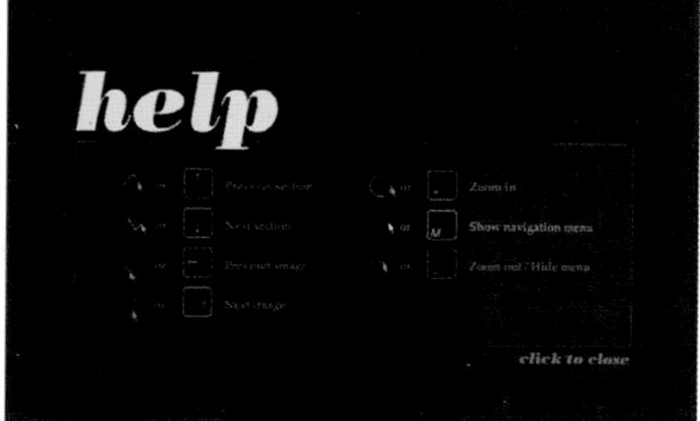
help
Zoom in
Show navigation menu
click to close

RENAISSANCE BSI

SOUTH AFRICA

www.renaissancebsi.co.za

2005

Concept

On this site the user can choose which level of the building they are interested in and explore it by means of the floor plans in order to find the information they are looking for easily. /// Auf dieser Site wählt der User eine interessante Etage des Gebäudes und erforscht über den Grundriss dessen Details. /// Sur ce site, l'utilisateur peut choisir l'étage de l'immeuble qui l'intéresse et le découvrir à l'aide de plans pour trouver facilement les informations qu'il recherche.

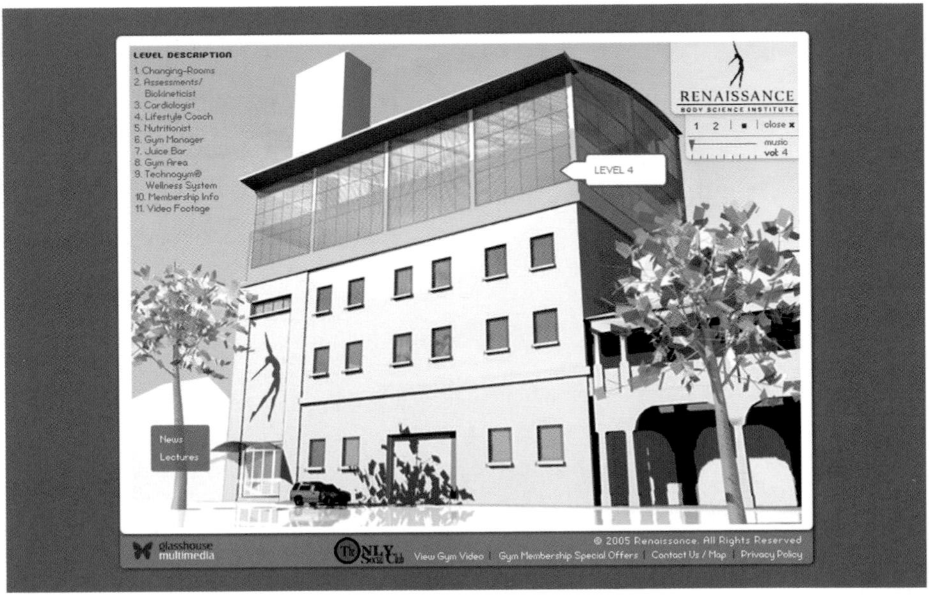

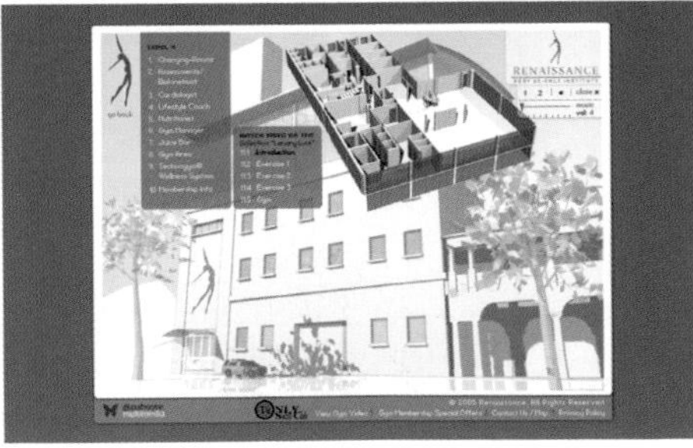

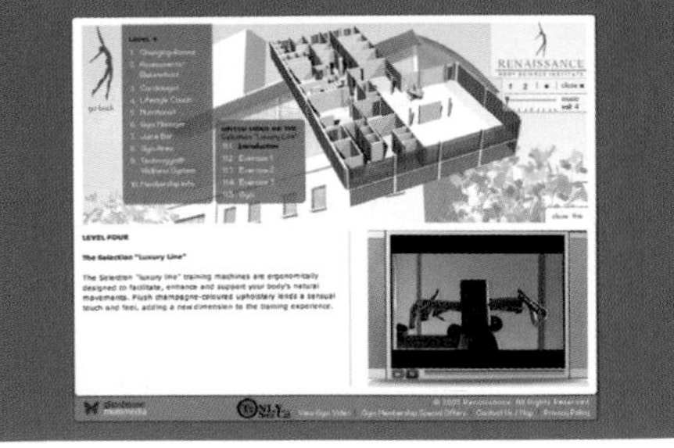

Info

DESIGN STUDIO: Glasshouse <www.glasshouse.co.za>. /// **DESIGN:** Cara Truter. /// **PROGRAMMING:** Cara Truter. /// **CLIENT:** Renaissance BSI. /// **TOOLS:** Adobe Photoshop, Adobe Flash, HTML. /// **AWARDS:** E-Creatives. /// **COST:** 90 hours.

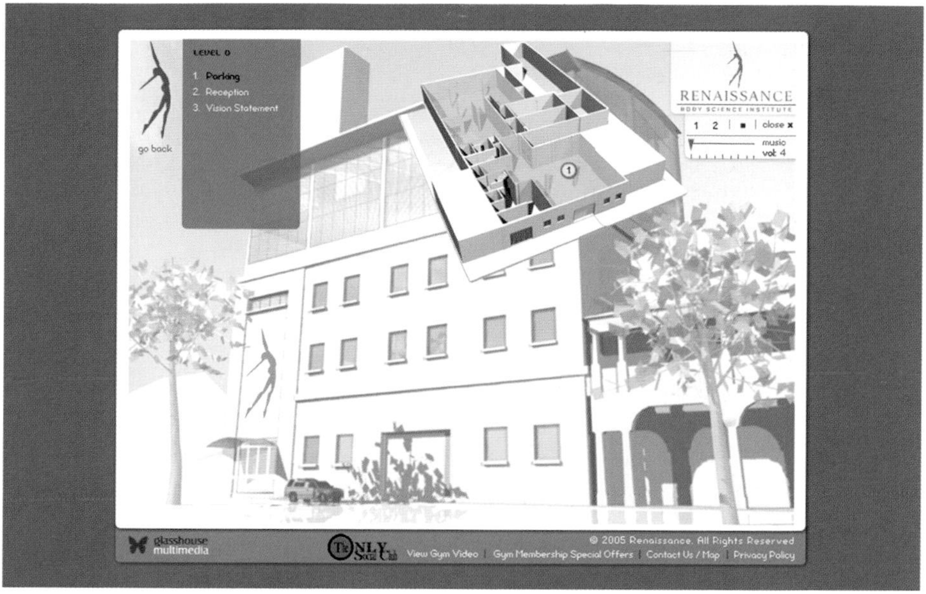

LEVEL 0
1. Parking
2. Reception
3. Vision Statement
go back
RENAISSANCE
BODY SCIENCE INSTITUTE
1 2 | ■ | close x
music
vol: 4
glasshouse multimedia
The ONLY Social Club
View Gym Video | Gym Membership Special Offers | Contact Us / Map | Privacy Policy
© 2005 Renaissance. All Rights Reserved

LEVEL 5
1. Excite™ Cardio
2. Outside Training Area
3. Kinesis™
4. Body Professionals
WATCH VIDEO ON
5.1 Kinesis Exercise 1
5.2 Kinesis Exercise 2
5.3 Kinesis Exercise 3
5.4 Kinesis Exercise 4
5.5 Kinesis Exercise 5
5.6 Kinesis Exercise 6
5.7 The Gym
go back
RENAISSANCE
BODY SCIENCE INSTITUTE
1 2 | ■ | close x
music
vol: 4
close this
LEVEL FIVE
Kinesis™
The Technogym® Kinesis™ equipment zone takes ergonomic design a step closer to absolute perfection. Kinesis™ is a tri-dimensional pulley system allowing for unlimited exercises and movements to improve strength, flexibility and balance, while stimulating the body and mind in a zen-like environment.
Kinesis is born out of the need to bring people closer to physical activity to improve the quality of their life. The inspiring principle is to rediscover the beauty of movement by means of free and natural movements.
glasshouse multimedia
The ONLY Social Club
View Gym Video | Gym Membership Special Offers | Contact Us / Map | Privacy Policy
© 2005 Renaissance. All Rights Reserved

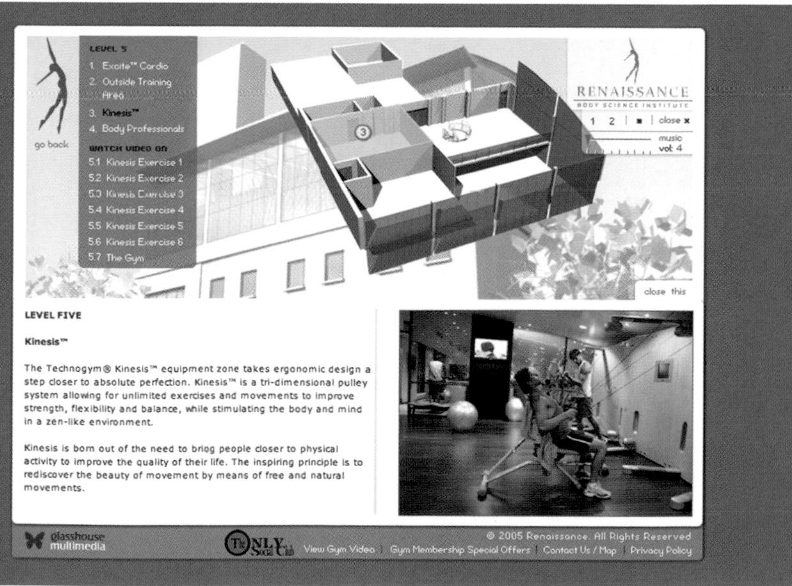

SAMSUNG MOBILE - MOBILE GRID

FRANCE

http://fr.samsungmobile.com/pid44/portables-samsung.html

2008

Concept

A complete and ergonomic grid which allows users to select, find, compare and also buy a new mobile phone. /// Mit diesem umfassenden und ergonomischen Raster können User neue Handys auswählen, vergleichen und auch kaufen. /// Une grille complète et ergonomique qui permet aux utilisateurs de sélectionner, de rechercher, de comparer et d'acheter un nouveau téléphone portable.

Info

Design Studio: Soleil Noir <www.soleilnoir.net>. /// **Design:** Pierre-Francois Hagège. /// **Programming:** Philippe Vignau, Francois Gillet. /// **Others:** Olivier Marchand (Project Manager). /// **Client:** Samsung France. /// **Tools:** Adobe Flash, Adobe Photoshop, XML. /// **Cost:** 1 month.

SHAKECONTROL

SPAIN

www.shakecontrol.com

2008

Concept

By dragging various characters the user can choose multiple-profile characterization: with different voices, upload your photo and record your message to send it to a friend. /// Indem der User verschiedene Typen aufs Handy zieht, wählt er aus mehreren Profilen mit verschiedenen Stimmen für das Gerät aus. Fotos können hochgeladen und eigene Botschaften an Freunde verschickt werden. /// En faisant glisser des personnages, l'utilisateur peut choisir une représentation avec plusieurs profils : avec diverses voix, il peut télécharger sa photo et enregistrer un message pour l'envoyer à un ami.

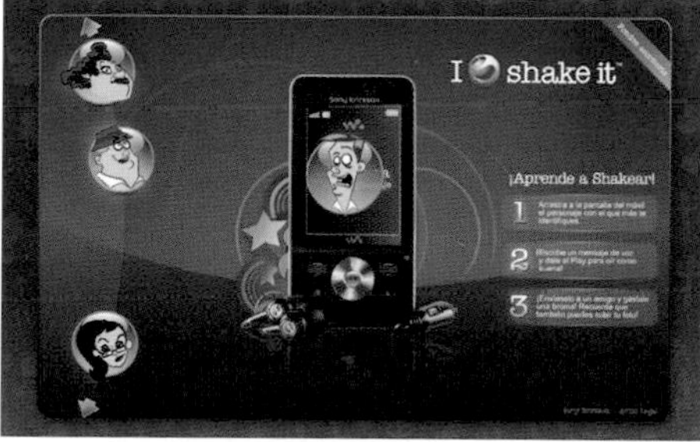

Info

DESIGN STUDIO: Medusateam <www.medusateam.com>. /// DESIGN: Medusateam. /// PROGRAMMING: Medusateam. /// CLIENT: Sony Ericsson. /// TOOLS: Adobe Flash, Adobe Photoshop. /// COST: 400 hours.

SILAS AND MARIA

UK

www.silasandmaria.com

2006

Concept

The idea of the navigation here is to take the user on a journey, by clicking on different images and immersing them in a different scenario. /// Dieser Navigation liegt das Konzept einer Reise zugrunde, bei der User auf verschiedene Bilder klicken und so in unterschiedliche Szenarien eintauchen. /// L'idée de la navigation consiste ici à faire voyager l'utilisateur, en cliquant sur différentes images et en le faisant entrer dans un autre scénario.

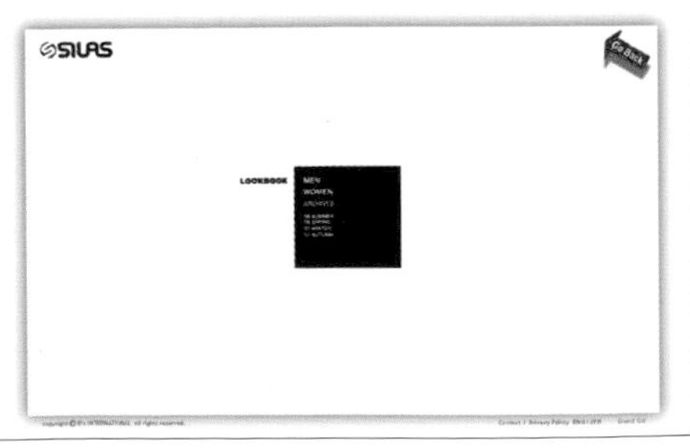

Info

Design Studio: Ever Growing Studio <www.evergrowing.net>. /// **Design:** Arron Bleasdale, Ben Sansbury. /// **Programming:** Arron Bleasdale. /// **Client:** Silas and Maria. /// **Tools:** Adobe Photoshop, Abobe Flash, Sound Studio. /// **Cost:** 160 hours.

SILAS
Go Back
LOOKBOOK
MEN
WOMEN

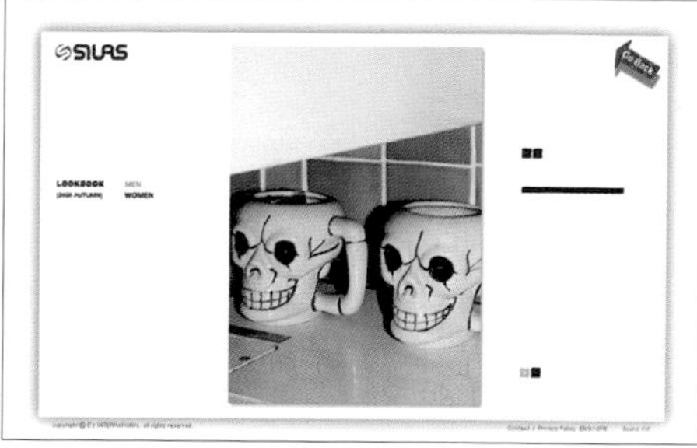
SILAS
Go Back
LOOKBOOK
MEN
WOMEN

SILAS
Go Back
Season Graphics
BACK
NEXT
Archives

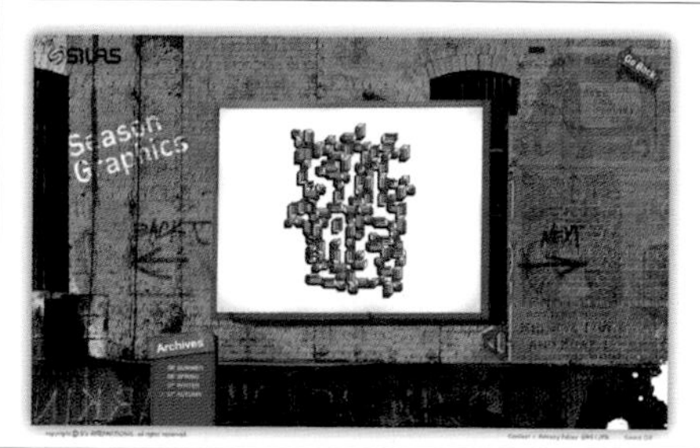
SILAS
Go Back
Season Graphics
BACK
NEXT
Archives

SILAS

SILAS
Go Back
SPECIALS

SILAS
Go Back
CITY OF LONDON

SILAS
Go Back
Making of Lookbook

SKY TOWER POLAND

POLAND

www.skytowerpoland.com

2008

Concept

To promote a real-estate initiative the interface offers a choice of presenter for this website. It also features a complex 3-D real-time rendering of the building showcased. /// Als Werbung für ein Immobilienunternehmen bietet das Interface dieser Website verschiedene Präsentatoren. Außerdem wird das Gebäude anhand einer komplexen 3-D-Darstellung vorgestellt. /// **Pour la promotion d'un projet immobilier, l'interface permet de choisir la présentation pour ce site Web. Elle montre aussi un rendu 3D complexe en temps réel du bâtiment présenté.**

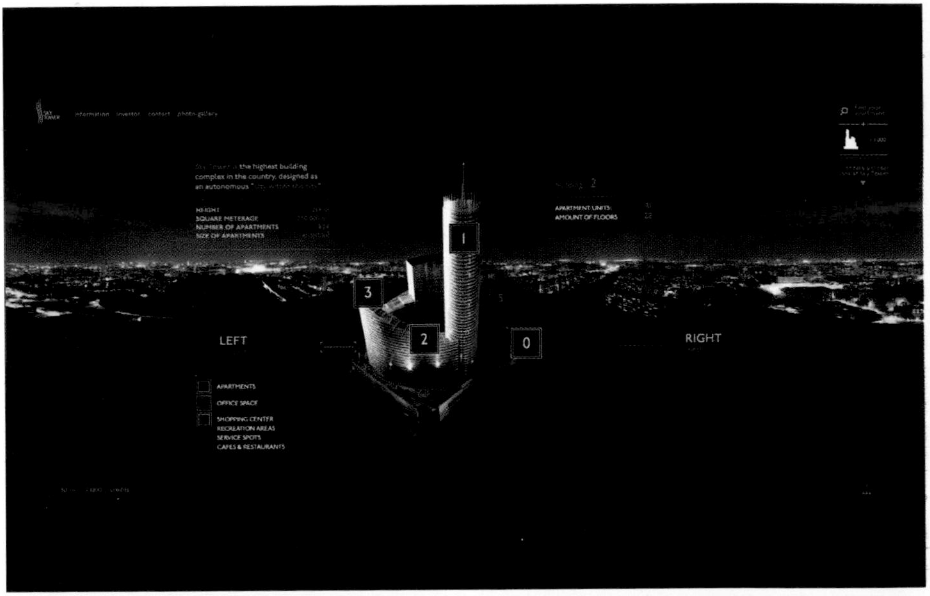

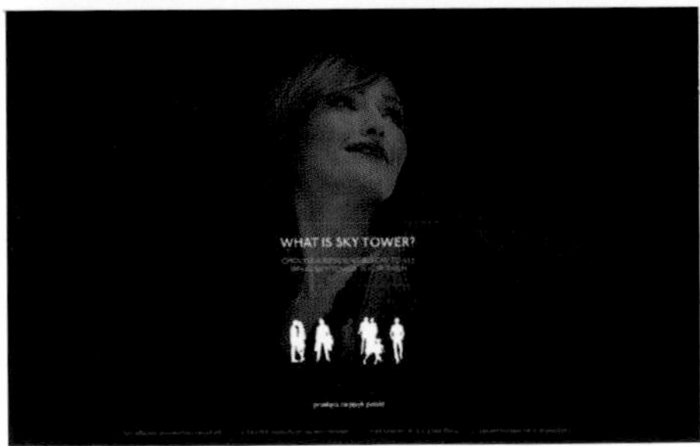

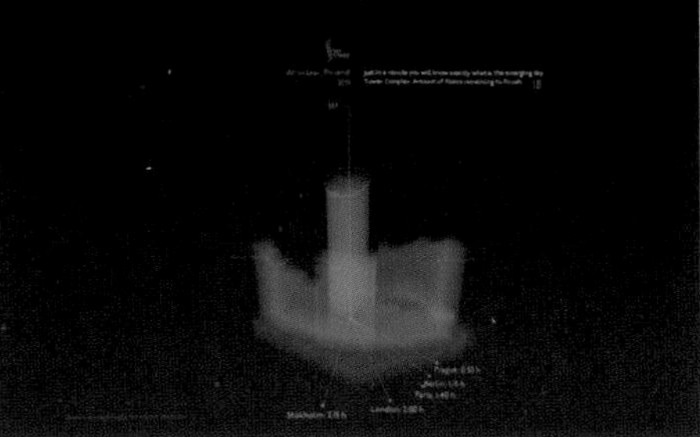

Info

Design Studio: Creative Agency: Max Weber <www.maxweber.com>; Motion Design: Odeon <www.odeon.com.pl>, Interactive Agency: Click5 <www.click5.pl>. /// **Design:** Grzegorz Mogilewski, Marcin Talarek, Piotr Tracki (Creative Direction); Grzegorz Mogilewski, Maciek Cecotka (Design). /// **Programming:** Jacek Zakowicz, Leszek Mzyk, Tomasz Kwolek, Wojtek Rymaszewski, Marcin Ryczan. /// **Others:** Maciej Dobrowolsk (Sound Design). /// **Client:** LC Corp. /// **Tools:** Adobe Flash, Adobe Photoshop, Adobe Illustrator.

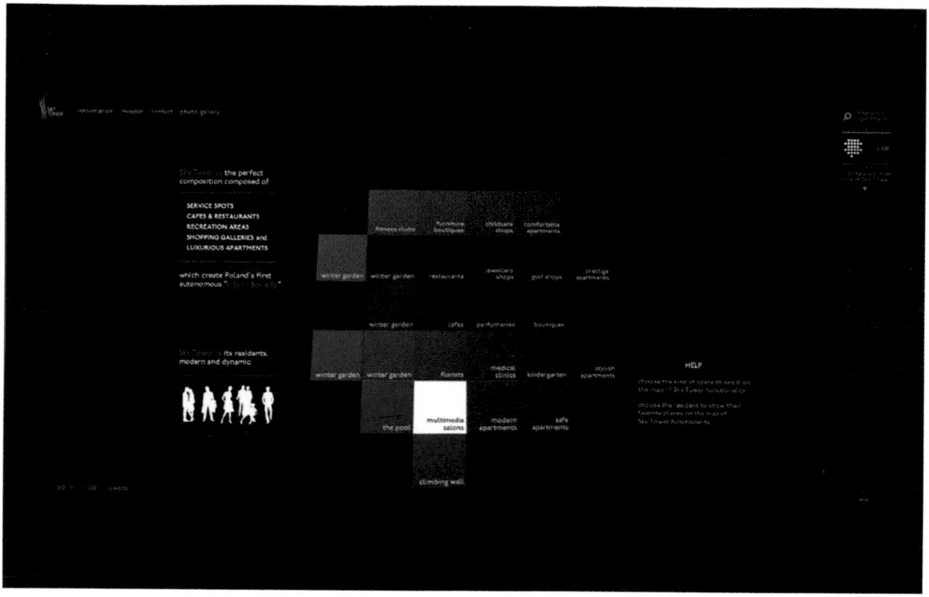

Sky Tower is the perfect composition composed of

SERVICE SPOTS
CAFES & RESTAURANTS
RECREATION AREAS
SHOPPING GALLERIES and
LUXURIOUS APARTMENTS

which create Poland's first autonomous

Sky Tower is its residents, modern and dynamic.

fitness clubs · furniture boutiques · childcare shops · comfortable apartments
winter garden · winter garden · restaurants · jewellery shops · golf shops · prestige apartments
winter garden · cafés · perfumeries · boutiques
winter garden · winter garden · florists · medical clinics · kindergarten · stylish apartments
the pool · multimedia salons · modern apartments · safe apartments
climbing wall

HELP

SNICKERS CROSS TÜRKIYE

TURKEY

www.snickers.com.tr/crossturkiye

2007

Concept

The event was about three roller-skaters skating across Turkey in two months, having the design of the site employ a 3-D street-sign navigation system to enhance the communication of concept and to make navigation easy. /// Bei diesem Event reisten drei Roller-Skater zwei Monate lang durch die Türkei. Das Site-Design vermittelt das Konzept über eine Navigation mit Verkehrszeichen in 3-D und vereinfacht so die Steuerung der Site. /// L'événement porte sur trois rollerskaters se déplaçant en Turquie pendant deux mois. Le design du site a recours à un système de navigation 3D à base de plaques de rues pour mieux transmettre le concept et faciliter la navigation.

Info

Design Studio: 2FRESH <www.2fresh.com>. /// **Design:** 2FRESH. /// **Programming:** 2FRESH. /// **Client:** MARS. /// **Tools:** Adobe Photoshop, Adobe Illustrator, Adobe Flash, Adobe Dreamweaver, Adobe After Effects. /// **Awards:** Creativity Award, Interactive Media Awards, Horizon Interactive Awards, Web Award. /// **Cost:** 1450 hours.

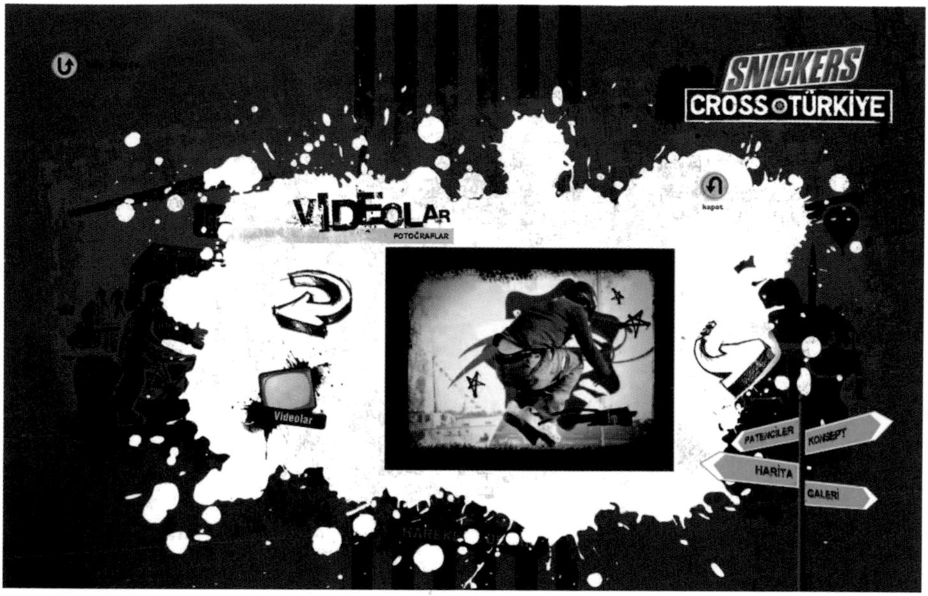

SNICKERS
CROSS TÜRKİYE

VİDEOLAR
FOTOĞRAFLAR

Videolar

PATENCİLER
KONSEPT
HARİTA
GALERİ

SNICKERS
CROSS TÜRKİYE

ETKİNLİKLER
YOL HARİTASI

Gelecek Etkinlikler

21 Mayıs Pazartesi
Şanlıurfa Mola

20 Mayıs Pazar
Kavşak Şanlıurfa40 km

19 Mayıs Cumartesi
Birecik Kavşak 42 km

18 Mayıs Cuma
Kavşak Birecik 18 km

17 Mayıs Perşembe

PATENCİLER
KONSEPT
HARİTA
GALERİ

SOLAR SPRING/SUMMER 2008

POLAND

www.solar-company.com.pl/08

2008

Concept

With this site users are transported to Tenerife with relaxing sounds and waves among which they have to find hot-spots presenting the latest fashion collection from Solar Company. /// Diese Site versetzt die User nach Teneriffa, wo sie bei entspannenden Klängen und Meeresrauschen Hotspots suchen können, die die aktuelle Collection der Solar Company präsentieren. /// Dans ce site, les utilisateurs sont transportés à Tenerife, avec bruits apaisants et vagues compris, et ils doivent trouver dans le paysage des zones sensibles présentant la dernière collection de Solar Company.

Info

Design Studio: Huncwot <www.huncwot.com>. /// **Design:** Arek Romanski, Lukasz Knasiecki. /// **Client:** Solar Company LTD. /// **Tools:** FreeHand, Flash, SQL. /// **Cost:** 140 hours.

SPIER SUSTAINABILITY

SOUTH AFRICA

www.spier.co.za/sustainability

2008

Concept

Users are able to immerse themselves in the site and are encouraged to interact through the use of a Flash environment which allows them to explore the eco-friendly, sustainable business from within the local community. /// Die User betreten die Site, um mit ihr herumzuspielen. Sie erforschen aus der lokalen Community heraus das über Flash umgesetzte Gelände der umweltfreundlich und nachhaltig wirtschaftenden Firma Spier. /// Les utilisateurs peuvent plonger dans le site et sont invités à interagir grâce à un environnement Flash qui leur permet d'explorer l'activité durable et respectueuse de l'environnement développée au sein de la communauté locale.

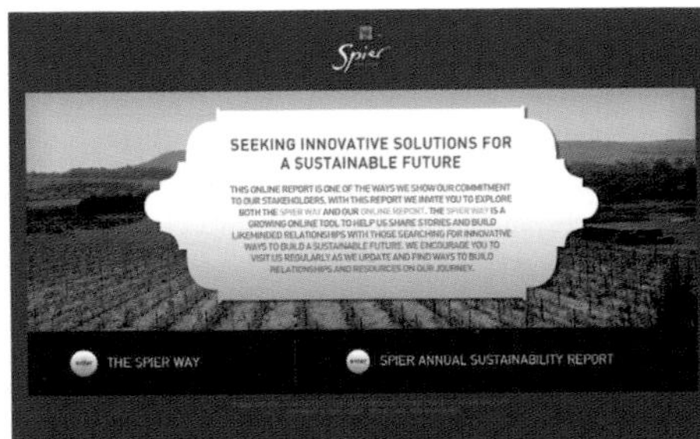

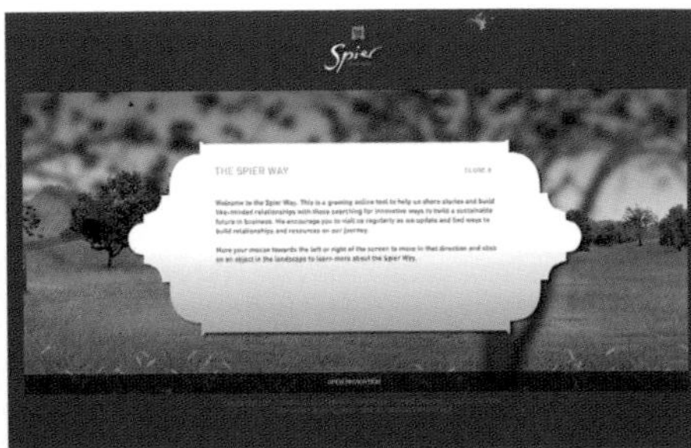

Info

Design Studio: HelloComputer <www.hellocomputer.net>. /// **Design:** Mark Tomlinson, Simon Spreckley. /// **Programming:** Kyle Ward, Mike Hayes. /// **Client:** Spier. /// **Tools:** Adobe Flash, Adobe Photoshop, Adobe Illustrator, Maya, PHP, XML, HTML, My SQL. /// **Awards:** Loerie Award (Experiential/Digital – Bronze). /// **Cost:** 160 hours.

Spier
CHEETAH OUTREACH & EAGLE ENCOUNTERS

Spier
SPIER CONTEMPORARY
Corporate Social Investment

Spier
CHEETAH OUTREACH AND EAGLE ENCOUNTERS
BACKGROUND
One of our most important values is to protect and conserve our natural environment and we address it in many ways, visible and invisible. We preserve our fynbos species that grow in our part of the Cape Floral Kingdom. We also believe in conservation on a larger scale, and in drawing attention to the plight of many wild creatures whose habitat is being destroyed.
CHALLENGE
In Africa, rapid industrialisation and a growing population means land once left wild and inhabited by animals is becoming tamed and often eroded by

Spier
SPIER CONTEMPORARY
BACKGROUND
The Africa Centre, an NGO supported by Spier, has taken responsibility for what was previously known as the Spier Arts Summer Season. The Africa Centre is a physical entity and an ongoing philosophical process. In time it will emerge as a multi-sited, multiple-usage space where the visual, intellectual and performance cultures of Africa are celebrated, studied and brought to life for diverse audiences in innovative ways.
www.africacentre.net
CHALLENGE
Part of its brief is to showcase, promote and develop emerging South

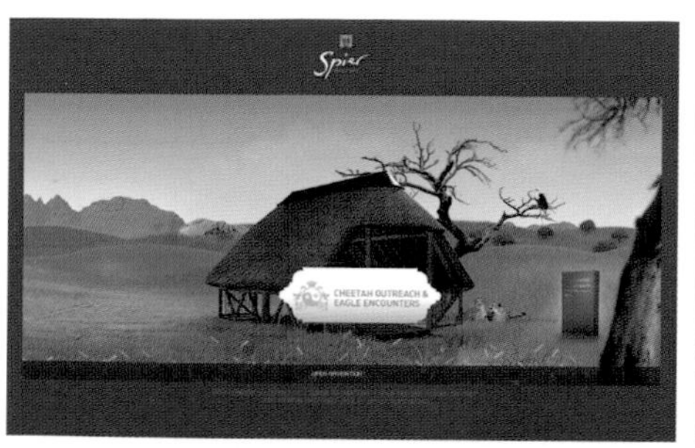

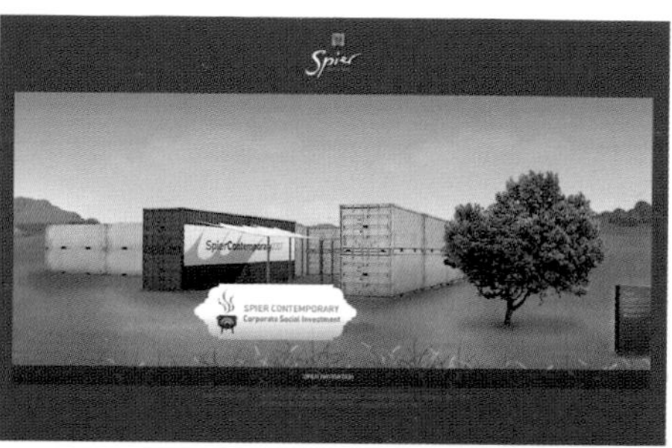

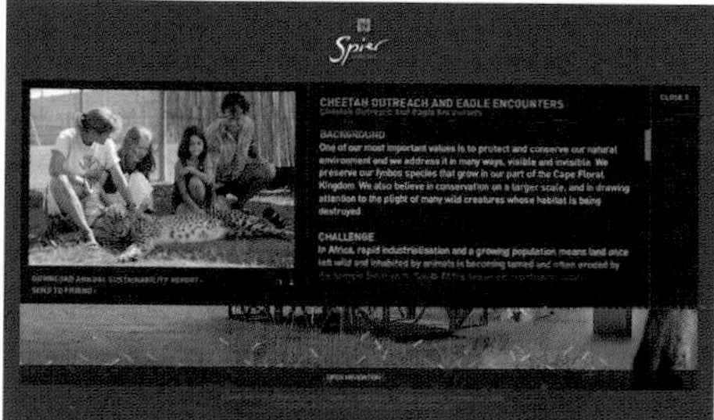

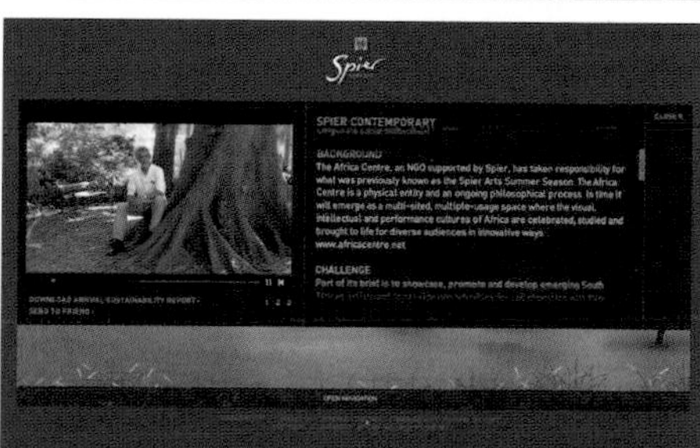

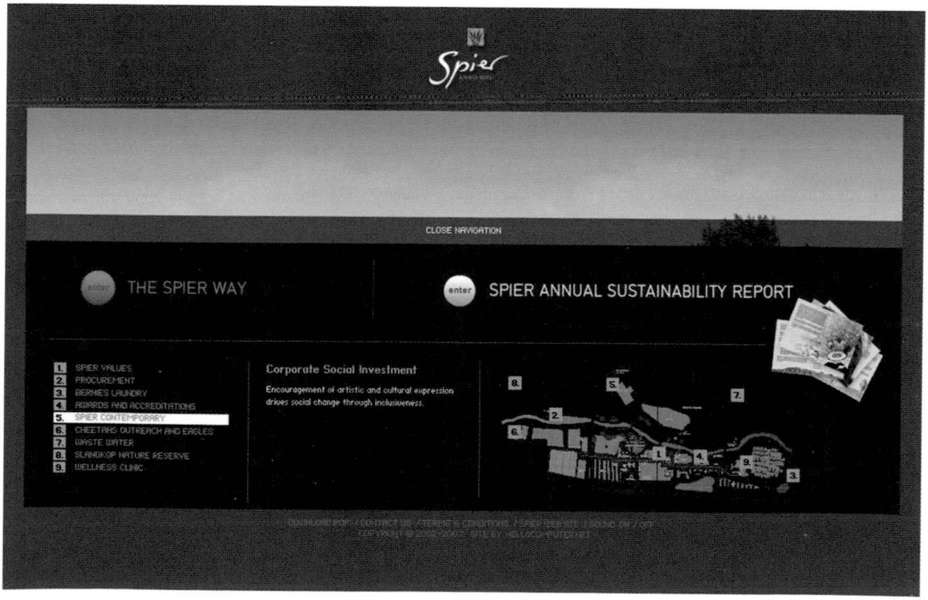

Spier
CLOSE NAVIGATION
enter THE SPIER WAY
enter SPIER ANNUAL SUSTAINABILITY REPORT
1. SPIER VALUES
2. PROCUREMENT
3. BERNIE'S LAUNDRY
4. AWARDS AND ACCREDITATIONS
5. SPIER CONTEMPORARY
6. CHEETAHS OUTREACH AND EAGLES
7. WASTE WATER
8. SLANGKOP NATURE RESERVE
9. WELLNESS CLINIC
Corporate Social Investment
Encouragement of artistic and cultural expression drives social change through inclusiveness.
8.
5.
7.
2.
6.
1.
4.
9.
3.

SPRINT SPEED FOR THE HOLIDAYS

USA

http://sprintholiday2.dev.domanistudios.com/2008

2008

Concept

An immersive Flash site, showcasing cellular phones, featuring a unique navigation system utilizing three levels of zooming camera movements. The site also featured an e-card creator, giving the user keyboard and mouse control over a 3-D skater. /// Eine fesselnde Flash-Site als Showcase für Handys mit einem einzigartigen Navigationssystem, das drei Zoomstufen bei den Kamerabewegungen einsetzt. Mit einem 3-D-Skater, der über Tastatur oder Mausbewegungen gesteuert wird, können auch e-Cards erstellt werden. /// Un site Flash immersif présentant des téléphones portables, avec un système de navigation unique qui repose sur trois niveaux de mouvements de zoom de la caméra. Le site fournit aussi un créateur d'e-cards, laissant à l'utilisateur le contrôle d'un skater 3D au moyen du clavier et de la souris.

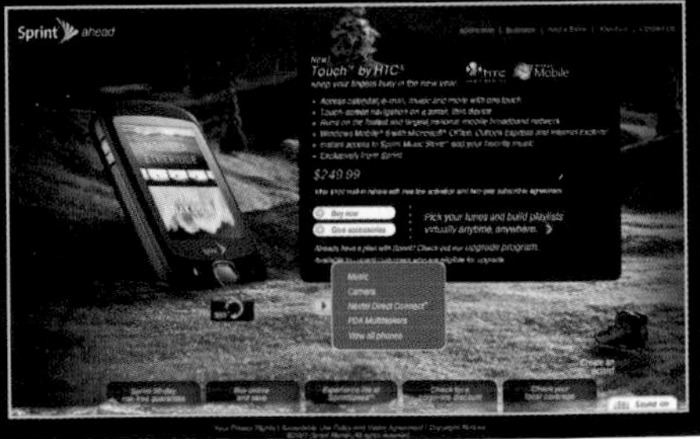

Info

Design Studio: Domani Studios <www.domanistudios.com>. /// **Design:** Goodby Silverstein & Partners; Domani Studios. /// **Programming:** Domani Studios. /// **Client:** Goodby Silverstein & Partners. /// **Tools:** Adobe Photoshop, Flash, Adobe After Affects, XML, HTML. /// **Awards:** 2008 One Show Interactive Awards (Merit).

Sprint ahead
Create some magic
at the speed of light
To design your card, start by choosing which
ice rink you want for your background.
Sprint.com | Business | Find a Store | About Us | Contact Us
Your Privacy Rights | Acceptable Use Policy and Visitor Agreement | Copyright Notices
©2007 Sprint Nextel. All rights reserved.

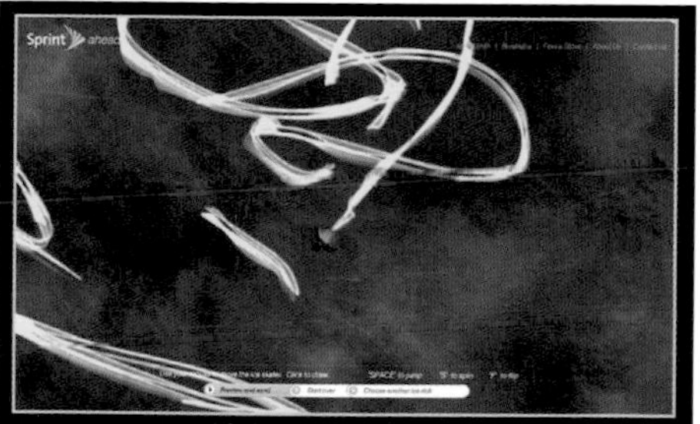
Sprint

Sprint ahead
2008: The year for SprintSpeed.™

Sprint ahead

Sprint ahead
BlackBerry® Pearl™ 8130
$199.99

STEPHEN YABLON ARCHITECT

USA

www.syarch.com

2006

Concept

Built on square grids, the architecture office is presented through a fast-animated navigation on one of the sides of a square. /// Auf einem quadratischen Raster aufbauend, präsentiert sich das Architekturbüro auf den quadratisch angelegten Flächen über eine flott animierte Navigation. /// Construit sur un quadrillage, le cabinet d'architecture est présenté grâce à une navigation d'animation rapide sur l'un des côtés d'un carré.

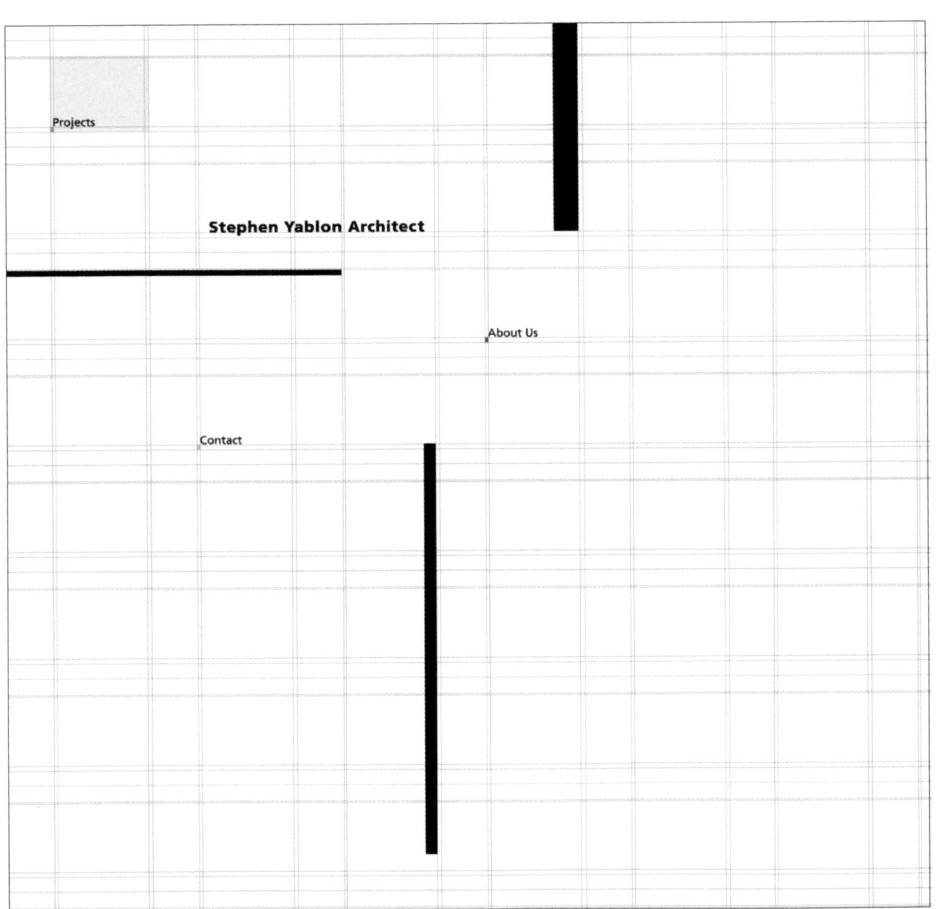

Info

DESIGN STUDIO: Knowawall, Inc. <www.knowawall.com>. /// **DESIGN:** Noah Wall. /// **PROGRAMMING:** Noah Wall, Sean Yeomans. /// **CLIENT:** Stephen Yablon Architect. /// **TOOLS:** Adobe Photoshop, Flash, PHP. /// **COST:** 30 Days.

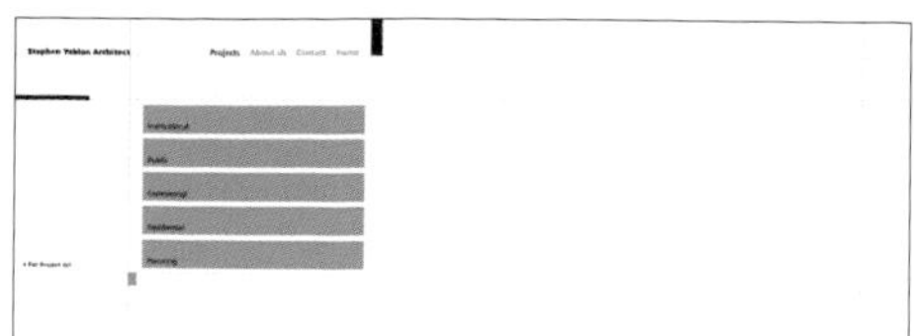

Stephen Yablon A

Betances Community Center   Bronx, New York

Stephen Yablon Architect

Commercial

Corporate Headquarters
AG Asset Management
Enterprice Community Partners
Cooper, Robertson & Partners
Angelo, Gordon & Co.
Sony New Technologies
Alson Capital Partners LLC
Vera Institute of Justice
AFD
Lawyer's Committee

Corporate Headquarters   Preston, England, Second Place International Competition

✚ **General Info** Project Data

SYA was a finalist in a competition sponsored by the Royal Institute of British Architects for the corporate headquarters of a real estate development firm in Northern England.

Our solution was a striking, low, sustainable, building that sweeps around the corner of its roundabout site and brings you into a courtyard that looks to the sky. The sleek form is clad on the south, east and west exposures in horizontal wood louvers on the which reduce heat gain while expressing its wooded site. The top of the building is covered by a green roof which insulates the building, captures rainwater and allows for its reuse.

The central feature is a large, covered, luminous, courtyard, a highly active town square which is the heart of the work experience. This space is surrounded on three sides by two floors of flexible workspace and a single floor of amenities not found nearby. The courtyard acts as the buildings lungs creating natural ventilation through operable panels in its glass roof.

Yablon Architect

STUDIO FM MILANO

ITALY

www.studiofmmilano.it

2008

Concept

With this dynamic system you can move through projects, exploring horizontal and vertical dimensions. /// Bei diesem dynamischen System kann man sich durch die Projekte bewegen und durch vertikales und horizontales Scrollen deren Dimensionen erforschen. /// Les menus du haut fonctionnent d'abord verticalement puis, pour chaque rubrique, une navigation horizontale est activée par défilement, ce qui permet à l'utilisateur de rechercher le contenu. Un système rapide et bien pensé lorsque la base de données contient un nombre élevé d'images.

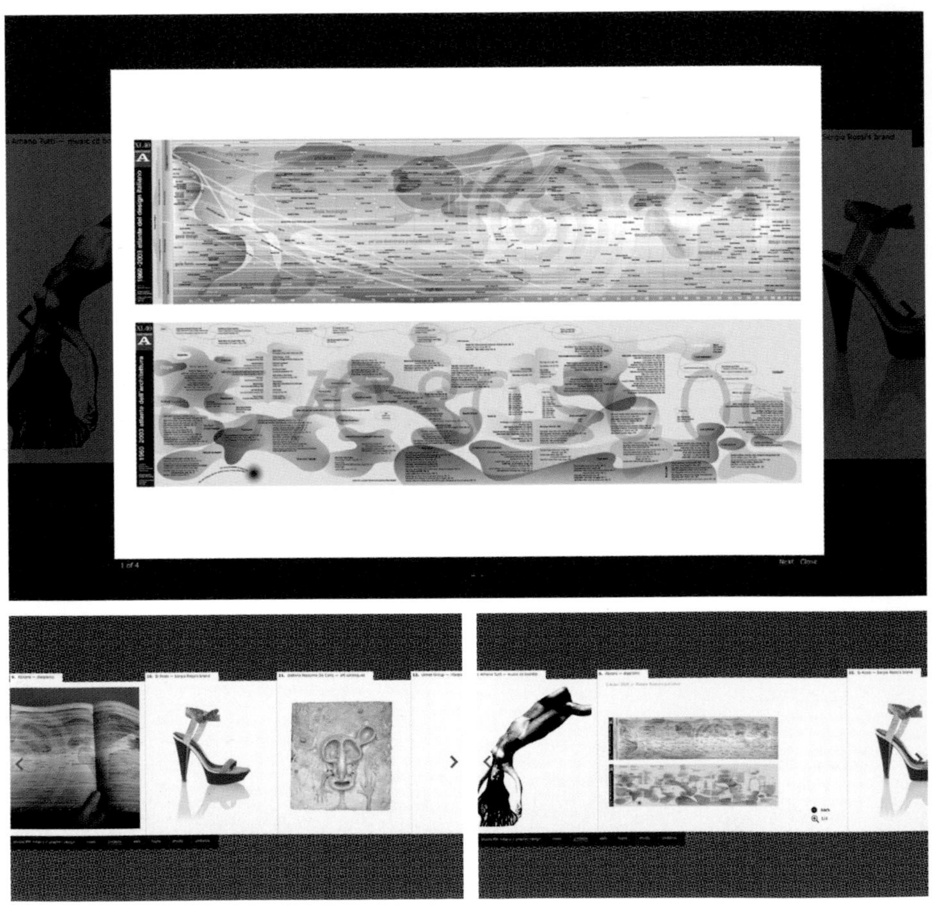

Info

DESIGN STUDIO: studio FM milano <www.studiofmmilano.it>. /// **DESIGN:** studio FM milano. /// **PROGRAMMING:** studio FM milano. /// **TOOLS:** ZenPhoto, JQuery.

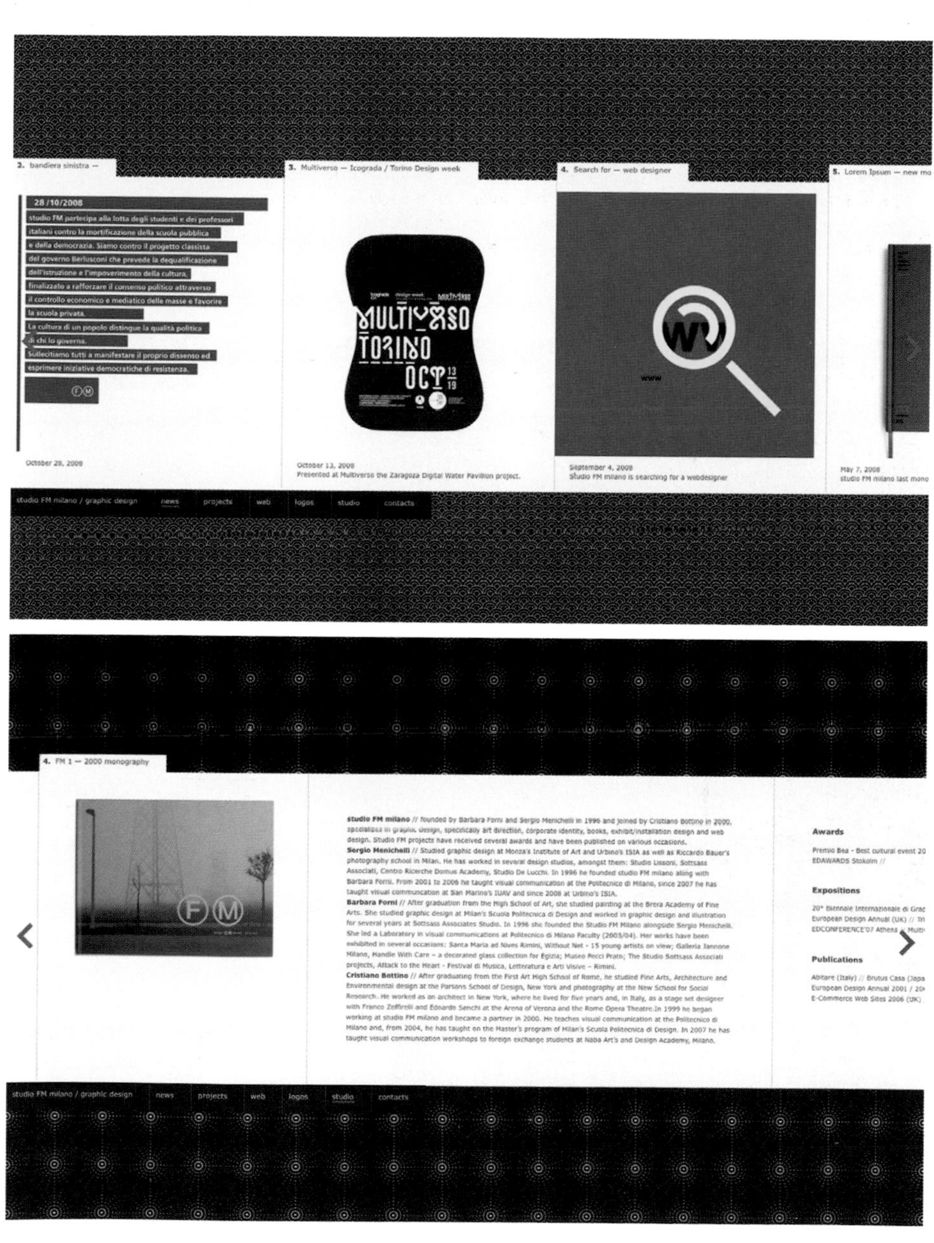

2. bandiera sinistra —
28 /10/2008
studio FM partecipa alla lotta degli studenti e dei professori
italiani contro la mortificazione della scuola pubblica
e della democrazia. Siamo contro il progetto classista
del governo Berlusconi che prevede la dequalificazione
dell'istruzione e l'impoverimento della cultura,
finalizzato a rafforzare il consenso politico attraverso
il controllo economico e mediatico delle masse e favorire
la scuola privata.
La cultura di un popolo distingue la qualità politica
di chi lo governa.
Sollecitiamo tutti a manifestare il proprio dissenso ed
esprimere iniziative democratiche di resistenza.
October 28, 2008
3. Multiverso — Icograda / Torino Design week
MULTIVERSO
TORINO
OCT 13 19
October 13, 2008
Presented at Multiverso the Zaragoza Digital Water Pavilion project.
4. Search for — web designer
www
September 4, 2008
studio FM milano is searching for a webdesigner
5. Lorem Ipsum — new mo
May 7, 2008
studio FM milano last mono
studio FM milano / graphic design
news
projects
web
logos
studio
contacts
4. FM 1 — 2000 monography
studio FM milano // founded by Barbara Forni and Sergio Menichelli in 1996 and joined by Cristiano Bottino in 2000, specializes in graphic design, specifically art direction, corporate identity, books, exhibit/installation design and web design. Studio FM projects have received several awards and have been published on various occasions.
Sergio Menichelli // Studied graphic design at Monza's Institute of Art and Urbino's ISIA as well as Riccardo Bauer's photography school in Milan. He has worked in several design studios, amongst them: Studio Lissoni, Sottsass Associati, Centro Ricerche Domus Academy, Studio De Lucchi. In 1996 he founded studio FM milano along with Barbara Forni. From 2001 to 2006 he taught visual communication at the Politecnico di Milano, since 2007 he has taught visual communcation at San Marino's IUAV and since 2008 at Urbino's ISIA.
Barbara Forni // After graduation from the High School of Art, she studied painting at the Brera Academy of Fine Arts. She studied graphic design at Milan's Scuola Politecnica di Design and worked in graphic design and illustration for several years at Sottsass Associates Studio. In 1996 she founded the Studio FM Milano alongside Sergio Menichelli. She led a Laboratory in visual communications at Politecnico di Milano Faculty (2003/04). Her works have been exhibited in several occasions: Santa Maria ad Nives Rimini, Without Net - 15 young artists on view; Galleria Jannone Milano, Handle With Care – a decorated glass collection for Egizia; Museo Pecci Prato; The Studio Sottsass Associati projects, Attack to the Heart - Festival di Musica, Letteratura e Arti Visive – Rimini.
Cristiano Bottino // After graduating from the First Art High School of Rome, he studied Fine Arts, Architecture and Environmental design at the Parsons School of Design, New York and photography at the New School for Social Research. He worked as an architect in New York, where he lived for five years and, in Italy, as a stage set designer with Franco Zeffirelli and Edoardo Senchi at the Arena of Verona and the Rome Opera Theatre.In 1999 he began working at studio FM milano and became a partner in 2000. He teaches visual communication at the Politecnico di Milano and, from 2004, he has taught on the Master's program of Milan's Scuola Politecnica di Design. In 2007 he has taught visual communication workshops to foreign exchange students at Naba Art's and Design Academy, Milano.
Awards
Premio Bea - Best cultural event 20
EDAWARDS Stokolm //
Expositions
20° Biennale Internazionale di Grac
European Design Annual (UK) // Tri
EDCONFERENCE'07 Athens // Multi
Publications
Abitare (Italy) // Brutus Casa (Japa
European Design Annual 2001 / 20
E-Commerce Web Sites 2006 (UK)
studio FM milano / graphic design
news
projects
web
logos
studio
contacts

SUBRAUMSTUDIO

GERMANY

www.subraumstudio.com

2007

Concept

The user can here explore Subraumstudio, a German agency specializing in industrial design, architecture and 3-D, through a unique mouseless interface. /// Der User erkundet hier über ein einzigartiges mausloses Interface die Website von Subraumstudio. Diese deutsche Agentur ist auf Industriedesign, Architektur und 3-D spezialisiert. /// **L'utilisateur peut découvrir Subraumstudio, une agence allemande spécialisée dans le design industriel, l'architecture et l'animation 3D, via une interface unique sans souris.**

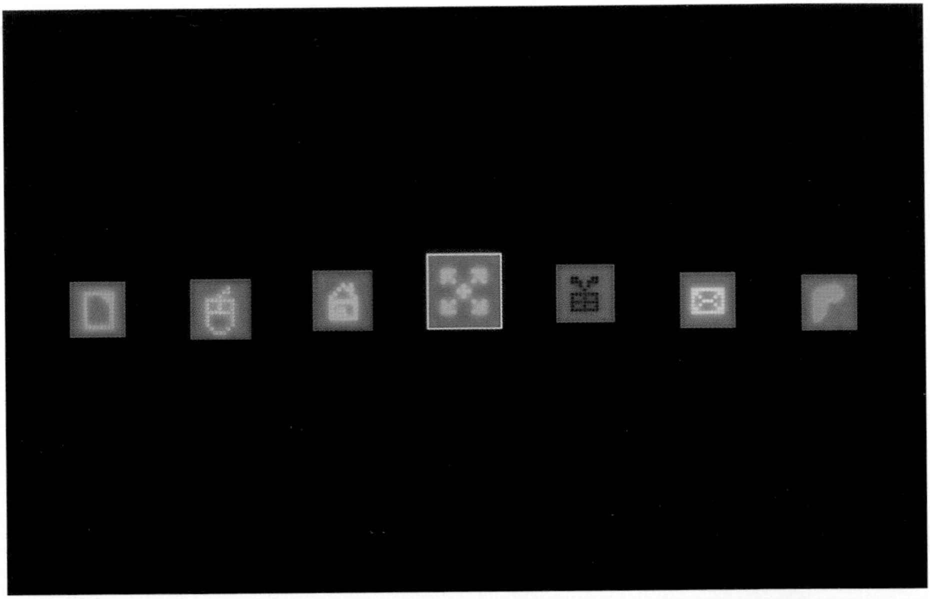

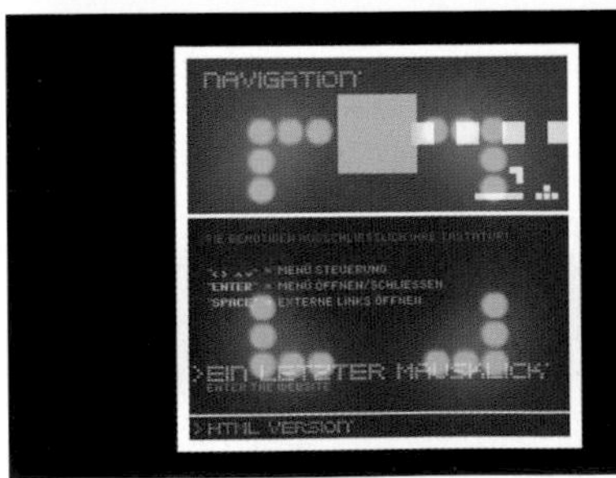

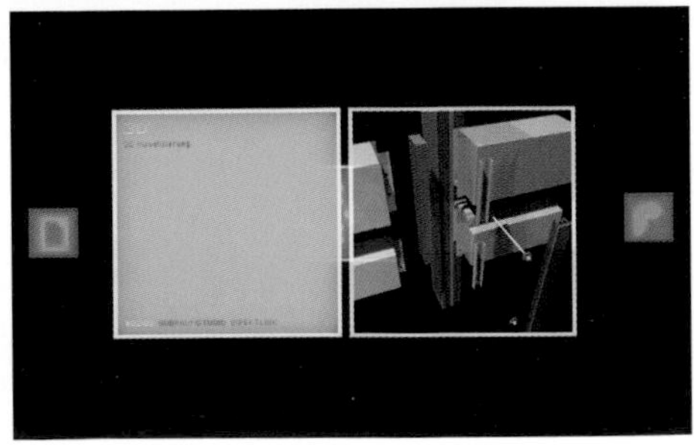

Info

Design Studio: NALINDESIGN <www.nalindesign.com>. /// **Design:** Andre Weier. /// **Programming:** Andre Weier. /// **Others:** Samuel Trebbin (Sound Design). /// **Client:** SUBRAUMSTUDIO. /// **Tools:** Adobe Flash, Adobe Photoshop, XML, PHP, CSS, JavaScript, htaccess, effective CMS. /// **Awards:** American Design Award (Gold), Suedwestfalen Award (Winner 2007/Best Experimental Website), coolhompages.com (Site of the Week), Creative Website Awards. /// **Cost:** 3 months.

TAKE AGENCY

GERMANY

www.takeagency.com

2008

Concept

The navigation is based on the idea of a strong horizontal arrangement, which leads the user through the site step by step. As an extra feature all info boxes are made so they may be dragged. /// Die Navigation basiert auf dem Konzept einer durchgängig horizontalen Anordnung, die den User Schritt für Schritt durch die Site führt. Als besonderes Feature können alle Info-Boxen auch mit der Maus gezogen werden. /// La navigation repose sur l'idée d'une organisation horizontale compacte, qui guide pas à pas l'utilisateur à travers le site. Comme fonction supplémentaire, toutes les zones d'information peuvent être déplacées par glissement.

Info

DESIGN STUDIO: Tilt Design Studio <www.tiltdesignstudio.com>. /// **DESIGN:** Marc Antosch, Felix Schultze. /// **PROGRAMMING:** Felix Schultze. /// **CLIENT:** Simon Reinitzer (Take Agency). /// **TOOLS:** Adobe Flash, ActionScript. /// **COST:** ca. 240 hours.

TDK RECORDING MEDIA EUROPE

GERMANY

www.tdk-media.eu

2007

Concept

A hierarchical dynamic navigation with virtually infinite depth and minimal screen footprint when not in use. The challenge was to reach the same look and feel the previous, Flash-based navigation achieved but without the constraints typical to a plug-in dependant solution. /// Diese hierarchische und dynamische Navigation ist praktisch unendlich tief und nimmt wenig Platz in Anspruch, wenn sie nicht benutzt wird. Die Herausforderung bestand darin, das gleiche Look & Feel wie die vorige, auf Flash basierende Navigation zu bekommen, aber ohne die Einschränkungen, die für eine von einem Plug-in abhängige Lösung typisch ist. /// Une navigation dynamique hiérarchique d'une profondeur quasiment infinie et avec un encombrement minimal de l'écran lorsqu'elle n'est pas utilisée. Le défi consistait à obtenir la même apparence que la navigation antérieure en Flash, mais sans les contraintes propres à une solution reposant sur un plug-in.

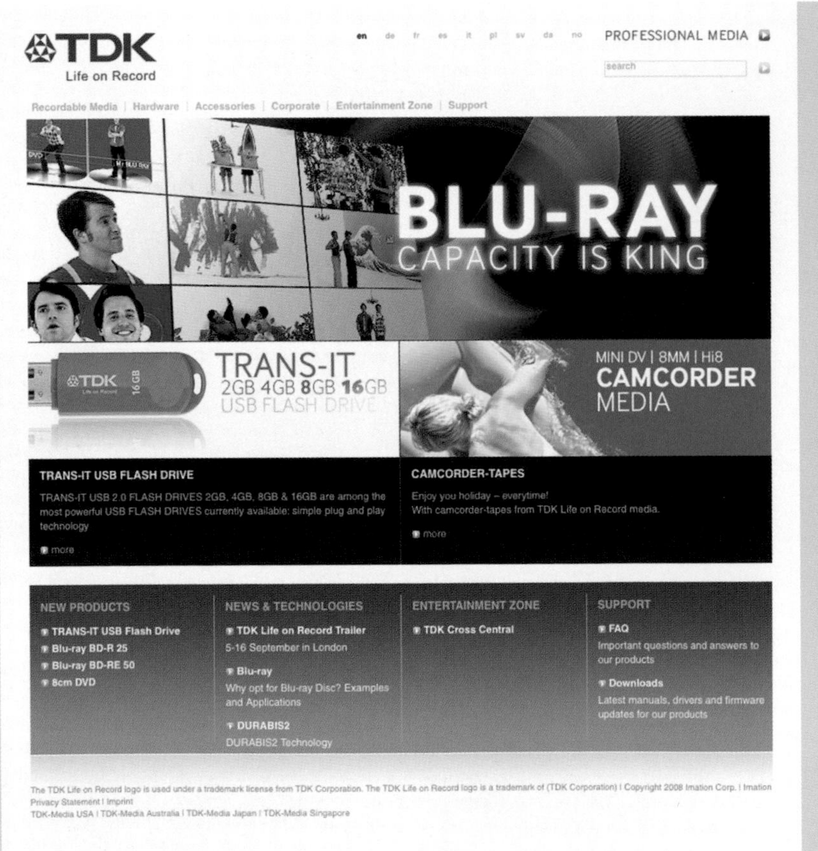

Info

DESIGN STUDIO: wysiwyg* software design gmbh <www.wysiwg.de>. /// **DESIGN:** Lars Emmelmann, Alexander Koch, Oliver Heib. /// **PROGRAMMING:** Norbert van Bebber, Pattrick Kreutzer, Mathias Wegerhoff. /// **CLIENT:** TDK Recording Media Europe. /// **TOOLS:** HTML, CSS, JavaScript, PHP, MySQL.

en de fr es it pl sv da no PROFESSIONAL MEDIA

search

Recordable Media | Hardware | Accessories | Corporate | Entertainment Zone | Support

Blu-ray | DVD | CD | MiniDisc | Audio Cassettes | Video Cassettes | Camcorder Cassettes

CD-R | CD-RW | Audio CD | High Capacity | Inkjet Printable | Lightscribe

HIGH CAPACITY RECORDABLE 800MB 90MIN

SEE ALSO:

- CD/DVD Marker
- CD/DVD/Blu-ray Optical Guid

Product recommendation:

High Capacity Recordable

HIGH CAPACITY RECORDABLE dramatically pushes today's limits of CD-R recording. Enjoy an extra 10 minutes of CD-Audio recording time per disc, or a full extra hour of your personal music from a six-disc car CD changer. Or, record your own videos with longer programming or higher-quality encoding for near-DVD picture quality. Just check the compatibility of your CD-R/RW writer, adjust the settings of your burning software and fully benefit from the High Capacity Recordable.

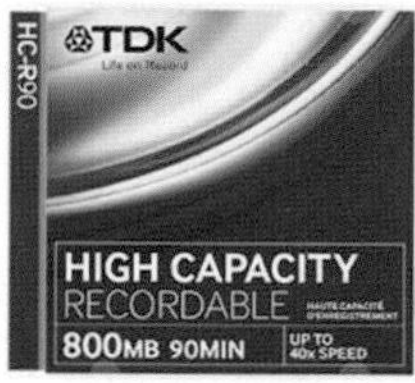

High Capacity CD

- Full 90 minutes/800 MB capacity.
- Recording Speed up to 40x.
- Available as: Single Jewel Case, 10 pack.

High Capacity CD Cakebox

- Available as: 25 pieces cakebox.

Note: Please note that all configurations of packaging may not be available in all countries. For further details please contact your local TDK Life on Record brand office.

top

THALIA

USA

www.thalia.com

2007

Concept

With a book-like interface, the navigation offers fully animated menus to match the entertaining characteristics of the website. /// Das Interface ist einem Buch nachempfunden. Die Navigation bietet komplett animierte Menüs, die zum unterhaltsamen Charakter der Website passen. /// **Avec une interface partant d'un livre, la navigation présente des menus entièrement animés à l'image du caractère ludique du site Web.**

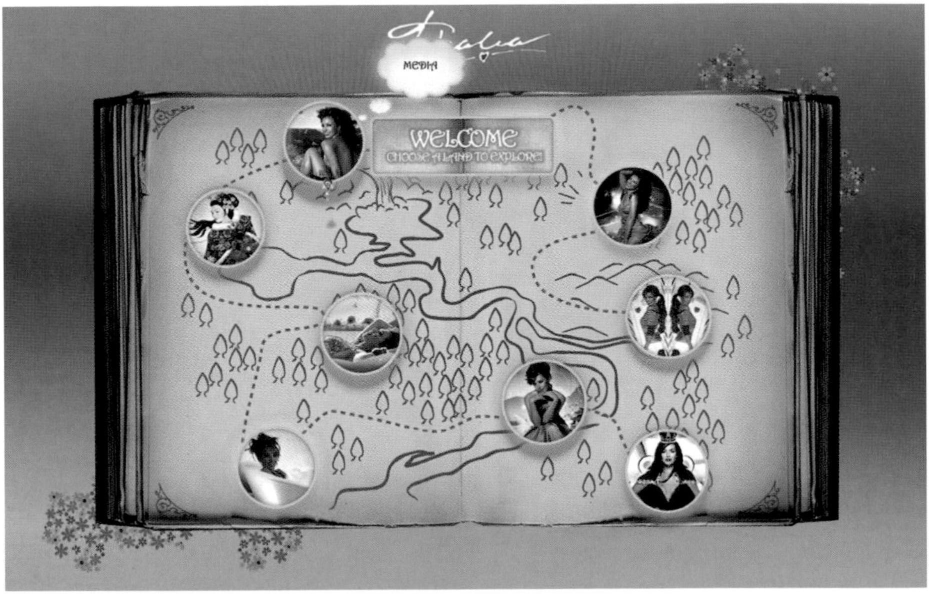

Info

Design Studio: BKWLD <www.bkwld.com>. /// **Design:** Jeff Toll. /// **Programming:** Ben Borowski. /// **Client:** Thalia. /// **Tools:** XML, HTML, Adobe Photoshop, Adobe Flash, PHP. /// **Awards:** Creative Website Awards, Latin Websites Awards.

T-RADIO
BACK TO NAVIGATION
DISCOGRAPHY
LYRICS
VIDEOS

T-RADIO
BACK TO NAVIGATION
PHOTO GALLERY

THE ASURA

GERMANY

www.the-asura.nalindesign.com

2005

Concept

An open-book interface in a very realistic composition. The navigation is built through the pictures and bookmarks: after clicking one of them, the cards pop out of the book and under the screen. /// Das Interface wird sehr realistisch als offenes Buch umgesetzt. Die Navigation ist aus Bildern und Lesezeichen aufgebaut: Wenn man auf eine Karte klickt, springt sie aus dem Buch hervor, und das Lesezeichen schiebt sich aus den Seiten heraus. /// Une interface avec un livre ouvert, d'une composition très réaliste. La navigation se fait à base d'images et de signets : lorsque l'utilisateur clique dessus, les photos surgissent du livre.

Info

Design Studio: NALINDESIGN <www.nalindesign.com>. /// **Design:** Andre Weier. /// **Programming:** Andre Weier. /// **Others:** Samuel Trebbin (Sound Design). /// **Client:** THE ASURA. /// **Tools:** Adobe Flash, Adobe Photoshop, text editor, XML, PHP. /// **Awards:** Web Design Library (Site of the Day), internetvibes.net, E-creative.net (Site of the Day). /// **Cost:** 3 months.

THE LUCKY STRIKES

UK

www.theluckystrikes.com

2008

Concept

Rather than using 'standard button' navigation, the user is encouraged to explore the website by interacting with certain objects which relate to the content of their particular section. /// Anstatt über eine Navigation mit Schaltflächen die Site zu erforschen, soll der User mit bestimmten Objekten interagieren, die sich auf den Content des jeweiligen Bereichs beziehen. /// À la place d'une navigation à base de boutons standard, l'utilisateur est invité à explorer le site Web en interagissant avec certains objets liés au contenu de leur section.

Info

Design Studio: RARE Design Associates <www.wearerare.com>. /// **Design:** Steve Simmonds, James Arnott. /// **Programming:** Steve Simmonds. /// **Client:** The Lucky Strikes. /// **Tools:** Adobe Flash, Adobe Photoshop, Adobe Illustrator. /// **Awards:** Y Design Awards 2000. /// **Cost:** 150 hours.

THE CORONA BEACH

USA

www.thecoronabeach.com

2008

Concept

The goal here was to craft a relaxing destination on the Internet. Dragging your mouse expands your view of the crystal waters. The interface functions as an extension of the environment. /// Das Ziel hier war, im Internet einen Ort der Entspannung zu schaffen. Durch Ziehen mit der Maus verschiebt sich der Blick auf die wundervolle Meeresbucht. Das Interface dient als Erweiterung der Umgebung. /// L'objectif était de concevoir une destination relaxante sur Internet. Le glissement de la souris révèle d'autres vues des eaux cristallines. L'interface fonctionne comme une extension de l'environnement.

Info

Design Studio: Big Spaceship <www.bigspaceship.com>; Cramer-Krasselt/Chicago <www.c-k.com>. /// **Design:** Big Spaceship, Cramer-Krasselt/Chicago. /// **Programming:** Big Spaceship. /// **Others:** Cramer-Krasselt. /// **Client:** Corona. /// **Tools:** Adobe Photoshop, Adobe Illustrator, Adobe After Effects, Flash, Flex Builder, ActionScript, Papervision 3D, Tween. /// **Awards:** Creativity Awards, FWA (Site of the Day), Web Awards (Outstanding Website).

Corona Extra
Corona Extra

Video
Desktop
Video
Gallery
Icons
Events
ENTER
"Bare Essentials"
go to the beach

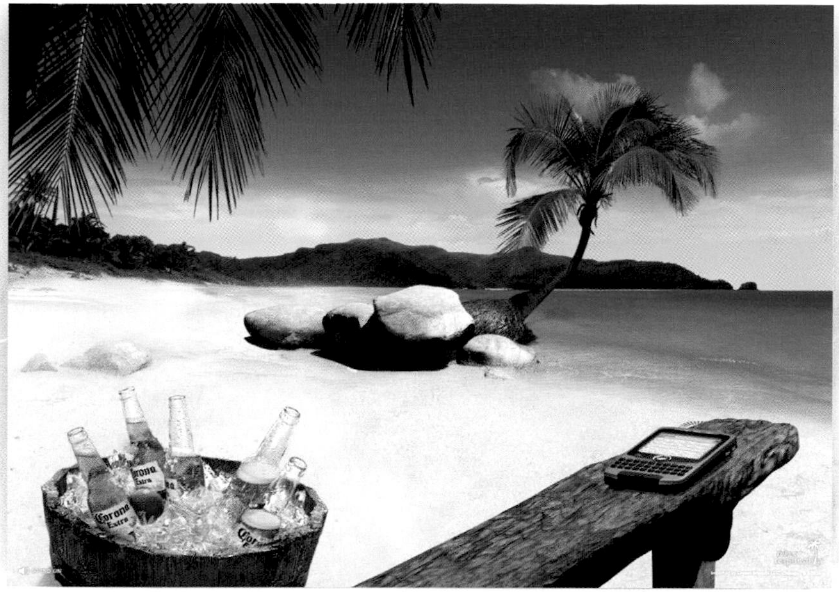

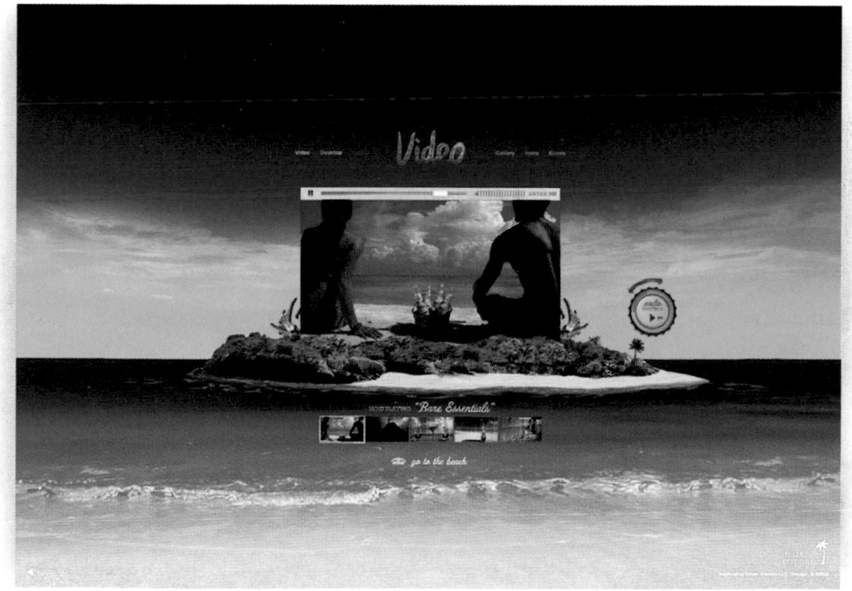

THE SPANIARD BAR

NORTH IRELAND

www.thespaniardbar.com

2007

Concept

In addition to a standard type navigation at the top the design integrated tangible objects or knick-knacks from the bar itself to encourage more interactive exploration of this content-managed microsite. /// Neben der Standardnavigation am oberen Rand integriert das Design konkrete Objekte oder Nippes von der Bar selbst, um den User zu ermutigen, diese über Content gemanagte Microsite aktiv zu erforschen. /// **Outre la navigation standard en haut, le design comprend divers objets ou gadgets pour une exploration plus interactive de ce microsite géré par le contenu.**

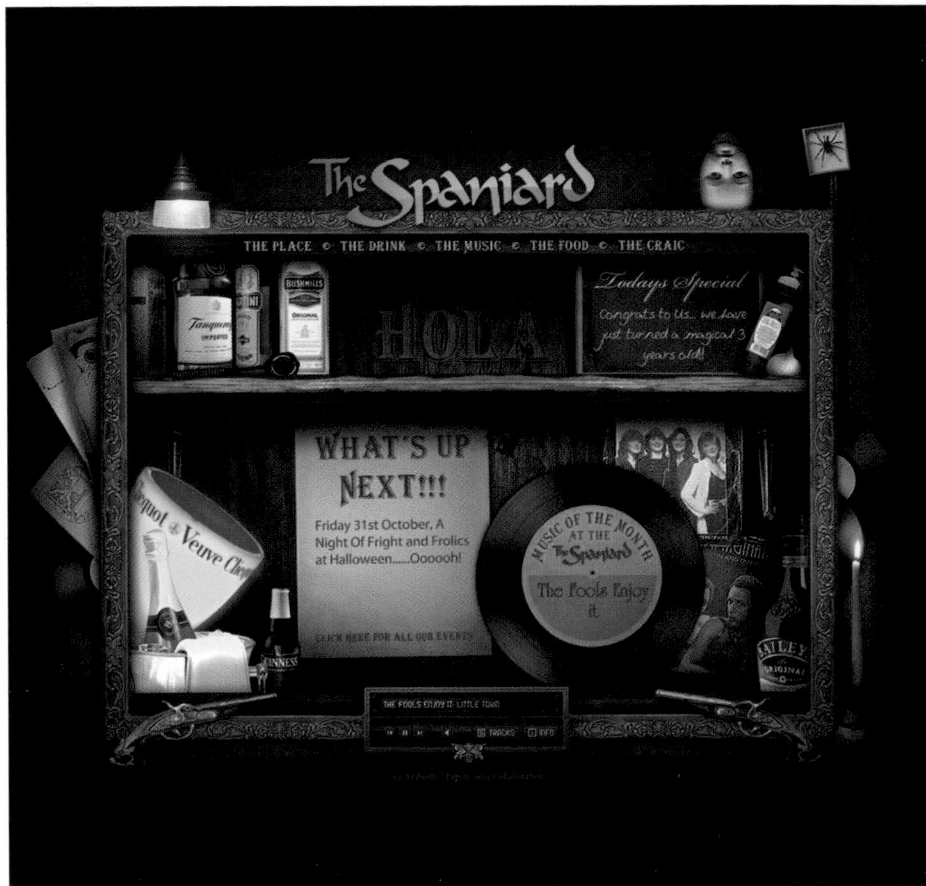

Info

Design Studio: Amberfly <www.amberfly.com>; Papermouse <www.papermouse.net>. /// **Design:** Richard Ryan, Peter Barr. /// **Programming:** Peter Barr, Radosław Gasiorek. /// **Others:** Michael Lee (3D/Animation) <www.biggun.tv>. /// **Client:** The Spaniard Bar. /// **Tools:** Adobe Flash, Adobe Photoshop, Adobe Illustrator. /// **Awards:** Dope Award, Flash Loaded, Faveup. /// **Cost:** 200 hours.

The Spaniard

The Spaniard

The Spaniard
THE PLACE • THE DRINK • THE MUSIC • THE FOOD • THE CRAIC
Available
Click to go Back
Sun-Wed 12-6pm, Thurs-Sat 12-8pm
Tortilla Espanola-Traditional Spanish Potato & Onion Omelette with Alioli
£3.95
Albondigas - Spicy pork meatballs with a tomato and almond sauce
£4.50
Chorizo - Sauteed Spanish Sausage
£4.50
mar - Salt and Chilli Squid
scroll

The Spaniard
WHATS THE SCORE

The Spaniard
MEMBERS NEWS
STAND UP COMEDY
MURIELS CAFE BAR

THE STARTER WIFE SOCIAL LIFE

USA

www.tswlife.com

2008

Concept

Users can create profile avatars, visit famous locations in Southern California, and find hidden rewards to build up points and then redeem them in order to dress their avatar. Plus, there are 10 Flash mini-games, one (each week) per episode. /// Die User erschaffen für ihre Profile Avatare, besuchen berühmte Sehenswürdigkeiten Südkaliforniens und suchen nach versteckten Belohnungen, um Punkte zu sammeln und diese für die Bekleidung ihres Avatars einzulösen. Außerdem gibt es zehn Flash-Minigames (eines pro Woche und Episode). /// **Les utilisateurs peuvent créer des avatars de profil, visitez des lieux célèbres du sud de la Californie et trouver des récompenses cachées pour accumuler des points et les échanger ensuite contre des vêtements pour habiller leur avatar. Sont aussi disponibles 10 mini-jeux en Flash, un (chaque semaine) par épisode.**

Info

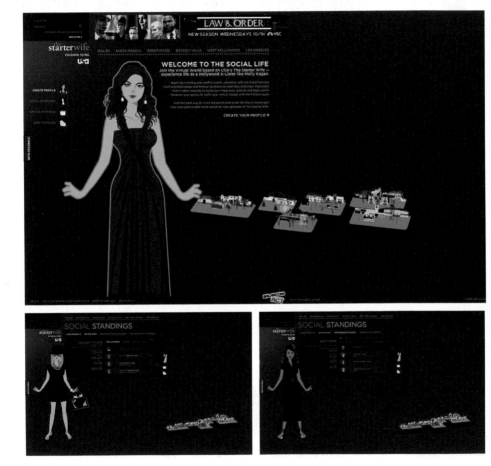

Design Studio: Freedom + Partners <www.FreedomandPartners.com>. /// **Design:** Vas Sloutchevsky (Chief Creative Officer), Matt Sundstrom (Creative Director), Annie Rudden (Illustrator). /// **Programming:** Robert Forras (Chief Technology Officer), Shea Gonyo (EVP Technical Director), Brian Kadar (Senior Developer/Interactive). /// **Others:** Mark Ferdman (Chief Executive Officer); Nicholas Kircos (Developer/Interactive/Motion/Games); Gicheol Lee (Developer/Interactive/Games). /// **Client:** NBC Universal (USA Network). /// **Tools:** Adobe Flash, Papervision 3D, MySQL, SmartFox Server, Java, JSP. /// **Cost:** 2,400 hours.

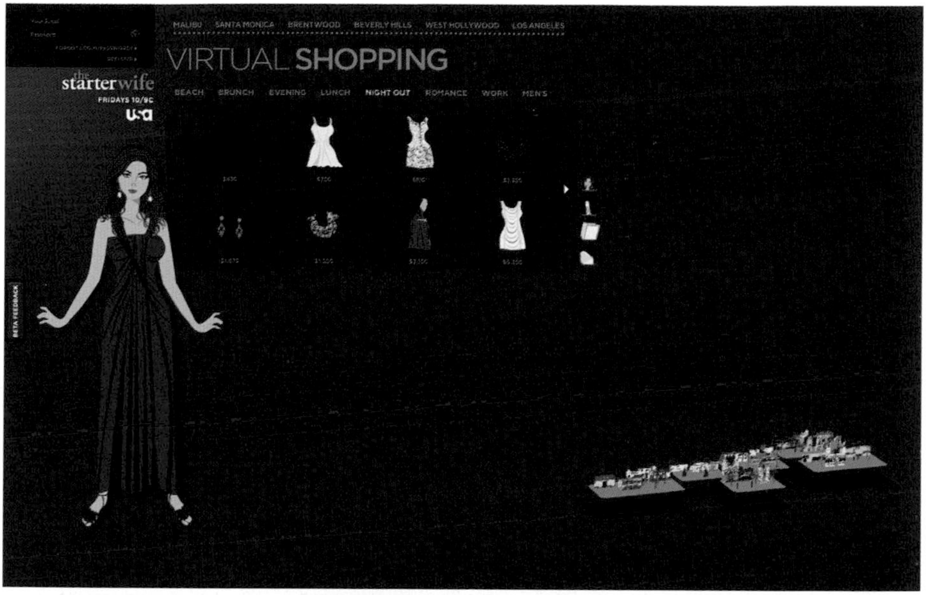

MALIBU SANTA MONICA BRENTWOOD BEVERLY HILLS WEST HOLLYWOOD LOS ANGELES

VIRTUAL SHOPPING

the starter wife
FRIDAYS 10/9C

BEACH BRUNCH EVENING LUNCH NIGHT OUT ROMANCE WORK MEN'S

BETA FEEDBACK

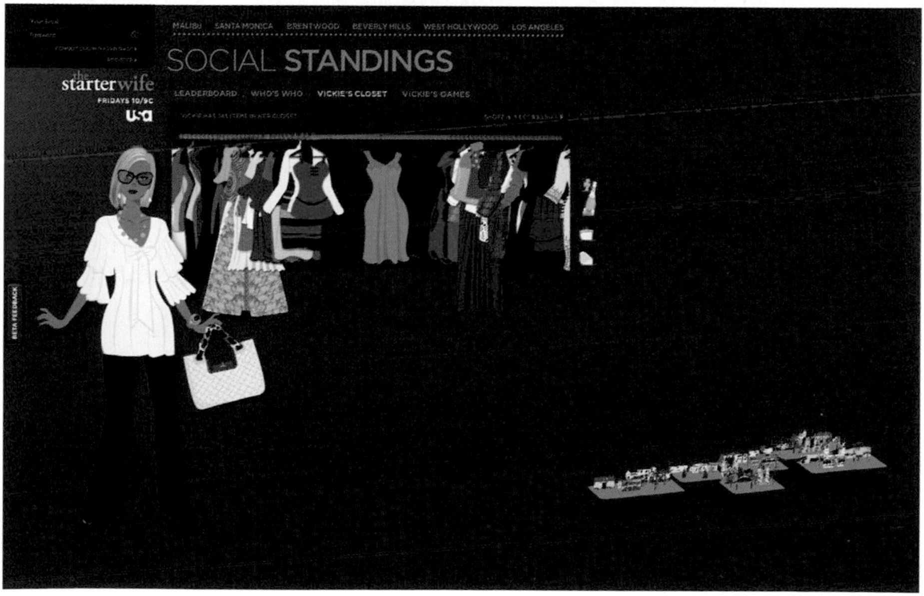

MALIBU SANTA MONICA BRENTWOOD BEVERLY HILLS WEST HOLLYWOOD LOS ANGELES

SOCIAL STANDINGS

the starter wife
FRIDAYS 10/9C

LEADERBOARD WHO'S WHO VICKIE'S CLOSET VICKIE'S GAMES

BETA FEEDBACK

THE WORLD WE LIVE IN

SOUTH AFRICA

www.glasshouse.co.za/flash

2008

Concept

The page allows users to experience Glasshouse and the world we live in, featuring a scroll-over horizontal navigation to invite users to move deeper and interact with the site through movement and games. /// Auf dieser Site erforscht der User Glasshouse und die Welt, in der wir leben. Die Scroll-over-Navigation lädt ein, sich auf der Site umzuschauen und sie näher zu untersuchen, um mit der Site über Bewegungen und Spiele zu interagieren. /// **La page permet aux utilisateurs de découvrir Glasshouse et le monde dans lequel nous vivons, avec une navigation horizontale par défilement pour inviter les utilisateurs à plonger dans le contenu et à interagir avec le site via des déplacements et des jeux.**

Info

DESIGN STUDIO: Glasshouse <www.glasshouse.co.za>. /// **DESIGN:** Wimpie Meyer, Mikey Pauls, Cara Truter. /// **PROGRAMMING:** Cara Truter, Chris Truter. /// **TOOLS:** Adobe Photoshop, Adobe Flash, ActionScript, XML. /// **AWARDS:** Strange Fruits, Fcukstar, E-Creative, Website Design Awards, Hot Webber Awards. /// **COST:** 400 hours.

Sato

STRATEGY

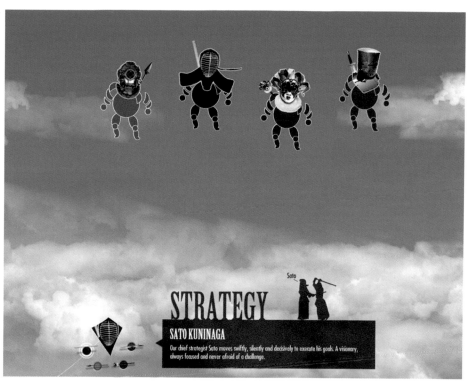

SATO KUNINAGA

Our chief strategist Sato moves swiftly, silently and decisively to execute his goals. A visionary, always focused and never afraid of a challenge.

THOMAS RUSCH

GERMANY

www.thomasrusch.com

2006

Concept

The navigation is fixed in the website's centre and from there it extracts itself vertically. /// Die Navigation ist in der Mitte der Site zentriert und klappt vertikal aus. /// La navigation est fixe au centre du site Web et se développe verticalement à partir de là.

Info

Design Studio: Tilt Design Studio <www.tiltdesignstudio.com>. /// **Design:** Marc Antosch, Guido von Schneider-Marientreu. /// **Programming:** Guido von Schneider-Marientreu. /// **Others:** Carsten Scholz (Sound Design). /// **Client:** Thomas Rusch. /// **Tools:** Adobe Flash, ActionScript. /// **Awards:** FWA (Site of the Day), Red Dot Communications Design Award, Designpreis der BRD 2008. /// **Cost:** ca. 160 hours.

TILT DESIGN STUDIO

GERMANY

www.tiltdesignstudio.com

2007

Concept

Navigation here is more than a means to an end, it's the main feature of the website. All work is arranged as square previews, which lead the user straight into the portfolio. As a special feature the user can filter projects. /// Die Navigation ist hier mehr als nur Mittel zum Zweck – sie ist das Haupt-Feature der Website. Alle Arbeiten sind als quadratische Previews arrangiert, die den User direkt ins Portfolio führen. Als besonderes Feature kann der User die Projekte nach Kriterien filtern. /// **La navigation, ici davantage un moyen qu'une fin, est la caractéristique principale du site. Tout le travail est organisé sous forme de volets de visualisation carrés qui mènent l'utilisateur directement au portfolio. Une fonction spéciale permet de filtrer les projets.**

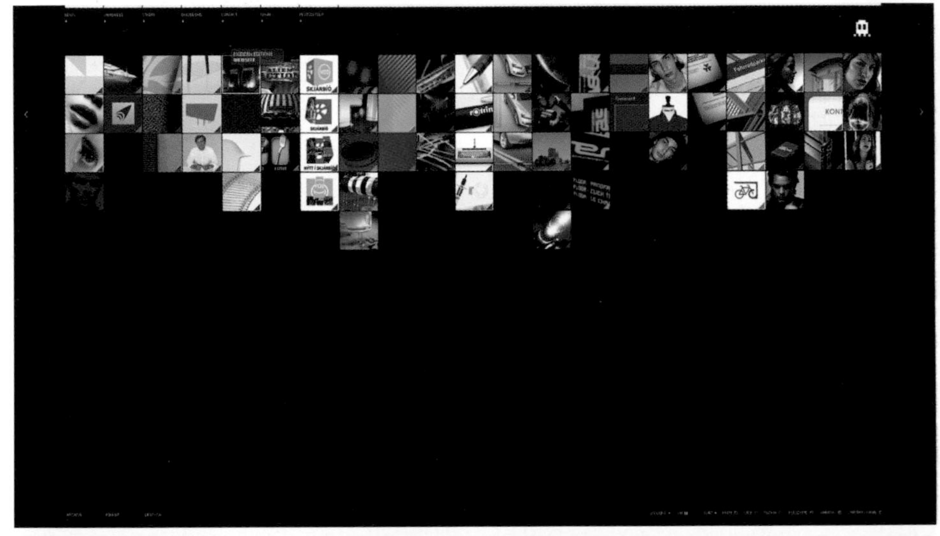

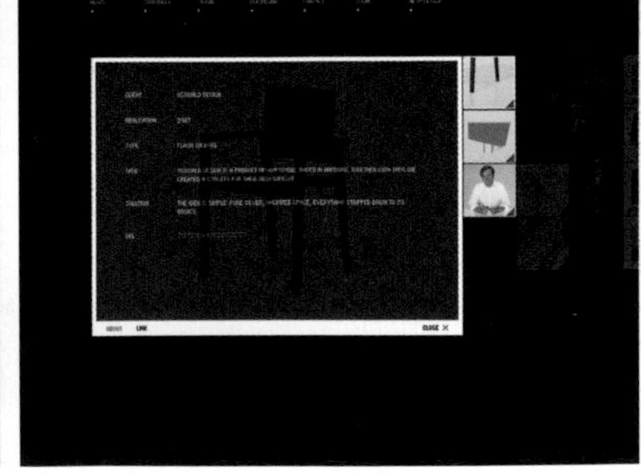

Info

Design Studio: Tilt Design Studio <www.tiltdesignstudio.com>. /// **Design:** Marc Antosch, Dominic Bünning, Ralph Heinsohn, Felix Schultze, Guido von Schneider-Marientreu (Creative Direction); Marc Antosch, Ralph Heinsohn (Art Direction). /// **Programming:** Felix Schultze, Guido von Schneider-Marientreu. /// **Others:** Sven Lütgen (Sound Design). /// **Client:** Tilt Design Studio. /// **Tools:** Adobe Flash, ActionScript. /// **Awards:** FWA (Site of the Day), DDC (Bronze), Designpreis der BRD 2008, Webby Award 2008. /// **Cost:** ca. 190 hours.

ABOUT
PEOPLE

MERRY X-MAS AND A HAPPY NEW YEAR
DDC BRONZE AWARD
ALIEN ACTION NOMINATED FOR EUROPRIX
ANOTHER FWA FOR TILT
NEW ROTRING WEBSITE ONLINE

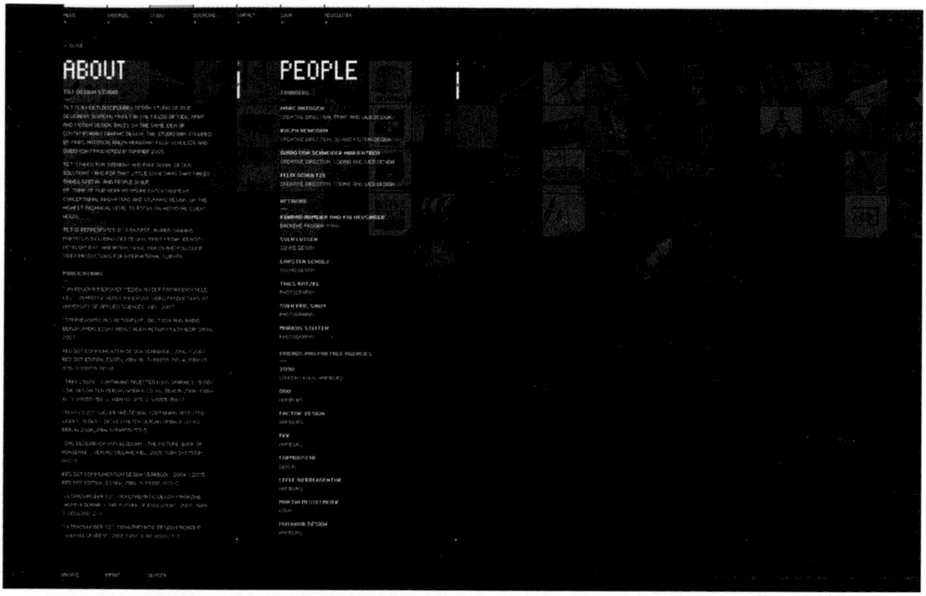

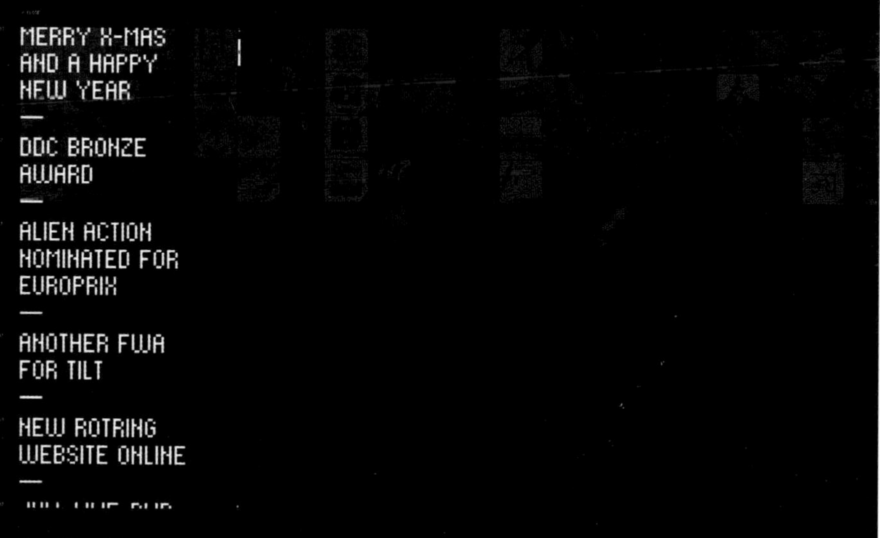

TRANSPARENT HOUSE

USA

www.transparenthouse.com

2008

Concept

The horizontal display of images on full-screen mode allows a view rich in detail thanks to the size of the images. The menu works straight through the topics with quick access to the content desired. /// Die horizontale Darstellung von formatfüllenden Bildern erlaubt dank der Größe der Bilder sehr detaillierte Einblicke. Das Menü arbeitet anhand der Themen schnörkellos, und man gelangt schnell zum gewünschten Inhalt. /// **L'affichage horizontal des images en mode plein écran offre une vue très détaillée grâce à leur taille. Le menu conduit directement aux rubriques, avec un accès rapide au contenu souhaité.**

Info

DESIGN STUDIO: Amberfly <www.amberfly.com>. /// **DESIGN:** Peter Barr. /// **PROGRAMMING:** Douglas Noble. /// **CLIENT:** Transparent House. /// **TOOLS:** Adobe Photoshop, Flash, PHP, MySQL, AMFPHP. /// **AWARDS:** Dope Award, Flash Loaded, faveup. /// **COST:** 250 hours.

LANGUAGE SEARCH LOGIN

HIGH VELOCITY

Welcome to
Transparent House
We Create The Reality

Featured
Work
JW Marriott
Article
Transparent House or In House

Latest
News
CREATE NUS
Half Street Interiors
JW Marriott, Indianapolis

Demo Reel

Transparent House
HOME SERVICES PORTFOLIO COMPANY NEWS / AWARDS / PRESS CONTACT
MINIMIZE

LANGUAGE SEARCH LOGIN

HIGH VELOCITY

Transparent House
HOME SERVICES PORTFOLIO COMPANY NEWS / AWARDS / PRESS CONTACT
MAXIMIZE

TYPE FACE MEDIA

SOUTH AFRICA

www.typefacemedia.co.za

2008

Concept The site is slim in content, but makes use of a quirky navigation tool that is unusual and surprising to the user. Further surprises are in store for the site visitor, which reflects the Typeface Media brand. /// Die Site ist inhaltlich recht schlank, verwendet aber ein schrulliges Navigations-Tool, das ungewöhnlich und für den User überraschend ist. Auf der Site warten weitere Überraschungen auf den User, die der Marke Typeface Media entsprechen. /// Le site compte peu de contenu mais utilise un outil de navigation original et surprenant. D'autres surprises attendent le visiteur du site, à l'image de la marque Typeface Media.

"any type of face you need"
FACE
about us
contact
what we do
?
type face
creative agency
media
typeface media, a creative agency
TYPEFACE MEDIA. (C) TYPEFACE 2008. ALL RIGHTS RESERVED = SITE BY STONEWALL+ = SOUND OFF

Info DESIGN STUDIO: Stonewall+ Digital Marketing <www.stonewall.co.za>. /// DESIGN: Adam Whitehouse, Damien Manual. /// PROGRAMMING: Umar Jakoet. /// OTHERS: Alastair Coombe, Andy Ellis, Piers Buckle (Concept/Creative Treatment). /// CLIENT: Type Face Media. /// TOOLS: Adobe Flash, Adobe Photoshop, XML. /// COST: 80 hours.

VIK MUNIZ

USA

www.vikmuniz.net

2007

Concept

The website of the Brazilian artist enables quick access to films, images, gallery exhibitions and all information about the artist from the menu on the right-hand side. /// Auf der Website des brasilianischen Künstlers kann man anhand des Menüs rechts schnell auf Filme, Fotos, Galerieausstellungen und alle Infos über den Künstler zugreifen. /// **Le site Web de l'artiste brésilien permet d'accéder rapidement à des films, des images, des galeries et à toutes les informations sur l'artiste depuis le menu sur le côté droit.**

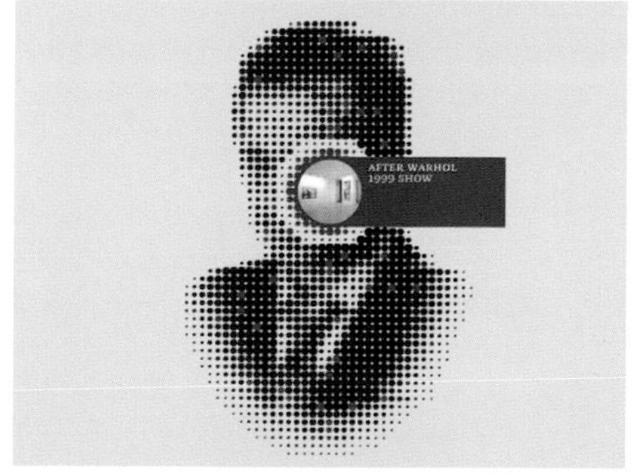

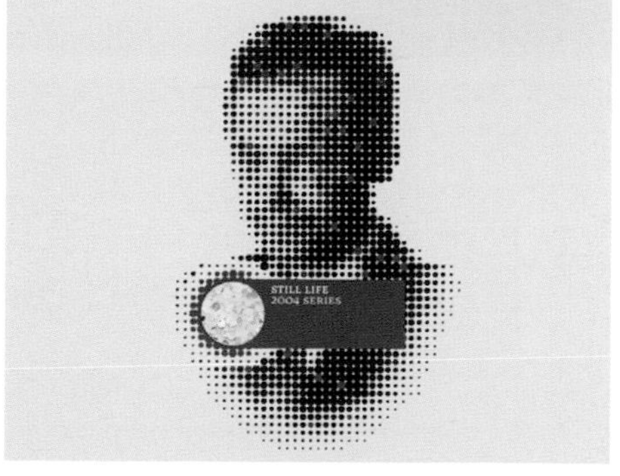

Info

DESIGN STUDIO: Knowawall, Inc. <www.knowawall.com>. /// **DESIGN:** Noah Wall. /// **PROGRAMMING:** Noah Wall, Sunil Kapila, Andrea Stein. /// **CLIENT:** Vik Muniz Studio. /// **TOOLS:** Adobe Photoshop, Adobe Illustrator, Adobe Flash, PHP. /// **COST:** 30 days.

VIRGIN MUSIC FESTIVAL

SOUTH AFRICA

www.virginfestival.co.za

2008

Concept

The navigation is made up of various icons representing content pieces, which reveal themselves through animation and sound burst. /// Die Navigation besteht aus verschiedenen Icons. Sie repräsentieren verschiedene Content-Bereiche, die mit Animationen und Sounds gezeigt werden. /// La navigation se compose de diverses icônes illustrant des éléments du contenu, qui se révèlent dans une explosion d'animation et de son.

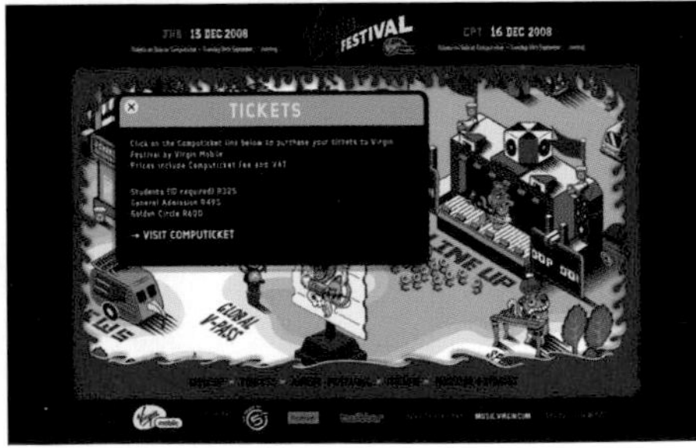

Info

DESIGN STUDIO: Stonewall+ Digital Marketing <www.stonewall.co.za>. /// DESIGN: Adam Whitehouse, Damien Manual, AMICOLLECTIVE (Illustration). /// PROGRAMMING: Umar Jakoet. /// OTHERS: Alastair Coombe, Evan Milton. /// CLIENT: Virgin. /// TOOLS: Adobe Flash, ActionScript, Adobe Photoshop, XML. /// COST: 80 hours.

JHB 13 DEC 2008
Virgin FESTIVAL
CPT 16 DEC 2008
LINE UP
ONE REPUBLIC
CPT TIME TBC
JHB TIME TBC
EDDY GRANT
CPT TIME TBC
JHB TIME TBC
SUGABABES
CPT TIME TBC
JHB TIME TBC
THE PARLOTONES
CPT TIME TBC
MUSIC.VIRGIN.COM

JHB 13 DEC 2008
Virgin FESTIVAL
CPT 16 DEC 2008
ABOUT
LOGISTICS
FAQ
USEFUL LINKS
SPONSORS
PRESS INFORMATION
TERMS AND CONDITIONS
LOGISTICS
How do I get there?
Johannesburg Botanical Gardens, Emmarentia is situated at the Emmarentia Dam
If you are coming on the N1 South, take the Beyers Naude Drive off-ramp, turn left and drive straight towards Roosevelt Park. Emmarentia Dam is opposite Westpark Cemetery. Details of parking areas will be provided in due course.
If you are coming on the N1 North, take the Beyers Naude Drive off-ramp, turn right and go straight towards Roosevelt Park. Emmarentia Dam is opposite Westpark Cemetery.
Westcoast Ostrich Ranch is just 25 minutes drive from Cape Town city centre. Take the N1 towards Durbanville, take the N7 exit then turn onto Van Schoorsdrif Road, Philadelphia.
Details of parking areas will be provided in due course
Is there car parking available?
MUSIC.VIRGIN.COM

VOYEUR STUDIO

MEXICO

www.voyeurstudio.net

2008

Concept

A website where you can navigate a structure based on videos, giving a unique experience to the user, and creating a different environment from other websites. /// Der User erforscht über Videos die Struktur dieser Website. Diese unvergleichliche Erfahrung unterscheidet sich deutlich von der Umgebung anderer Websites. /// **Un site Web dans lequel vous pouvez parcourir une structure à partir de vidéos, ce qui offre une expérience unique à l'utilisateur et crée un environnement différent des autres sites.**

Info

Design Studio: 3indesign Media Solutions <www.3indesign.com>. /// **Design:** Edgar Francisco Solano Chavez, Eduardo Aguilar, Jair Barrón, Pablo Vega, Ricardo Espinosa. /// **Programming:** Edgar Francisco Solano Chávez, Ricardo Espinosa. /// **Others:** Voyeur Studio: Gustavo Dueñas, Graziella Reynosa. /// **Client:** Voyeur Studio. /// **Tools:** Adobe After Effects, Adobe Photoshop, Flash. /// **Cost:** 260 hours.

Voyeur
MENU PRINCIPAL
PORTAFOLIO 01
PORTAFOLIO 02

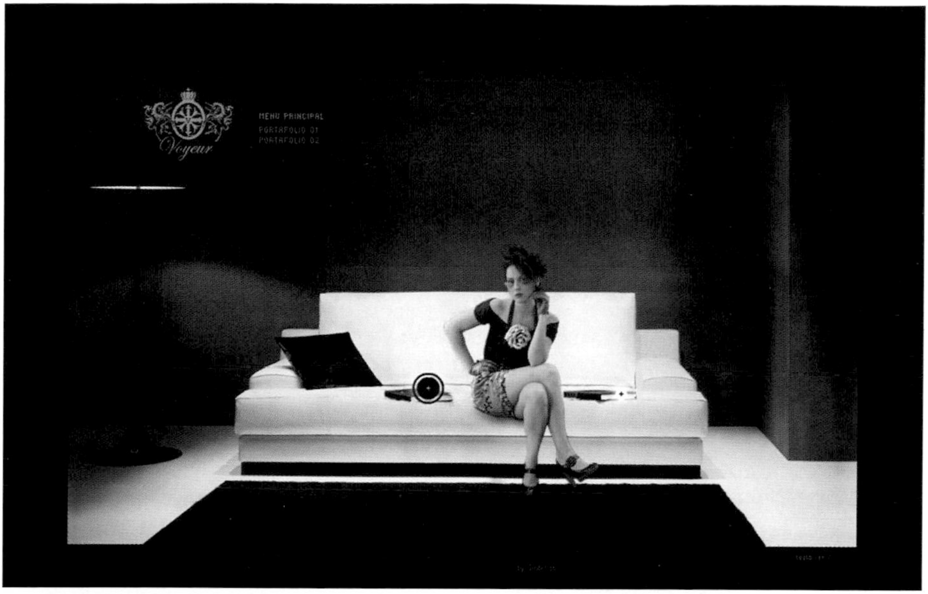

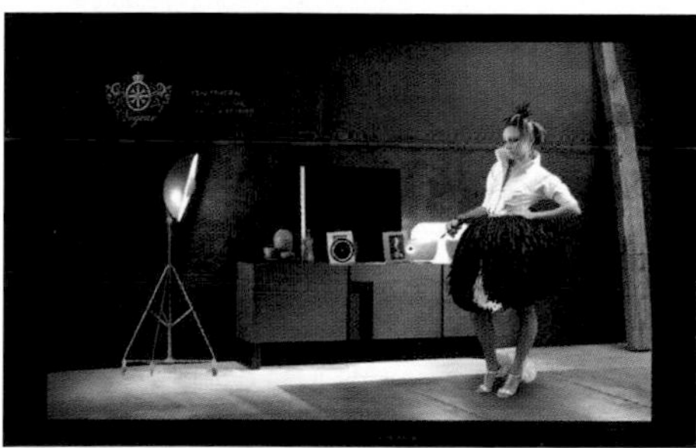

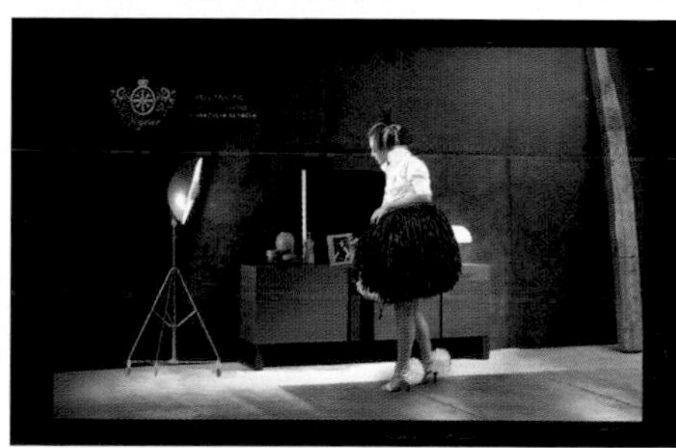

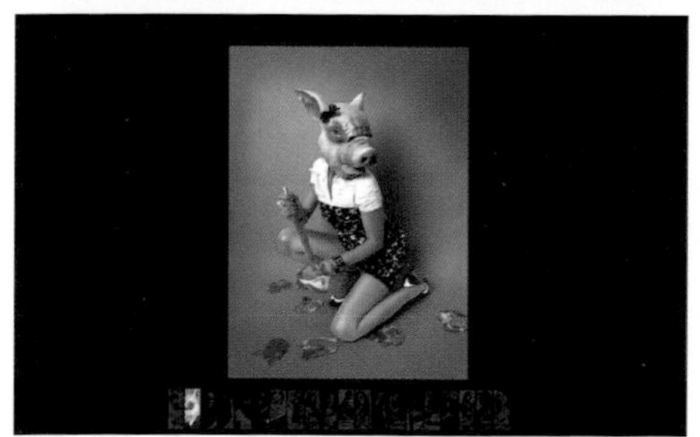

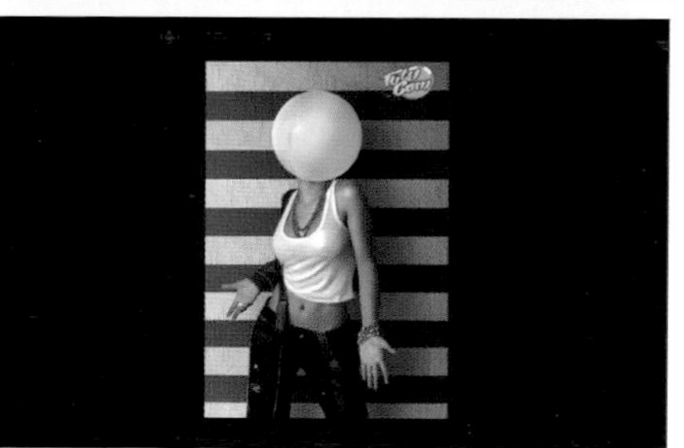

WE ARE THE WORLD

BELGIUM

www.wimvanhenden.be/flash

2008

Concept

This website is an installation that displays real-time what people are looking for on the Internet. If you are not using the navigation it disappears, which shifts the focus much more toward the imagery. /// Diese Website ist eine Installation, die in Echtzeit ausgibt, wonach Menschen im Internet suchen. Wenn die Navigation nicht verwendet wird, verschwindet sie, was den Fokus mehr auf die bildliche Darstellung verschiebt. /// Ce site Web est une installation montrant en temps réel ce que les gens recherchent sur Internet. Si vous n'utilisez pas la navigation, elle disparaît, ce qui a pour effet de faire ressortir les images.

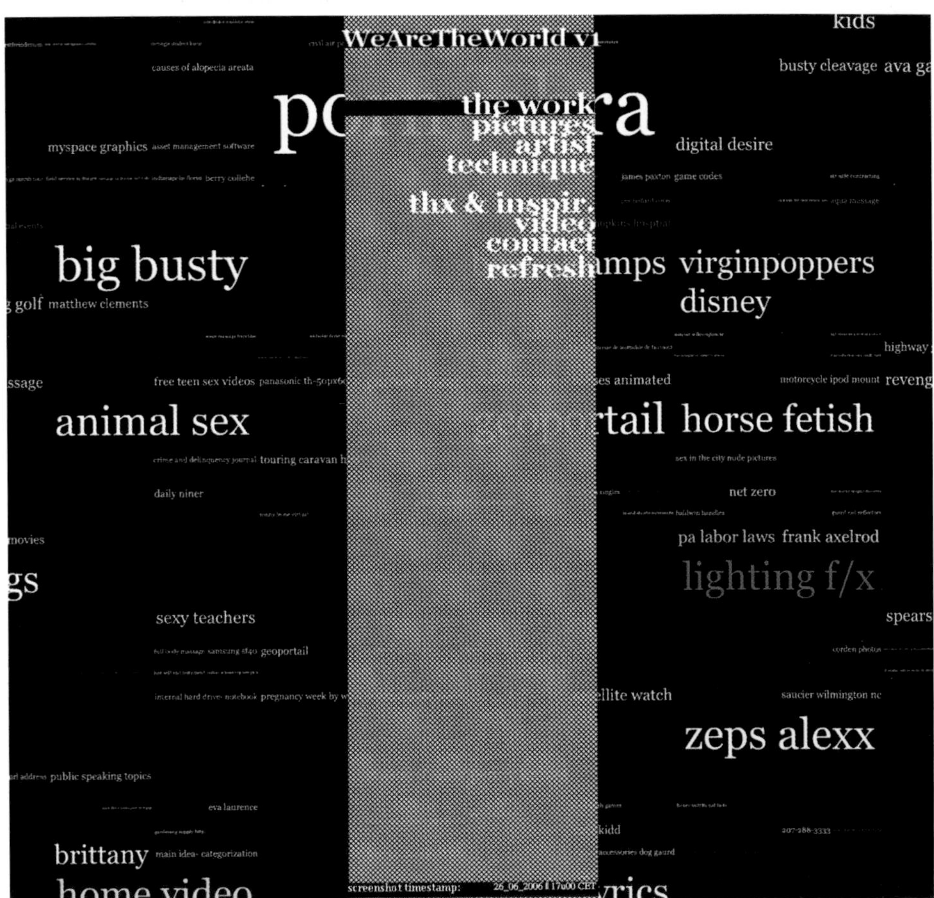

Info

Design Studio: Wim Vanhenden <www.wimvanhenden.be>. /// **Design:** Wim Vanhenden. /// **Programming:** Wim Vanhenden. /// **Client:** Wim Vanhenden. /// **Tools:** Adobe Flash, Adobe Photoshop, XML, FDT for coding. /// **Cost:** 42 hours.

Culture Club Ghent

Culture Club Ghent

Culture Club Ghent

Prints @ The Guesthouse Antwerp

WHY DO YOU REMEMBER?

BRAZIL

www.whydoyouremember.com

2007

Concept

The website creates a human experience database with a fully interactive interface to create custom contents and to support communication between users. /// Diese Website schafft eine Datenbank menschlicher Erfahrungen mit einem vollständig interaktiven Interface, um eigene Inhalte zu schaffen und die Kommunikation zwischen den Usern zu unterstützen. /// **Le site Web crée une base de données d'expériences humaines avec une interface entièrement interactive pour générer un contenu personnalisé et gérer la communication entre les utilisateurs.**

Info

DESIGN STUDIO: Arterial <www.arterial.tv>; Tátil Design < www.tatil.com.br>. /// **DESIGN:** Arterial: Chris Calvet, Marcos Leme (Design/Architecture); Tátil Design: Fred Gelli, Pat Pinheiro, Roberta Gamboa, Lorena Castelan, Claudia Niemeyer (Art Direction). /// **PROGRAMMING:** Luciano Bonachella <www.bonacode.com>. /// **OTHERS:** Rico Gelli (Photography); Barbara Judd (Music Concrete). /// **CLIENT:** Tátil Design. /// **TOOLS:** Adobe Flash, ActionScript, PHP. /// **COST:** 3 months.

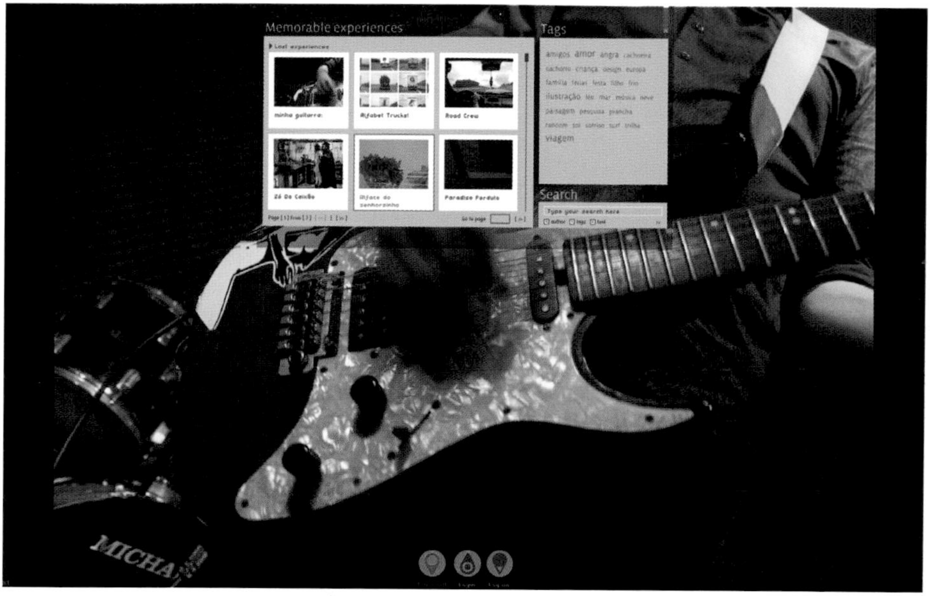
Memorable experiences
Last experiences
minha guitarra:
Alfabet Trucks!
Road Crew
Zé Do Caixão
Paradise Perdido
Tags
amigos amor angra
criança design europa
ilustração
viagem
Search
Type your search here
MICHA

What is the project?
[+] Rules
[+] Credits
Why
do you
remember
tátil

WORLD OF MR. COGITO

POLAND

www.herbert2008.pl/cogito

2008

Concept

Navigation is based on the virtual desk of Zbigniew Herbert, one the most famous Polish poets of the 20th Century. Everything is slowly moving, interactive items and fragments of sentences float freely over the desk. /// Die Navigation basiert auf einer virtuellen Nachbildung des Schreibtischs von Zbigniew Herbert, einem der berühmtesten polnischen Dichter des 20. Jahrhunderts. Alles bewegt sich langsam, und interaktive Elemente und Satzfragmente gleiten frei über den Tisch. /// **La navigation repose sur le bureau virtuel de Zbigniew Herbert, l'un des poètes polonais les plus célèbres du XXe siècle. Toutes les animations sont lentes et des éléments interactifs et des extraits de phrases flottent librement sur le bureau.**

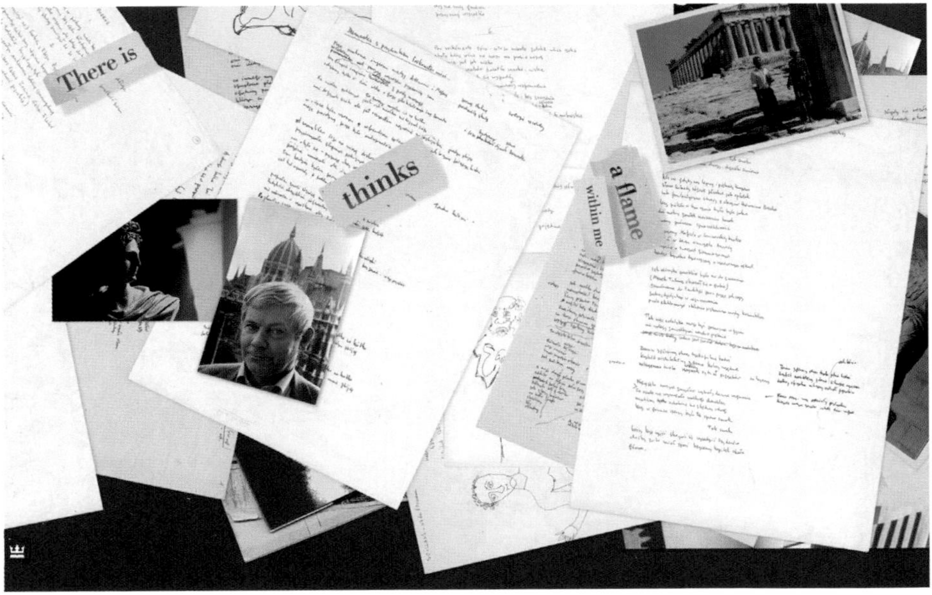

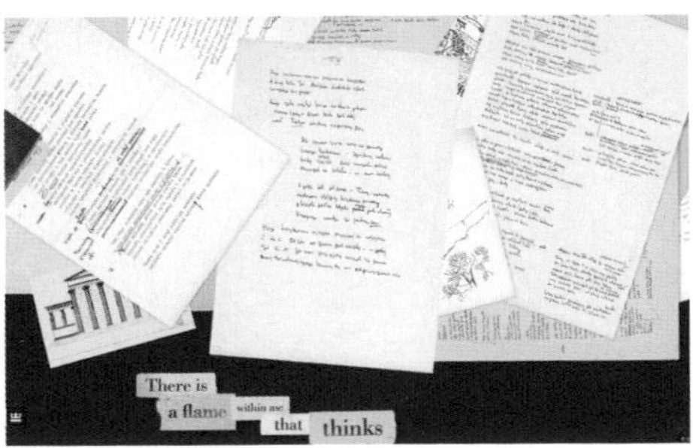

Info

Design Studio: Huncwot <www.huncwot.com>. /// **Design:** Arek Romanski, Lukasz Knasiecki. /// **Client:** National Library of Poland. /// **Tools:** Adobe Photoshop, Flash, SQL. /// **Cost:** 120 hours.

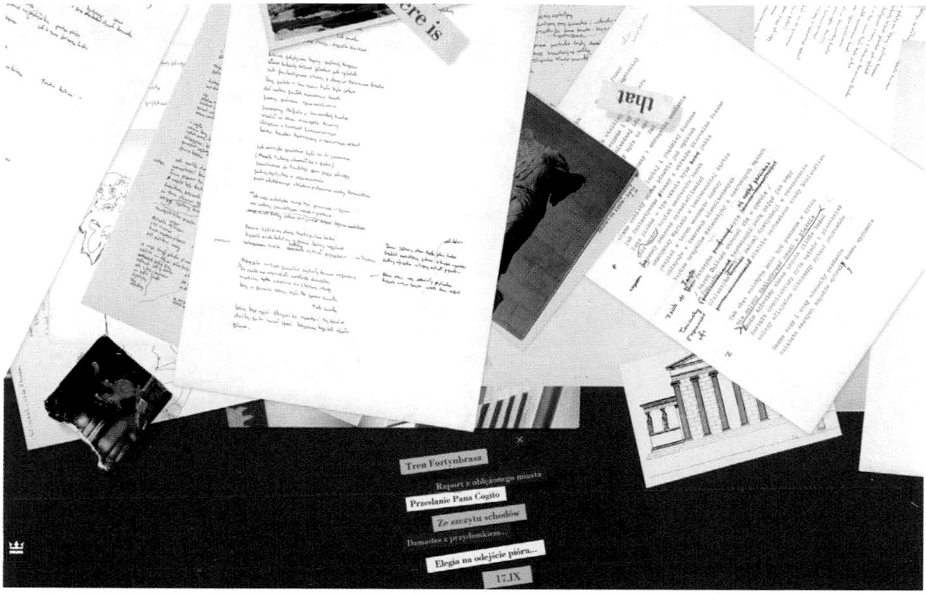

here is
that
Tren Fortynbrasa
Raport z oblężonego miasta
Przesłanie Pana Cogito
Ze szczytu schodów
Damastes z przydomkiem...
Elegia na odejście pióra...
17.IX

thinks

that
a flame

that
think

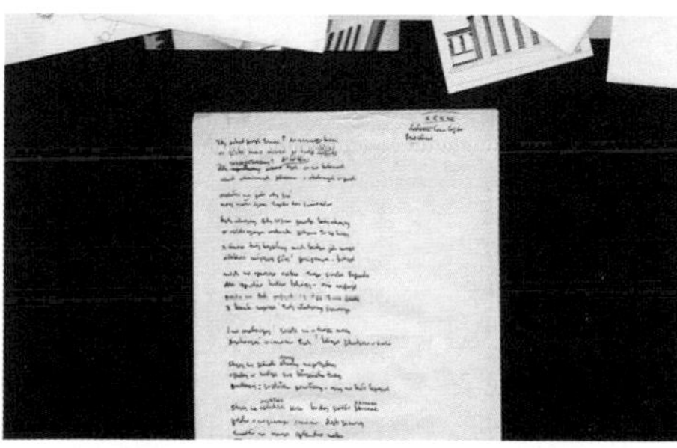

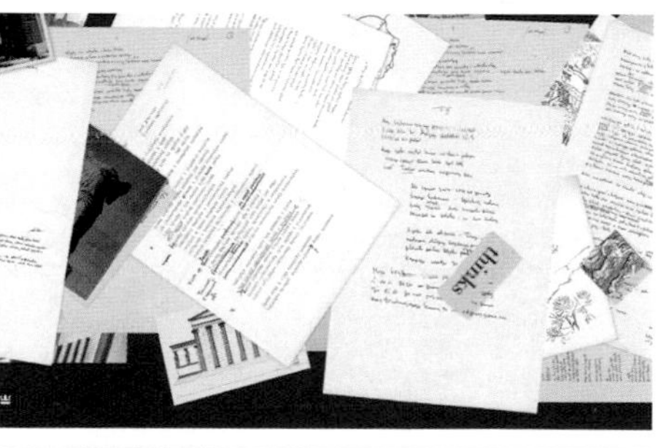

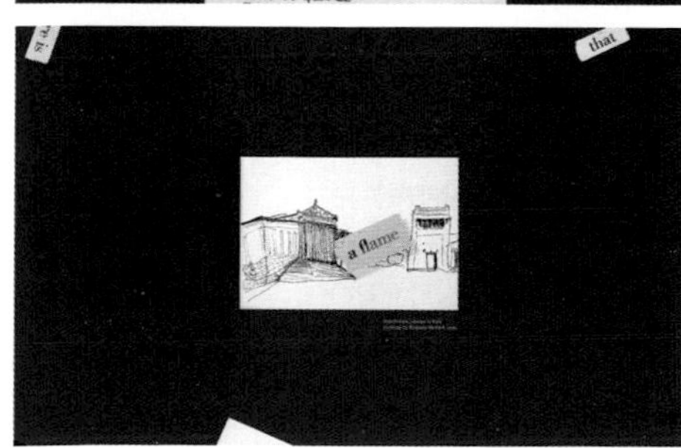

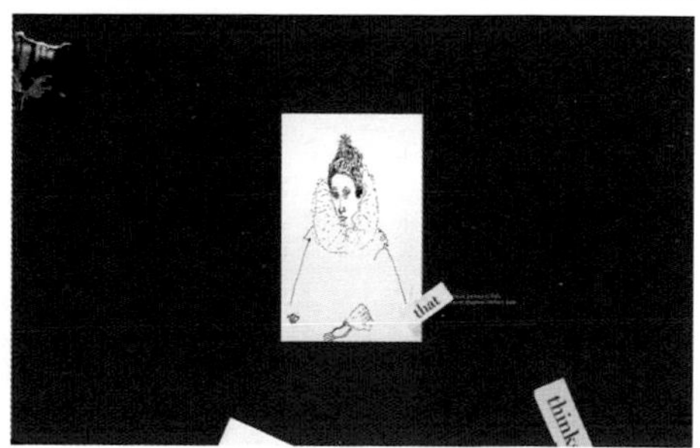

WORSE THAN A FAIRY TALE

USA

www.worsethanafairytale.com

2007

Concept

The beautiful illustrated backgrounds form the menu, dividing them into three layers and a horizontal movement. /// Die wunderschön gestalteten Hintergründe bilden das Menü, das aus drei Schichten und einer horizontale Bewegung besteht. /// **Les arrière-plans superbement illustrés composent le menu et se divisent en trois couches, avec un déplacement horizontal.**

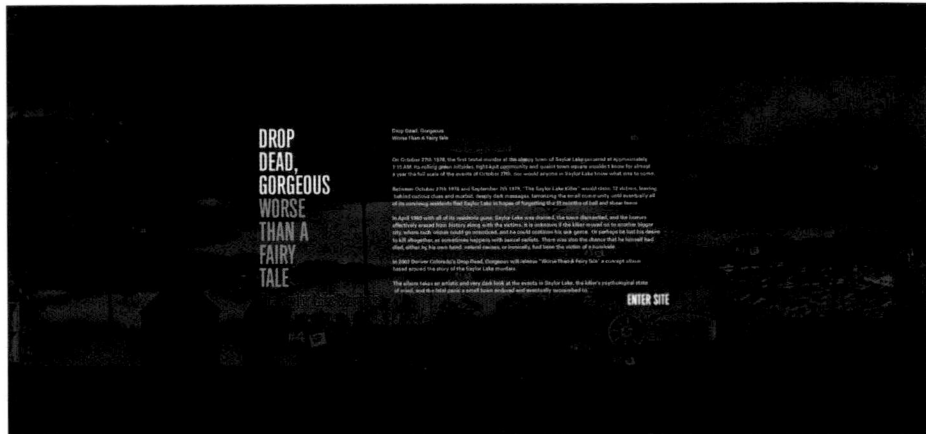

Info

Design Studio: BKWLD <www.bkwld.com>. /// **Design:** Jeff Toll. /// **Programming:** Phuong Nguyen. /// **Client:** Suretone Records. ///
Tools: XML, HTML, Adobe Photoshop, Adobe Flash, PHP.

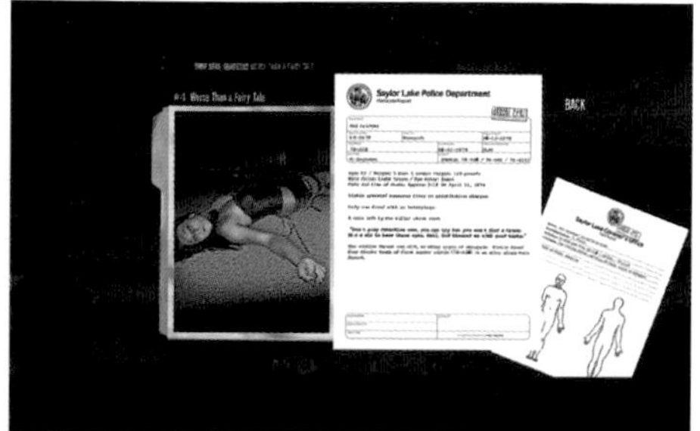

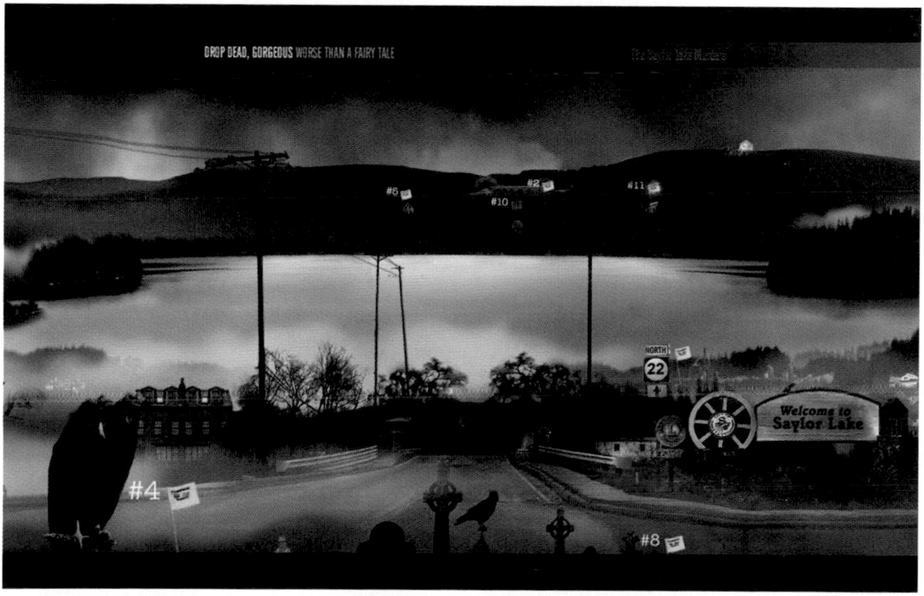

DROP DEAD, GORGEOUS WORSE THAN A FAIRY TALE

The Saylor Lake Murders

#5
#2
#11
#10
NORTH
22
Welcome to Saylor Lake
#4
#8

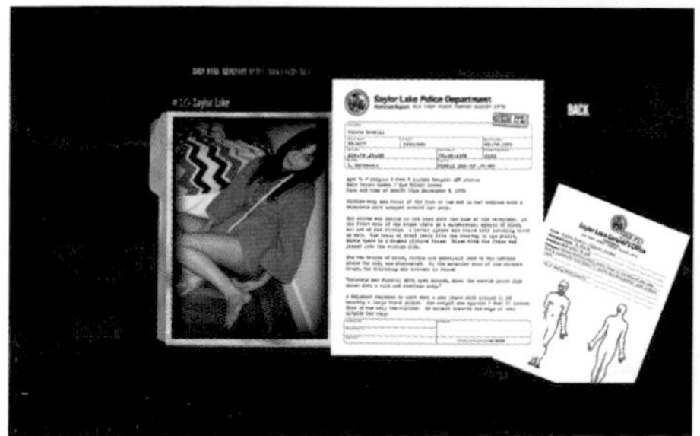

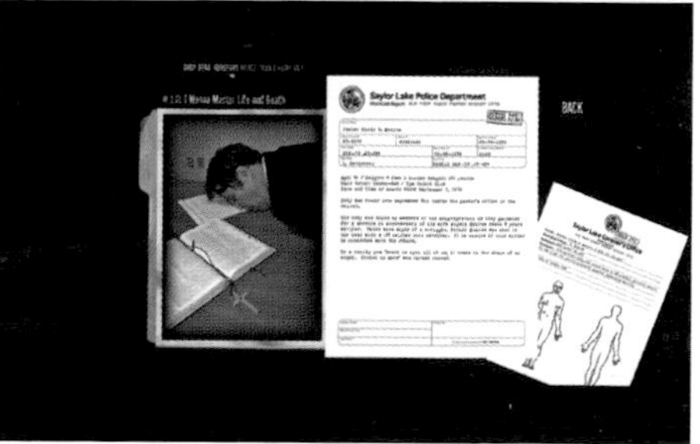

WHALEFOOTAGE

GERMANY

www.whalefootage.org

2007

Concept

All the films can be viewed in full-screen mode. Parallel to this, the user can navigate intuitively between the various film sequences by rolling over the flip-book-like preview pictures. /// Alle Filme können bildschirmfüllend betrachtet werden. Parallel kann der User auch intuitiv zwischen den verschiedenen Filmsequenzen navigieren, indem er mit der Maus nach Art eines Daumenkinos über die Vorschaubilder fährt. /// **Tous les films peuvent être vus en mode plein écran. Par ailleurs, l'utilisateur peut naviguer de façon intuitive parmi les diverses séquences en déplaçant le curseur sur des volets de visualisation en forme de folioscope.**

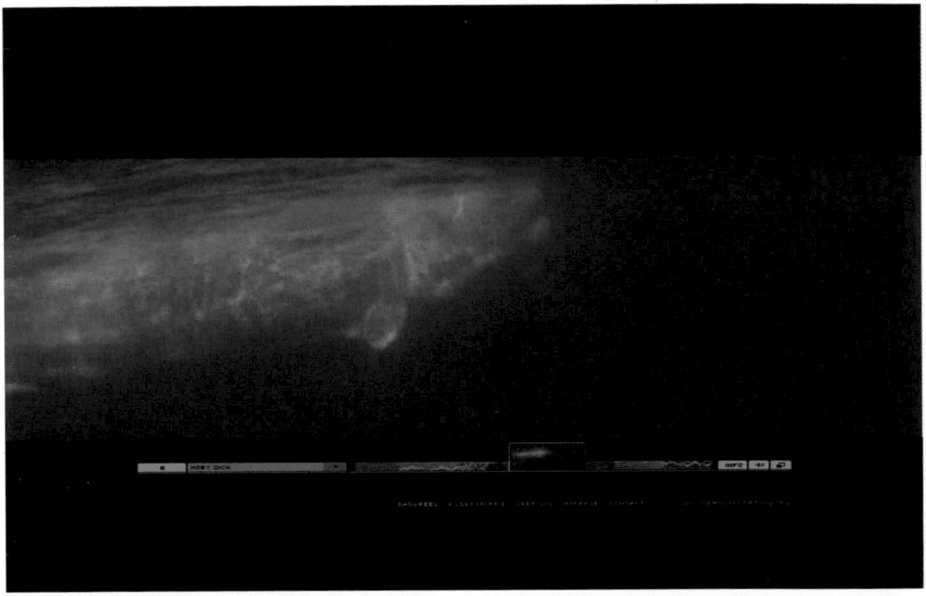

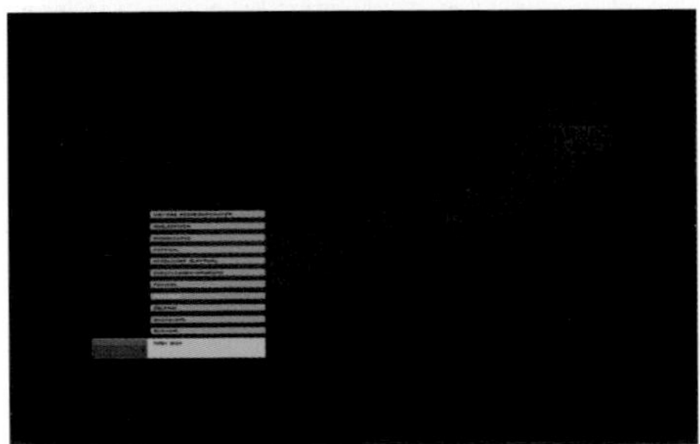

Info

Design Studio: Scholz & Volkmer GmbH <www.s-v.de>. /// **Design:** Heike Brockmann (Creative Direction); Philipp Bareiss (Art Direction). /// **Programming:** Peter Reichard (Technology Direction); Florian Finke. /// **Others:** Peter Reichard, Philipp Bareiss, Duc-Thuan Bui (Concept); Dieter Paulmann, Tanja Winkler (Copy); Jörg Remy (Sound Design). /// **Client:** Okeanos (Foundation for the Sea). /// **Tools:** PHP, JavaScript, ActionScript, Perl, Flash, MySQL, RedFive Streaming Server, imageMagick, ffmpeg. /// **Awards:** FWA (Site of the Day); Webby Awards (Honoree); iF Communication Design Award (Gold); New York Festivals Innovative Advertising Awards (Finalist).

ZHANNA

SPAIN

www.zhannamusic.com

2008

Concept

The navigation shows an introduction from the artist, a rotoscope animation of her mouth talking. The interface design adapts to any screen size, optimizing the legibility, the bright graphics, animations, and the background pictures of the artist. /// Die Navigation zeigt als Einführung eine Rotoskopie-Animation des sprechenden Mundes der Sängerin. Das Interface-Design passt sich jeder Bildschirmgröße an. So werden Lesbarkeit, die kräftigen Grafiken, Animationen und Hintergrundbilder der Künstlerin optimiert. /// La navigation montre une introduction de l'artiste, une animation au rotoscope de sa bouche en train de parler. Le design de l'interface s'adapte à n'importe quelle taille d'écran, avec une optimisation de la lisibilité, des graphiques vifs, des animations et des images en arrière-plan de l'artiste.

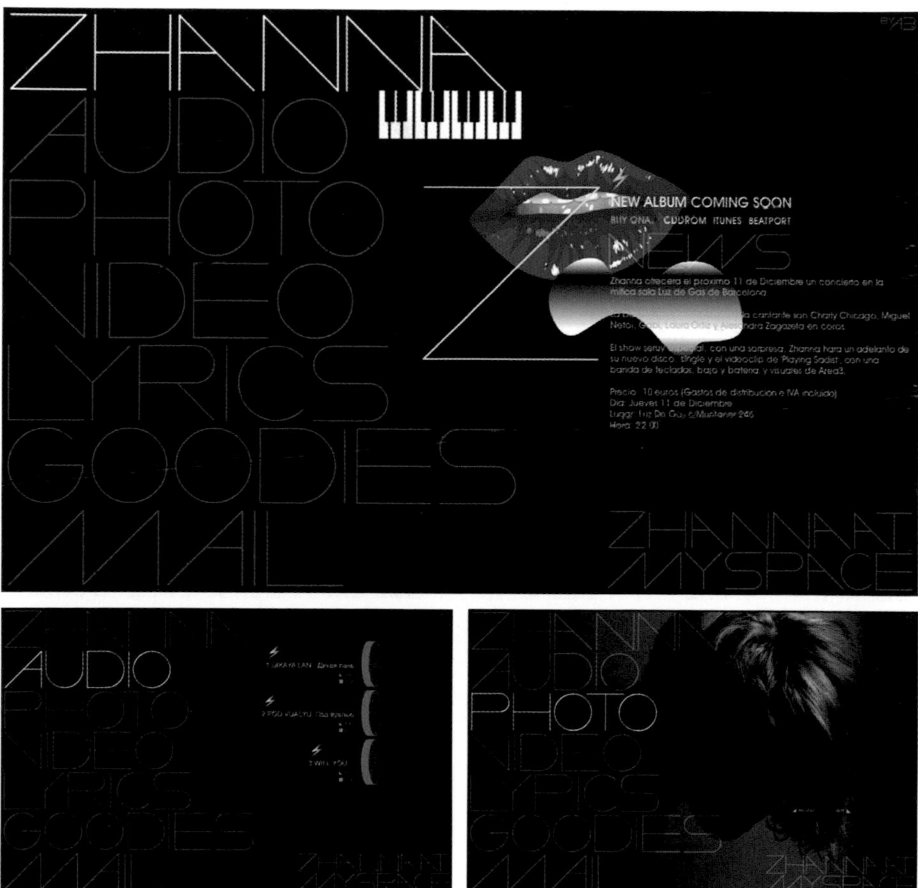

Info

Design Studio: area3 <www.area3.net>. /// **Design:** Sebastián Puiggrós, Claudio Molina, Stephano Dinamarca, Chema Longobardo. /// **Programming:** Federico Joselevich, Sebastián Puiggrós. /// **Client:** Zhanna. /// **Tools:** Adobe Flash, Adobe Illustrator. /// **Cost:** 420 hs.

CREDITS

Dear readers, it is a pleasure to be able to bring you this title which focuses entirely and specifically on elegant and intelligent ways to navigate websites. As with previous titles in this general field we have had a really hard time deciding which examples we would have to leave out, particularly with having to select from websites employing such a wide variety of approaches and objectives. The thinking around navigation systems is not only becoming a hotter subject but is developing into a more complex and diverse interface between designers and website users, making it a fascinating and challenging area for all professionals in the field to learn more about. The quality of work possible and the availability of resources are now reaching a point where designers have almost all the freedom they ever hoped for.

Any navigation system nowadays needs to go through a design process which includes the original briefing, project strategy, a conceptual development phase, video production, special film-shooting sections, special effects, soundtrack, illustration, customized content management, and so on, an increasingly involved process in its own right This book is intended to serve as a reference for anyone interested in working at the highest levels online, which today is relevant to almost all businesses and professionals. The challenges undertaken by these design studios, the complexity of the work they carry out, and the demanding clients they handle will leave no doubt that the featured works in this book are a ready reference for the most up-to-date examples of navigation systems at the cutting edge.

We have had the good fortune to work with some great contributors in putting together this book, starting with Matthew Clugston, from Clusta in Birmingham, UK, on the navigation system developed for Publicis, employing the computer's webcam to relay orientation. The second case is from Mark Johnson, from Sequence, who has written about the Torchwood Hub interface design. The last case study is from Dylan Tran, from Fahrenheit Studios, and examines an overall approach to the subject. Apart from these, we were delighted to receive tons of submissions from the large body of creative workers involved in transforming how we find our way round in cyberspace. We extend our thanks to them all in this book, whether featured or not, for the huge contribution they are making in the web-design community.

As ever my special thanks to Daniel Siciliano Brêtas, the designer of the series and my right hand, for making the whole process once again work so smoothly, and to our production man Stefan Klatte for his continuing design work on the book, as fresh and efficient as a future-looking topic such as this deserves.

I hope you enjoy navigating this collection as much as we enjoyed assembling it!

Julius Wiedemann

IMPRINT

Web Design: Navigation

To stay informed about upcoming TASCHEN titles, please request our magazine at www.taschen.com/magazine or write to TASCHEN, Hohenzollernring 53, D-50672 Cologne, Germany, contact@taschen.com, Fax: +49-221-254919. We will be happy to send you a free copy of our magazine which is filled with information about all of our books.

Design & layout: Daniel Siciliano Brêtas
Production: Stefan Klatte
Editor: Julius Wiedemann
Editorial coordination: Daniel Siciliano Brêtas

English revision: Chris Allen
German translation: Katrin Kügler (Equipo de Edición), and Jürgen Dubau
French translation: Valérie Lavoyer (Equipo de Edición)

Printed in Italy
ISBN: 978-3-8365-0496-6

TASCHEN is not responsible when web addresses cannot be reached, if they are offline or can be viewed just with plug-ins.

Guidelines for Online Success Eds. Rob Ford, Julius Wiedemann / Softcover, 336 pp. / € 29.99 / $ 39.99 / £ 24.99 / ¥ 5.900

Web Design: Flashfolios Ed. Julius Wiedemann Flexi-cover, 192 pp. / € 6.99 / $ 9.99 / £ 5.99 / ¥ 1.500

Web Design: Video Sites Ed. Julius Wiedemann Flexi-cover, 192 pp. / € 6.99 / $ 9.99 / £ 5.99 / ¥ 1.500

"These books are beautiful objects, well-designed and lucid." —*Le Monde*, Paris, on the ICONS series

---

"Buy them all and add some pleasure to your life."

60s Fashion Ed. Jim Heimann
70s Fashion Ed. Jim Heimann
African Style Ed. Angelika Taschen
Alchemy & Mysticism Alexander Roob
Architecture Now! Ed. Philip Jodidio
Art Now Eds. Burkhard Riemschneider, Uta Grosenick
Atget's Paris Ed. Hans Christian Adam
Bamboo Style Ed. Angelika Taschen
Barcelona, Restaurants & More Ed. Angelika Taschen
Barcelona, Shops & More Ed. Angelika Taschen
Ingrid Bergman Ed. Paul Duncan, Scott Eyman
Berlin Style Ed. Angelika Taschen
Humphrey Bogart Ed. Paul Duncan, James Ursini
Marlon Brando Ed. Paul Duncan, F.X. Feeney
Brussels Style Ed. Angelika Taschen
Cars of the 70s Ed. Jim Heimann, Tony Thacker
Charlie Chaplin Ed. Paul Duncan, David Robinson
China Style Ed. Angelika Taschen
Christmas Ed. Jim Heimann, Steven Heller
James Dean Ed. Paul Duncan, F.X. Feeney
Design Handbook Charlotte & Peter Fiell
Design for the 21st Century Eds. Charlotte & Peter Fiell
Design of the 20th Century Eds. Charlotte & Peter Fiell
Devils Gilles Néret
Marlene Dietrich Ed. Paul Duncan, James Ursini
Robert Doisneau Jean-Claude Gautrand
East German Design Ralf Ulrich/Photos: Ernst Hedler
Clint Eastwood Ed. Paul Duncan, Douglas Keesey
Egypt Style Ed. Angelika Taschen
Encyclopaedia Anatomica Ed. Museo La Specola Florence
M.C. Escher
Fashion Ed. The Kyoto Costume Institute
Fashion Now! Eds. Terry Jones, Susie Rushton
Fruit Ed. George Brookshaw, Uta Pellgrü-Gagel
Greta Garbo Ed. Paul Duncan, David Robinson
HR Giger HR Giger
Grand Tour Harry Seidler
Cary Grant Ed. Paul Duncan, F.X. Feeney
Graphic Design Eds. Charlotte & Peter Fiell
Greece Style Ed. Angelika Taschen
Halloween Ed. Jim Heimann, Steven Heller
Havana Style Ed. Angelika Taschen
Audrey Hepburn Ed. Paul Duncan, F.X. Feeney
Katharine Hepburn Ed. Paul Duncan, Alain Silver
Homo Art Gilles Néret
Hot Rods Ed. Coco Shinomiya, Tony Thacker
Grace Kelly Ed. Paul Duncan, Glenn Hopp
London, Restaurants & More Ed. Angelika Taschen
London, Shops & More Ed. Angelika Taschen
London Style Ed. Angelika Taschen
Marx Brothers Ed. Paul Duncan, Douglas Keesey
Steve McQueen Ed. Paul Duncan, Alain Silver
Mexico Style Ed. Angelika Taschen
Miami Style Ed. Angelika Taschen
Minimal Style Ed. Angelika Taschen
Marilyn Monroe Ed. Paul Duncan, F.X. Feeney
Morocco Style Ed. Angelika Taschen
New York Style Ed. Angelika Taschen
Paris Style Ed. Angelika Taschen
Penguin Frans Lanting
Pierre et Gilles Eric Troncy
Provence Style Ed. Angelika Taschen
Safari Style Ed. Angelika Taschen
Seaside Style Ed. Angelika Taschen
Signs Ed. Julius Wiedeman
South African Style Ed. Angelika Taschen
Starck Philippe Starck
Surfing Ed. Jim Heimann
Sweden Style Ed. Angelika Taschen
Tattoos Ed. Henk Schiffmacher
Tokyo Style Ed. Angelika Taschen
Tuscany Style Ed. Angelika Taschen
Valentines Ed. Jim Heimann, Steven Heller
Web Design: Best Studios Ed. Julius Wiedemann
Web Design: Best Studios 2 Ed. Julius Wiedemann
Web Design: E-Commerce Ed. Julius Wiedemann
Web Design: Flash Sites Ed. Julius Wiedemann
Web Design: Interactive & Games Ed. Julius Wiedemann
Web Design: Music Sites Ed. Julius Wiedemann
Web Design: Video Sites Ed. Julius Wiedemann
Web Design: Portfolios Ed. Julius Wiedemann
Orson Welles Ed. Paul Duncan, F.X. Feeney
Women Artists 20th & 21st Cent. Ed. Uta Grosenick

ICONS